W9-DFK-557

MONTANA
Century

100 Years in Pictures and Words

MONTANA Century

100 YEARS IN PICTURES AND WORDS

EDITED BY MICHAEL P. MALONE

© 1999 by Falcon® Publishing, Inc., Helena, Montana
All rights reserved.
Printed in Korea.
Second printing, 1999.

Photo credits

Cover: St. Helena Cathedral, *John Lambing*; grain elevator, *Bruce Selyem*; Anaconda Range, *Michael Sample*; Boss Ribs, *Herbert Titter, courtesy of the Montana Historical Society*; loggers, *courtesy of the Montana Historical Society*

Back cover: Rodeo rider, *courtesy of the Brandt Family*; grizzly, *Daniel J. Cox*; Makoshika State Park, *Michael Sample*; Greene sisters, *courtesy of Vivian Purdy*

Title page: Horse in road, *Joanne M. Berghold*

Previous page: Lake McDonald, Glacier National Park, *Salvatore Vasapolli*

This page: George Bird Grinnell (1849–1938) poses on a glacier—perhaps even the one that bears his name—in Glacier National Park. In 1910, this naturalist, author, and friend of the Blackfeet was instrumental in convincing Congress to preserve the spectacular glacier country as a national park. *Photo courtesy of the Montana Historical Society*

Next page: Swan Range near Bigfork, *John Reddy*

Table of contents: Tepees, *Chuck Haney*; "Montana Street," *Michael Crummett*; Boss Ribs, *Herbert Titter, courtesy of the Montana Historical Society*; Billings mural, *Michael Crummett*; sheep, *Michael Crummett*; rainbow trout, *Michael Sample*; Eastern Montana homesteader Janet Williams with trapped coyote pup, 1911, *Evelyn J. Cameron, courtesy of the Montana Historical Society*; blanket-flower, *Michael Sample*

Library of Congress Cataloging-in-Publication Data

Montana century / Michael P. Malone, editor.
      p.   cm.
      Includes bibliographical references and index.
      ISBN 1-56044-827-X (hc.)
      1. Montana—History—20th cntury. 2.
Montana—History—20th century Pictorial works.   I.
Malone, Michael P.
F731.M743 1999   99-27502
978.6'033--dc21   CIP

Project Editor: Gayle Shirley
Production Editor: Larissa Berry
Book design by Michael Cutter and Jeff Wincapaw
Cover design by Jeff Wincapaw

For extra copies of this book, please check with your local bookstore or write Falcon, P.O. Box 1718, Helena, MT 59624. You may also call Falcon toll-free at 1-800-582-2665 or visit our website at www.Falcon.com.

CONTENTS

MONTANA IN THE TWENTIETH CENTURY

MONTANA AT THE OUTSET OF THE NEW CENTURY

During the century that elapsed between the late 1890s and the late 1990s, the Treasure State of Montana traveled a challenging and often tortuous road that took it from raw frontier to the modern entity we know today. Similar roads were followed by Montana's sister states; but few, if any, of those sister states experienced such extreme highs and lows, booms and busts, as did Montana in the twentieth century. It has been an interesting journey, one that sometimes took the state to the center of the American experience but more often found it on the outer margins of the national scene.

Americans have loved, over the years, to talk and dream of the "last frontier," whenever and wherever it may have been. Montana can, in fact, make a very good claim to whatever honors come with the title. By about any definition, the newborn "Treasure State" entered the new century a true "frontier." The 1900 census found a mere 243,329 people inhabiting a sprawling landmass of fully 145,556 square miles, which made for a remarkably low ratio of 1.67 inhabitants to the square mile. Only a few years earlier, historian Frederick Jackson Turner had created a sensation when he declared the American frontier closed. The 1890 census, he noted, had revealed the existence of no coherent frontier line, with "frontier" defined as broad areas with two or fewer residents to the square mile. In this context, Montana was very much an outlier, a vast frontier as of yet barely "opened."

Montana was even more a near-wilderness frontier than these singular statistics indicated, for its population lay overwhelmingly in the mountainous southwestern region, where it had begun gathering back in the 1860s mining rushes. In the ensuing years, the bustling and dynamic mining city of Butte had risen not only to supremacy in Montana but also to supremacy among all the West's metal mining "camps." It was a fascinating and isolated outpost of ethnic-urban America in the faraway Rockies. Flanking it were the smelting and refining complexes at Anaconda and Great Falls, the lumbering center of Missoula, the small capital city of Helena, and farming towns like Deer Lodge, Bozeman, and Kalispell.

Reflecting the dominance of mining in Western Montana, the state was heavily ethnic, especially Irish, and thereby Catholic in religion and Democratic in

BY MICHAEL P. MALONE

Opposite: Workers at the dawn of the century use horse power to haul a massive load of lumber from the woods of Western Montana. Mining and smelting—with their voracious appetites for construction timbers and fuel—kept loggers and lumber mills in the state busy during the early 1900s. *Photo courtesy of the Montana Historical Society*

political ' loyalty. Not surprisingly, the governmental institutions of the new state, created mainly during the frenzied legislative session of 1893, were clustered in an arc around Butte: the capital in Helena; the four units of higher education in Missoula, Dillon, Butte, and Bozeman; the penitentiary in Deer Lodge, and so forth.

The eastern plains of Montana lay remarkably open and unpopulated at the dawn of the new century. The state's diverse population of Indians had by now entered upon the dreary course of reservation life, isolated and largely forgotten by white Americans. They lived on three huge reservations north of the east-flowing Missouri River: the Blackfeet, Fort Belknap (Gros Ventre and Assiniboine tribes), and Fort Peck (Assiniboine and Sioux) Reserves—as well as on the Crow and Northern Cheyenne Reservations south of the Yellowstone River and the Salish-Kootenai Reserve in northwestern Montana.

Two cities commanded the east-central region: Great Falls in central Montana, whose economy was linked heavily with that of Butte to the south, and Billings on the Yellowstone River, a rail and irrigated

farming hub. Otherwise, only a scattering of small rail and ranching communities like Miles City in the southeast and Havre and Glasgow on the northern Hi-Line punctuated this huge swath of windswept prairie, plateaus, and pine ridges. Agriculture ruled supreme here, as it still does today, but almost entirely in the form of ranching, much of it still on the open range and on isolated tracts of irrigated river bottom, for example around Billings and Glendive.

This new state offered a genuine case study of life on the "last frontier." Homesteaders had not yet arrived in appreciable numbers, and the very fragile, boom-and-bust economy rested upon the narrow base of a surging mining complex in the west and a scattered ranching domain in the east. Railroads, primarily the Northern Pacific in the south and the Great Northern along the Hi-Line, aimed mainly at crossing rather than serving the state; nevertheless, they provided both vital services and important employment opportunities to centers like Billings-Laurel, Livingston, and Havre. In the west, a wasteful but robust lumbering business centered around Missoula and in the Clark Fork and Flathead Valleys, mainly as ancillary enterprises to mining and railroading; similarly focused were deep coal mines located primarily east of Great Falls and around Red Lodge in south-central Montana.

The western and eastern sectors of Montana, so often contrasted over the years, in fact had much in common. Both relied overwhelmingly upon the extraction of natural resources, and with the singular exception of copper refining, neither added much value to the natural product. Cattle left the state by rail for finishing in the Midwest, and the wool clip from the largest population of sheep in America—six million head—likewise was shipped to woolen mills far away. Miners and ranchers, smelter workers and rail workers, Montanans worked with their hands, harvesting the products of the land, seemingly isolated and insulated from the world beyond. But then as now, they were not insulated, as the sweeping events of the next two decades were about to reveal.

Opposite: By 1900, Butte was one of the most prominent metal-mining camps in the West. This photo—looking north from East Park Street—dramatically illustrates the mix of homes, businesses, mines, and smelters that made the Mining City such a gritty and dynamic industrial town. *Photo courtesy of the World Museum of Mining*

Above: A Glendive-area man hauls four tons of freshly sheared wool to market. At the dawn of the century, Montana's sheep industry was at its peak and the state boasted the largest population of woolies in the nation: almost six million head. *Photo courtesy of the Frontier Gateway Museum*

Left: A distinguished statesman and Crow leader, Plenty Coups (1848–1932) skillfully led his people from the days of the buffalo into the complex 20th century. After his death, the title of tribal chief was retired and a state park was established at Pryor to honor his memory. *Photo courtesy of the Western Heritage Center*

THE CLOSING OF THE FRONTIER: 1900–1920

The first two decades of the twentieth century would prove to be the most hectic of its entirety. During these seminal years, two momentous historic occurrences combined to form much of the personality of modern Montana: the climax and denouement of the "copper wars" that had begun during the last years of the preceding century and the great homestead rush that thrust the east-central reaches of the state into the modern world.

Montana's epic "War of the Copper Kings" had flared throughout the 1890s, the first decade of statehood, beginning in Butte as a baronial fight between William Andrews Clark, the West's most affluent mining magnate, and Marcus Daly, the iron-fisted master of the gargantuan Anaconda Copper Mining Company. Its high points, or more correctly low points, included the bribery of legislators in 1893, when Clark unsuccessfully tried to gain election to the U.S. Senate by buying votes, and the mass spending of mining money in the 1894 capital fight, when Helena barely fended off Daly's attempt to move the capital to his "company town" of Anaconda. In 1899 and 1900, this episodic fight reached its nadir as Clark again bought up legislative votes and this time won a Senate seat, only to be forced to resign in 1900 when his sordid "man-buying" antics were brought to light in Washington, D.C. Daly died the same year.

Things got even more complicated in 1899 when executives of the Standard Oil Company, led by Henry Rogers and William Rockefeller, bought control of the giant Anaconda Company and made it the centerpiece of an eastern-based holding company called Amalgamated Copper. Through Amalgamated, they hoped to monopolize the entire copper industry, just as they had done earlier with oil. As the much-feared "Standard Oil Crowd" moved into Montana in alliance with Daly and the Anaconda, seeking to gain control of all Butte mining companies, it immediately caused enormous problems.

The first four years of the new century, 1900 through 1903, witnessed the most dramatic political confrontation in the history of the state—indeed, in the history of about any state. In the political campaign of 1900, Clark joined forces with a younger and fast-rising mining king, F. Augustus Heinze, to rouse opposition to the Amalgamated by attacking it as an evil monopolist and by winning the favor of their own workers by granting them an eight-hour workday. The pair bought newspapers across the state to serve their ends, and the Amalgamated countered with purchases of its own. Employing every trick from brass bands to broadsides pillorying the "trust" as an inhuman, monopolistic monster, Clark and the clever Heinze stunned Rogers and the other lords of Standard Oil by turning Montana voters decisively against them. Clark won a legislative majority that, this time, would elect him to the Senate sans bribes, and Heinze gained secure control of the city government of Butte, including two of the three district judges.

Heinze needed control of the courts, for he was by now engaged in a full-scale legal-political struggle with the Wall Street–based lords of Standard Oil for control of the Butte Hill. Too complex even to summarize here, this "Battle for Butte" involved massive litigation, in which Heinze's sway over both the judges and an angry public served him well, as did underground skirmishing between miners of both sides and political-journalistic onslaughts. However, though the anti-trust "progressives" succeeded for a time, in the end the Amalgamated could not be thwarted.

Rogers and his Montana machine, mainly the old Daly-Anaconda minions, first neutralized Clark, who now held his long-sought seat in the U.S. Senate, by the simple ploy of forcing him to join them by threatening to contest his election once again. They then broke the power of Heinze and his progressive allies by dramatically shutting down the Amalgamated's entire Montana operation in the fall of 1903. As a stunned state and nation watched, Amalgamated Copper dictated the terms under which it would allow the dominant share of Montana's work force to regain employment. It stipulated that the governor must call a special session of the legislature, and the lawmakers must enact a judge disqualification law that would break the hold of Heinze upon the Butte courts. After initially resisting this corporate extortion, Governor Joseph Toole called the special session, and the bullied legislators passed the law. A "sovereign" state had been thoroughly manhandled by a rogue super-corporation.

Amalgamated now brought almost the entire Montana metal mining industry under its control. Despite promises to the contrary, Heinze and his brothers sold their holdings to Amalgamated in 1906; but when they set out to invest their ten- to twelve-million-dollar profit on Wall Street, their Standard Oil foes quickly fleeced them. Senator Clark sold the larger part of his Butte operations in 1910 and now spent most of his time and money elsewhere, from Paris to New York to Los Angeles. Finally, in 1915, the holding company of Amalgamated Copper was disbanded under pressure of new federal tax and regulatory policies, and all of its holdings were grouped under the name of its largest operating company, Anaconda.

The newly independent colossus of Anaconda—with its cohort of mines, smelters, refineries, and lumber, coal, and rail affiliates; its corporate twin Montana Power Company, which had been formed in 1912 by Anaconda executives; and a chain of newspapers that included all but one of the state's major dailies (the *Great Falls Tribune*)—towered over the scantily populated state like some primeval beast. Indeed, Montana became the most oft-cited example of a state overwhelmingly dominated by a single corporation. Only tiny Delaware, in the embrace of Dupont, seemed a rival for this dubious honor. Admittedly, such a characterization was overdrawn and stereotypical; but it bore considerable truth, and Anaconda's heavy hand would palsy the Treasure State's political life until the 1970s.

Meanwhile, a separate and much larger train of events was under way that would even more emphatically remake the socioeconomic landscape of Montana. For years, the encroaching line of the farmers' frontier had hovered far to the east, just short of the hundredth meridian in the eastern Dakotas. The high, dry, and windswept Missouri

Plateau west of that line simply seemed too inhospitable to permit widespread cropping; only the grazing of cattle and sheep and the limited growth of irrigated crops along the fertile river bottoms, it would seem, could ever endure here.

However, by the close of the first decade of the new century, things were beginning to change rapidly. A cycle of more abundant rain and snowfall, combined with rising commodity prices, beckoned farmers westward onto the dry, shortgrass prairies. New farm technologies, such as steam tractors and grain seeding drills, came on the market at low prices fostered by mass production. In 1909, Congress passed the Enlarged Homestead Act, which in this part of the country doubled the size of homesteads from 160 to 320 acres. The Chicago, Milwaukee, St. Paul & Pacific Railway built through central Montana from 1906 through 1909 and began a massive campaign to advertise the region. Quickly, the railroads dominated by the indomitable Jim Hill—the Great Northern, Northern Pacific, and Burlington lines—followed suit, as did other promoters, such as towns, newspapers, and land hawkers.

As a result, in the decade following 1908, Montana witnessed the last great land rush in American history. The homesteaders, or "honyockers" as they were sometimes called by derisive stockmen, came from all points of the compass, particularly from the Upper Midwest, usually debarking by rail from the Twin Cities. Many came originally from the British Isles, Canada, Scandinavia, and Germany. They came in large numbers, boosting the census population from 376,053 in 1910 to 548,889 in 1920, and the number of farms and ranches from 26,214 to 57,677. They claimed 25 million acres during the fourteen years beginning in 1909 and established 114,620 homesteads; in many cases, more than one member of a family filed. They also secured other large acreages from the Northern Pacific Railroad and other realtors. In little more than a decade, they made their adopted land the most homesteaded state in the Union.

The big Northern Plains land rush brought with it

Above: In 1913, a homesteader unloads his worldly goods—including horses, cows, and chickens—directly off a boxcar at Sumatra, in what is now Rosebud County. Between 1910 and 1920, more than 100,000 homesteaders flocked to Montana, making this the most homesteaded state in the Union. Many came in response to massive promotional campaigns launched by the railroads. *Photo by Henry Syverud, courtesy of the Montana Historical Society*

Opposite: Early in the century, Butte was one of the strongest bastions of labor in America and no stranger to labor strife. In June 1914, a battle between factions of the Butte Miners Union—fanned by the Anaconda Company—led to the dynamiting of the union hall. This photo shows the hall the day after the blast. *Photo courtesy of the Montana Historical Society*

the most revolutionary changes the state has ever seen. The Democratic-Catholic mining communities of the west were quickly joined by Protestant-Republican farming and ranching communities in the east—a westward extension of the Upper Midwest. In sharp contrast to the scattered, old, male-dominated ranching towns like Miles City and Malta, the new farm towns, such as Chester, Glasgow, and Plentywood, bore the evidence of a strong female and family presence and aspired to be traditional and dynamic communities. Longing to be county seats, they spearheaded the drive to divide the state's huge counties and then to divide them again, leaving Montana with fifty-six, some of which would prove to be insufficiently populated to grow in the future. The homestead families and communities faced a hard existence, but they were profoundly optimistic that they could reform society, as they attempted to do by voting in statewide prohibition in 1916.

The outbreak of World War I in 1914 coincided with the peak year of homestead entries in Montana, and the war boom resulted in even higher prices for farm-ranch commodities. America's entry into the war in 1917–1918, in effect, overlay one boom with another in a final surge of land taking. Indeed, the prosperity caused by the Great War boosted all sectors of the Treasure State economy, packing logging camps with exploited and restive workers and pushing Butte's populace momentarily to more than eighty thousand. Regrettably, the brief interlude of war also produced a wave of labor-socialist unrest and a much greater wave of superpatriotic repression, which remarkably culminated in a Sedition Act passed by the legislature in 1918 that literally outlawed criticism of the government! The federal government used the Montana law as the model for its own 1918 Sedition Act, sometimes characterized as the most sweeping violation of civil liberties in the history of the nation.

Then, suddenly, the boom ended. A terrible cycle of drought began in 1918 and deepened to catastrophic proportions in 1919, accompanied by high winds that created a regional "dust bowl." At the same time, high commodity prices collapsed. The result was a massive socioeconomic crisis. Thousands of pioneer farmers simply packed up and left, and more than two hundred banks failed—more than half the total in the state. Montana's farms and ranches lost half the valuation of their lands. While the nation at large passed through a sharp but brief recession after the war, Montana and the interior West suffered a downturn that went deeper and lasted longer, until nearly mid-decade. In fact, the Treasure State was the only state to lose population in the 1920s, and this would be the only decade in its history during which it would register a net loss.

This terrible postwar depression of 1919 to 1922 appears, in retrospect, to be the major turning point in Montana history, the true close of the frontier and the birth of modern times. Hitherto a land of beckoning opportunities, Montana now became an afflicted region that saw its population, especially its rural population, fading away, that came to fear the future and feel threatened by change. The "roaring" 1920s thus dawned upon a state at once stricken by agricultural depression and saddled by the dominance of a big, backward corporation that seemed intent upon manacling it to the past.

HARD TIMES: 1920–1940

For most Americans, the 1920s were a time of unprecedented prosperity, a prosperity that was rudely eclipsed by the Great Depression that began in 1930 and persisted throughout most of the "dirty thirties." But for Montanans, the 1920s were harder. The depression that followed the First World War gave way to only a brief interlude of rainfall and prosperity during the middle and late 1920s, and then came a much longer and harder time of troubles.

By now a predominately agricultural state, Montana clearly displayed its modern profile by this time. Crop agriculture—mainly devoted to wheat and barley and centered in such favored regions as the "Golden Triangle" north of Great Falls, the Judith Basin, and the far northeast—was balanced by livestock operations, devoted primarily to cow-calf cattle operations and dwindling numbers of sheep. Growing numbers of operators both farmed and ranched; many stockgrowers raised hay crops such as alfalfa on irrigated bottomlands.

Certain major trends of modern, post-frontier agriculture first surfaced during the 1920s. Since homesteading had moved a far denser population onto these arid lands than they could sustain, the farming population and the number of farms and ranches began inexorably to shrink, from nearly sixty thousand units then to fewer than thirty thousand today. As homesteads were abandoned, they were consolidated into larger holdings, and the capitalization of these growing acreages also grew rapidly as farmers and ranchers invested in new technologies that ranged from mobile combines to gasoline and diesel tractors and other more sophisticated equipment. Even when the drought cycle ended in mid-decade, agriculturists here and elsewhere still paradoxically faced the low product prices that came with greater efficiency and the resulting overproduction.

Otherwise, the Treasure State economy evolved very little during the years between the world wars. As the Butte mines dug deeper and depleted the prime ore bodies, Anaconda shifted its primary focus southward to Mexico and especially to Chile, where it acquired the great Guggenheim family holdings at Chiquicamata in 1923. Soon, the majority of its product came not from Montana but from south of the border. Meanwhile, the coal mines at Red Lodge and elsewhere steadily reduced operations in the face of competition from petroleum products, and lumber production in the west remained static and added little value to product. The new natural products of these years were oil and natural gas, with the state's pioneer fields opening during the 1920s, especially in north-central Montana at Cut Bank and in the Kevin-Sunburst area. This isolated state continued to attract almost none of the burgeoning manufacturing and commercial growth that characterized much of the nation at this time.

Politically, the 1920s similarly marked the emergence of a modern, post-frontier profile. During the first two decades of the century, the new state had witnessed

On Independence Day 1919, a victory parade wends its way through the streets of Great Falls. Montanans enthusiastically celebrated both the Allied victory in World War I and the prosperity that they hoped and expected would follow. But the coming decade proved instead to be a time of troubles. Half of all farm mortgages would foreclose by 1925, and half of all commercial banks would fail. *Photo courtesy of the Cascade County Historical Society*

sharp encounters between right and left. Like other states, Montana had produced a robust, reformist "progressive" movement aimed at broadening public participation in government with direct-democracy measures like the initiative and referendum and, in 1914, with women's suffrage. Led by U.S. Senators Joseph Dixon (Republican) and Thomas J. Walsh (Democrat), the progressives had fought back against the heavy corporate role in politics. A powerful radical sector even thrived on the left, highlighted by labor socialists who momentarily captured the city governments of Butte and Anaconda. But World War I fostered a strong patriotic-conservative resurgence that continued to prevail during the postwar decades.

The years encompassing World War I and its aftermath were among the most frenzied in the political history of Montana. The radical left faced severe repression due mainly to its opposition to war. In the gubernatorial election of 1920, perhaps the most heated in state history, two anti-Anaconda candidates faced one another: Republican Joseph Dixon and the fast-rising Burton K. Wheeler, the candidate of both the Democrats and the agrarian, radical Nonpartisan League. Dixon won and initiated a sweeping program of reform. He lost his bid

After representing Montana in both houses of Congress, Republican Joseph M. Dixon (1867–1934) was elected governor in 1920. Characterized as an "earnest, capable, and honest man" by one historian, Dixon pushed for tax reform and led a fight to force the state's mining interests to pay their fair share of taxes. *Photo courtesy of the Montana Historical Society*

for re-election in 1924, but his initiative raising the taxation on mines won approval of the electorate. He is still remembered by some today as the best governor in the state's history.

The return of a brief prosperity in the mid-1920s brought with it a return to political calm and conservatism. Working with legislatures concerned about little more than holding down taxes and expenditures, stand-pat Democratic Governor John Erickson, whose good

looks and relaxed style made him a three-term favorite, had an easy time of it while the good times lasted. However, despite the surface calm, these years also marked the emergence of the modern Montana profile in politics, just as they did in the economic sector.

While the behemoth Anaconda Company, its team of lobbyists and newspapers, and its Montana Power Company affiliate anchored the right or conservative side of the spectrum, so, too, did other less heralded corporate interests, such as the Northern Pacific and Great Northern railroads and small lumber and oil firms. More importantly, agriculture also added vast weight to Montana conservatism, especially through such potent organizations as the Montana Stockgrowers and Montana Wool Growers Associations and the state Farm Bureau. Conservatives, both Republican and Democrat, relied upon such support, abetted as everywhere else by main-street, middle-class citizens in towns and cities. Now, as usual, they held sway over the legislative and executive branches of government in Montana.

If the heavy hand of Anaconda put a near-unique twist on Montana politics, so did the remarkable strength of the labor-left. As the socialists and other radicals lost their sway after the war, more moderate but still outspoken progressives and reformers gathered up much of their support, especially through the organizational strength of mining, smelting, and Rail Brotherhood unions and through the Farmers Union, the primary state organization of smaller operators that was becoming the state's largest agrarian group.

During the 1920s and for many years thereafter, even as conservatives ruled supreme in state government, liberal Democrats definitely had the edge in congressional representation, especially in the U.S. Senate. This trend first emerged in the 1922 election, when outspoken Burton K. Wheeler recovered from his gubernatorial defeat of two years before to join the already well-established Thomas Walsh in the Senate. The two Montana Democrats won national praise and blame for spearheading the exposure of scandal in the administration of President Warren G. Harding. They worked closely together until Walsh's death in 1933, just before he was to become U.S. attorney general under President Franklin Roosevelt.

This peculiar pattern of a liberal profile in national government and a conservative profile in state government, sometimes referred to as "political schizophrenia," had parallels in other western states but was particularly striking in Montana. No doubt it can be explained in part by the special heed that corporate interests paid to such state issues as regulation and taxation, as well as to the fact that labor-liberal power blocs were concentrated in a few urban locales, such as Butte, Great Falls, and Missoula. This enabled them to accumulate their strength in statewide contests, but they could not often control local rural contests. Conservatives, on the other hand, reached more broadly and easily into every legislative district. This schizoid pattern would not truly dissipate until the late 1980s. Prior to Conrad Burns's Senate victory in 1988, only *one* Republican had ever won popular election to the U.S. Senate from Montana since the general voting public had begun selecting senators in 1911.

The brief interlude of prosperity from roughly 1923 to 1930 abruptly dissipated with the onslaught of the Great Depression, triggered by the Wall Street crash in the autumn of 1929. By 1930 and 1931, the severe downturn in the national economy combined with another drought and low commodity prices to drive this state, like all its sisters, into the most severe depression in history. Wheat prices fell by four-fifths of their 1920 value to thirty-two cents a bushel by 1932; cattle prices dropped by two-thirds to $3.34 per hundredweight by 1934. With the collapse of the electrical and fabrication markets, the blue-chip corporation of Anaconda saw its stock values fall from $175 a share to an incredible $3 a share. Manufacturing employment fell catastrophically from nearly fifteen thousand workers in 1929 to just over six thousand in 1933. Thousands of Montanans looked desperately to the Red Cross, with its minuscule contributions, for help.

The dimensions of this greatest of American economic crises proved far too great for the anemic state governments to handle. As property taxes dried up, law-makers in Helena came up with little more by way of solution than to slash expenditures and initiate in 1931 a small tax on incomes, the beginning of the modern state income tax. Meanwhile, the administration of President Herbert Hoover offered not much more in federal assistance to the needy. That came only in 1933 with the accession to the presidency of Franklin D. Roosevelt and his New Deal program of direct federal intervention, the most dynamic period of governmental activism in American history.

Through its sweeping, hectic blitz of funding, regulatory, and reform initiatives, the New Deal changed the economy and government of Montana and other states forever. During the six years beginning in 1933, Uncle Sam pumped in more than $381 million and loaned another $142 million to the Treasure State, making it the second most subsidized state per capita in the Union. Why? Mainly because Montana was a classic western "acreage state," with few people and lots of land, resources, and federal property.

The new federal role and bankroll impinged upon this remote state in a myriad of ways and through a myriad of new agencies. For example, the Agricultural Adjustment Administration was soon paying ten million dollars annually to take cropland out of production, while the Taylor Grazing Act of 1934 finally allowed stockgrowers to lease public land. A host of different "relief" agencies, most notably the Works Progress Administration, offered federal jobs to the unemployed—affecting nearly one-fourth of all Montana homes by 1935. While the new Social Security Act began providing pension funds for the retired, the Rural Electrification Administration brought light and power to the countryside, and the Civilian Conservation Corps employed young men to preserve the environment.

Various New Deal agencies were responsible for the construction of many Montana structures, from schools to airports to dams. Many are still in use. By far the greatest, in fact the greatest in the nation, was the giant, earth-filled Fort Peck Dam, completed in 1940. Featured on the cover of the very first issue of *Life* magazine, this enormous project employed more than ten thousand people at the height of construction in 1936. It came to symbolize the new mood of the New Deal, a statement of national purpose and government initiative.

The New Deal did not end the depression in Montana or in the nation at large, but it did bring substantial relief and recovery. Beyond that, it both expanded the federal role here and energized the state government in Helena, which, for example, had to come up with matching funds to secure federal relief and other dollars. While nine-tenths of all states would eventually turn to sales taxes to cover the burgeoning costs of government, Montana then and now has refused to do so, relying instead upon its historic property taxes and its depression-born income tax.

Politically, the New Deal swung the support of the populace heavily toward the Democratic Party of Roosevelt, and henceforth the Democrats represented the party of liberal reform and the Republicans the party of conservatism. The remarkable popularity of Roosevelt and the New Deal, reflected in four landslide election triumphs for the president, made this the greatest period of one-party domination in the state's political history.

Democrats truly reigned supreme at all levels into the war years of the early 1940s. At the top of the pyramid in Montana stood senior U.S. Senator Burton K. Wheeler, a strong Roosevelt supporter who received in return such political prizes as the Fork Peck project. Wheeler eventually fell out with the president, opposed entry into World War II, and was defeated in 1946 after a Senate career of nearly a quarter of a century during which he wielded greater political power than any other Montanan ever has. Wheeler also collided with his new Senate colleague James Murray, an outspokenly liberal New Deal Democrat who would remain in office until 1961.

Genuine recovery, stability, and prosperity returned to Montana only with the Second World War, 1939–1945. Appreciable rainfall and the high commodity prices of wartime meant good times for those farmers and ranchers who had held on through the long hard times; their larger and more heavily capitalized agricultural units, with their trucks, tractors, mobile combines, and electrified homes, were starting to resemble those we know today. From the deep mines of Butte to the scattered lumber camps of the west to the isolated oil fields of the north, the state's other natural products

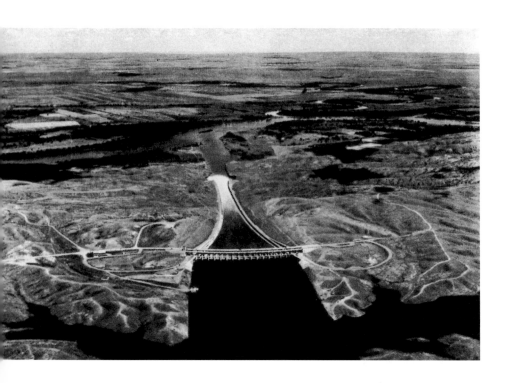

Left: This aerial view of the Fort Peck Dam on the Missouri River reveals the vast scale of the New Deal project, the largest undertaken in Montana during the Great Depression. At the peak of construction in 1936, the project employed more than 10,000 laborers. *Photo courtesy of the Western Heritage Center*

Opposite: U.S. Senator Burton K. Wheeler (1882–1975) was a leading progressive from Montana. In 1924, he ran for vice president on a Progressive Party ticket headed by "Fighting Bob" La Follette of Wisconsin. Wheeler was the first nationally known politician to back Franklin D. Roosevelt for president, but he led the opposition to Roosevelt's court-packing plan of the 1930s. *Photo courtesy of the Montana Historical Society*

industries boomed as well—even coal, although the terrible Smith Mine disaster of 1943 near Red Lodge, which cost the lives of seventy miners, served as a grim reminder of the dangers of this old livelihood.

Yet, as often happens, what failed to occur proved to be more significant than what actually did take place; for Montana, like the neighboring rural Dakotas, Wyoming, and Idaho—but unlike states with large urban centers such as Colorado and Utah—failed to attract the large defense industries drawn westward by war. It attracted only the Army Air Corps facilities at Great Falls, which became Malmstrom Air Force Base after the war. Thus, although this state like all others witnessed mass migrations of people, particularly those headed for military service or for better jobs elsewhere, it did not have its economy or its social order remade by this greatest of all wars and dislocations.

Politically, the war years produced a conservative reaction to the heady liberalism of the New Deal 1930s. The Democrats lost control of state government to Republican Sam "Model T" Ford, a political moderate who stood off the rightists in his own party and held power through an alliance with the conservative faction of the Democrats. The latter took their lead from maverick Senator Burton K. Wheeler, who was now estranged from the liberals in his own party. It was a time when, even more so than usual, party labels meant precious little in Montana.

INTO THE MAINSTREAM: 1945–1970

The quarter-century extending roughly from the end of World War II in 1945 into the early 1970s encompassed the era of maximum American prosperity and dominance of the modern world order. Seemingly quiet by earlier standards, these years nonetheless saw a steady movement in Montana toward shedding late-frontier traits such as corporate domination and a near-complete reliance upon extractive industries, and movement into the robust, middle-class American mainstream. The movement was, and is, far from complete, for the Treasure State remains a place of small cities and minimal suburbs, sparse industry, and a small middle class. Yet the movement has proven to be both profound and enduring in its impact.

The big postwar prosperity found full expression in Montana. Agricultural productivity and profitability soared with new generations of mechanization, new hybrid grains, super-chemical fertilizers and pesticides, and especially continuing aid from Uncle Sam. To the dismay of those who saw diversification as the only hope for the future, the Treasure State remained firmly focused upon range-feeder cattle grazing supplemented by a declining sheep industry, and upon spring and winter wheat supplemented by barley and hay crops. The state added very little value to the product of its dominant industry, but it proved to be a robust producer year-in and year-out, ranking midway among the top ten states in both beef and wheat output. However, the paradox that first appeared in the 1920s continued into the second half of the century: mounting production created surpluses and low prices, even as farm-ranch units grew bigger and the numbers living upon them steadily dwindled.

Other leading extractive industries evolved in very different ways. Once the backbone of the state, Butte mining lived on, but now as an obviously declining industry. Deepening shafts, diminishing higher-grade ores, and high-priced union labor made for pessimism as cheap South American copper flooded the markets. In 1955, to the amazement of many, Anaconda began open-pit mining right on the edge of the city, and the Berkeley Pit grew steadily over the years, eventually displacing all vein mining and becoming the crucible that now holds the world's largest body of toxic water. Meanwhile, Anaconda itself eventually entered the twentieth century, no longer preoccupied with Montana, and sold off its newspapers and moderated its heavy-handed lobbying methods.

Contrarily, the lumber industry evolved upward and outward during the postwar era. During the mid-1950s, the Hoerner and Waldorf companies built a major new pulp plant west of Missoula, which signaled a major step forward. They converted what had heretofore been a simple and wasteful lumber business into a true wood-products industry, producing not only cut lumber but also plywood, particleboard, cardboard liners, and other manufactured products. Indeed, the wood-products industry became, and has remained, the state's leading manufacturing industry. Unfortunately, it also caused environmental problems, most notably clearcutting, erosion, and a major air pollution problem in Missoula.

As mining and agriculture lost employment, the small Montana petroleum industry, both oil and natural gas, mushroomed in importance. The major development proved to be the opening of the great, deep-lying Williston Basin, whose western reaches extended into far Eastern Montana. Billings boomed through the 1950s as a refining and pipeline center and became, by 1960, the

state's largest city. During the 1960s, new fields opened, such as the Riger Ridge natural gas field in the north and the Belle Creek oil field in the southeast; but by then, the industry had stabilized as a classic extractive industry, with high value of product and low employment. While not a major petroleum state like Texas or Oklahoma, Montana is still an important one, where the industry counts heavily, for example in tax yields.

However, the main economic growth lay not in the traditional extractive industries, but elsewhere. Tourism had been only a marginal factor in Montana prior to mid-century, but now as elsewhere throughout the land, the new prosperity, the flood of cheap gasoline, and the building of new and better highways quickly made it a major business, especially in summer. Soon, gaudy "strips" radiated out of all larger towns, studded with gas stations, restaurants, and motels; and the traffic to

The Anaconda Company's vast Berkeley Pit, shown here about 10 years after it opened in 1955, swallowed large chunks of Butte's historic uptown before it was abandoned in the early 1980s. As the amount of copper ore diminished in the "Richest Hill on Earth," the efficiency of open-pit mining allowed Anaconda to keep producing. Today, with the underground pumps shut down, the pit is filling with toxic groundwater. *Photo courtesy of the Montana Historical Society*

Yellowstone and Glacier National Parks reached into the millions. Tourism, with its many low-paying and seasonal jobs, became a mainstay of the state economy, eventually ranking second only to agriculture as a source of dollars.

Even more important in broadening the Treasure State economy was the national trend toward growth in the non-manufacturing sectors of retail trade, "service," and government employment. As the role of the federal government continued to grow after the New Deal, thousands of its employees worked not only for such

stewardship agencies as the Bureaus of Reclamation and of Land Management and the Forest and National Park Services, but also at Malmstrom Air Force Base in Great Falls and, by the early 1960s, at the ominous missile silos that surrounded it. State employment, particularly in Helena and the university and college towns, also grew rapidly, as did the contingents of local government employees, particularly teachers. The tens of thousands now working in retail trade and in such varied services as health care, law, and accounting, simply reflected broader trends throughout the country.

Left: Workers install an intercontinental ballistic missile (ICBM) silo in Toole County in 1966. About 200 ICBM silos are scattered across north-central Montana, and before the close of the Cold War, Montana was jokingly known as one of the world's leading nuclear powers. *Photo by Jack Gilluly, courtesy of the Montana Historical Society*

Opposite: One of Montana's most respected politicians, Mike Mansfield served as majority leader in the U.S. Senate for 16 years—longer than any other senator. At the age of 73, he was named ambassador to Japan. Widely acknowledged to be one of America's great statesmen, Mansfield retired from public office in 1988. *Photo courtesy of the Montana Historical Society*

As population filtered out of the agrarian country-side and out of the extractive industries, it steadily grew in most of the state's small cities. By 1960, the Treasure State registered for the first time an "urban" majority of 50.2 percent of the populace—although, admittedly, most Americans would hardly consider this an urban place by any standard. The population grew at a much slower pace than that of the nation as a whole, from 559,456 in 1940 to 591,024 in 1950, 674,767 in 1960, and 694,409 in 1970. Only in the prosperous 1950s did Montana really experience robust growth, as reflected especially in the hectic 41.4 percent rise in the population of Yellowstone County (Billings).

The population profile shifted markedly during these years from the old, frontier pattern to the modern. Due to a relative lack of economic opportunities, the frontier pattern of a young, heavily male populace increasingly gave way to an hourglass pattern: a bulge of young and old with a relative paucity of the middle-aged, drawn elsewhere by opportunity. A state that had been so dominated by farmers and ranchers and by blue-collar mining, lumber, and rail workers now witnessed a burgeoning white-collar middle class that occupied the small suburbs of small cities and shopped in new centers such as Holiday Village Mall in Great Falls, Rimrock Mall in Billings, and Southgate Mall in Missoula.

Here as elsewhere, this prosperous quarter-century marked a new plateau of national mainstreaming. So notable in such a remote place as Montana, this trend had already begun with national print media, automobiles, movies, and radio. Now it advanced much more rapidly with mass highway and air travel, television, and eventually satellite and computer communications. All of these innovations, and others as well, broke down the old regional peculiarities and melded all Americans more nearly into one broad mass. For good or bad, the archetypal Montanan—epitomized by Helena's Gary Cooper as a tough but virtuous stoic—gave way to the mid-century American type, heavily concerned with conforming to middle-class standards and expectations.

Naturally enough, the economic and social stabiliza-tion of these years brought political stability as well. This trend was personified by a truly remarkable politician: Mike Mansfield, a quiet, pipe-smoking college professor and moderately liberal Democrat who went to the U.S. House in 1943 and the Senate in 1953. From 1961 until his retirement from Congress in 1977, Mansfield served as Senate majority leader, the longest such tenure in American history. Mansfield's style matched that of popular Republican President Dwight Eisenhower. He practiced a consensual politics, seeking calm and avoiding confrontation and bringing home lots of federal "pork," such as Hungry Horse, Canyon Ferry, Yellowtail and Libby Dams, thus capturing Republican as well as Democratic votes.

The "schizophrenic" pattern of a liberal presence in Congress matched by a conservative predominance at home continued unabated during these years. Serving with Mansfield in the Senate were, first, the aging New Deal Democrat Jim Murray and then the fiery progressive Lee Metcalf, a representative from the western district in the 1950s who then served as junior senator from 1961 until his death in 1978. Unlike Mansfield, Metcalf directly attacked the corporate "interests" at home and barely held on to his seat. In Congress, the western district remained in steadfastly liberal Democratic hands, those of Metcalf and Arnold Olsen, while the eastern district reflected the domination of agriculture with the likes of conservative Republicans Wesley D'Ewert and "Big Jim" Battin.

In remarkably sharp contrast, conservatives of both parties—but mainly Republican—ruled quietly at home.

In the large and ungainly legislature, whose membership exceeded 150 (making for one of the lowest ratios of representatives to constituents in America), rural areas easily predominated, especially through seniority; and farm-ranch representatives worked easily with corporate representatives and lobbyists against their beleaguered liberal foes. The rapidly growing cities faced mounting discrimination from this rural over-representation; and when the legislature itself refused to face the problem, the courts began in 1965 to mandate reapportionment. Meanwhile, a procession of Republican governors similarly reflected Montana's preference for conservatism at home: J. Hugo Aronson (1953–1961), Donald Nutter (1961–1962), and Tim Babcock (1962–1969).

Attempting to explain this political schizophrenia is a challenge. Admittedly, other western states have demonstrated similar dichotomies. But Montana's case is especially graphic, and its liberal presence in Washington made it seem by the late 1960s to be an outlier in an increasingly conservative and Republican West. From today's brief vantage, it would seem obvious to conclude that conservatism not only is but was the dominant strain, more broadly based and thus amply expressed in the legislature and in local government. Their numbers heavily attrited by blue-collar-union layoffs and by the steady erosion of progressive small farmers, the liberals could, nonetheless, frequently win statewide levies, especially when Democrats in Congress had the majority and thus the wherewithal to channel big bucks back to Montana; but they had to work mainly from confined bases in Butte-Anaconda, Missoula, Great Falls, and a few smaller locales.

Strip farming, also known as strip cropping, helps stop fierce prairie winds from carrying away precious topsoil. Introduced in Montana during the dust bowl days of the 1930s, strip farming was first developed in the prairie provinces of Canada. It is the most popular dry-land farming technique used today.
Photo by Stuart S. White

BOOM AND BUST: THE 1970S AND 1980S

The most recent rendering of the familiar Treasure State pattern of "boom and bust" occurred only yesterday, with a sudden upsurge in the agricultural and energy sectors of the economy followed by an equally abrupt shakeout. We live today in the aftermath and the influence of these formative events.

The situation of Montana as it entered upon the hectic decade of the 1970s appeared dichotomous, varying according to one's vantage. From an insular perspective, the state was relatively stable and even prosperous: the days of depression and depopulation seemed safely in the past, and most of the citizenry seemed better off than ever before. However, from a national viewpoint, things appeared differently. Montana looked to be a static, slow-growth state in a booming United States, a state sharing little in the new manufacturing and service industries that had lifted the nation to world dominance in the previous quarter-century. Now, suddenly, all that seemed to change.

Two engines drove the big boom that began during 1972–1973, one agricultural and the other energy. Following a major "wheat deal" in which the administration of President Richard Nixon sold stored surpluses to the Soviet Union, wheat and commodity prices rose spectacularly. Montana farmers enjoyed both bountiful harvests and prices of more than four dollars a bushel; cattlemen prospered, too, watching inventories climb by seventy-five percent and values more than double by the mid-1970s over those of a decade earlier. All of a sudden, the state's dominant livelihood soared to an unprecedented level of prosperity, and farmer-ranchers invested enthusiastically in new land and equipment.

The big energy boom of 1973 resulted from an embargo slapped on oil exports from Arab and other producing nations to the United States, which resulted in shortages and sky-high prices. To Montanans, the main result was not so much long lines at the gas stations as a sudden leap in both oil-gas and coal production and

in the taxes that the state reaped from them. Wildcatters swarmed over both Eastern and Western Montana, now enamored of the deep and difficult folds of the "overthrust belt" along the east slope of the Rockies, and the ever-deepening Williston Basin became again by the late 1970s one of the hottest prospecting locales in the country. By the crest of the boom in 1981, annual petroleum production reached a remarkable and unprecedented $1.45 billion.

However, the Treasure State's greatest energy asset is not oil and gas but rather coal, of which it holds fully thirteen percent of American reserves in shallow and easily mined seams, mainly in the southeast below the Yellowstone River. Montana's small coal mining industry, dominated by railroads and by Anaconda, had nearly dwindled away. Now, it suddenly came roaring back as big companies like Westmoreland, Decker, and Peabody began shoveling coal onto unit trains for shipment mainly to the Midwest, and as Montana Power's Western Energy subsidiary erected two giant, 350-megawatt, coal-fired plants at its burgeoning company town of Colstrip. From an output of only seven million tons in 1971, Montana's coal harvest leaped to thirty million tons by 1980. While some welcomed this big-time development, many others bemoaned it as a looming socioenvironmental disaster.

These dramatic developments, as historian Harry Fritz has aptly noted, broke upon a political climate already rumbling with change. For many years, critics had underscored the cumbersome antiquity of the state's 1889 constitution; and following a special election of delegates in 1971, the long campaign for reform climaxed with the assemblage at Helena early in 1972 of a notably progressive and capable gathering of delegates to draft a

Faced with a worldwide energy crisis, a handful of utility companies built four coal-fired generating plants at Colstrip in the 1970s and 1980s. Montana has some of the largest coal reserves in the nation, but as the tonnage taken from the Colstrip mines increased dramatically, alarmed Montanans lobbied the legislature to enact tough environmental protection laws.
Photo by Duncan R. Skinner, courtesy of the Boslaugh Family

new constitution. The document they produced introduced a number of dramatic changes, most importantly provisions to strengthen the powers of the governor, to modernize the legislature by mandating annual sessions and single-member districts, and to enhance democracy by making it easier for the voters to enact and repeal laws by direct initiative and referendum. Following a heated contest, the voters approved the new constitution by the hairbreadth margin of 116,415 to 113,883. Tellingly, the rising cities generally supported the change, while the conservative countryside opposed it.

Interestingly, the preamble of the new constitution expresses gratitude to the deity for the "quiet beauty of our state, the grandeur of our mountains, the vastness of our rolling plains." Partly as a reaction to the specter of proliferating coal development, a robust environmentalist movement surfaced dramatically in the Treasure State, spearheaded both by national organizations like the Sierra Club and the Wilderness Society and by such locally based groups as the Northern Plains Resource Council. The environmental movement has gained strength over the ensuing quarter-century and has ever more heatedly challenged the state's traditional extractive industries.

The new environmentalism melded with a generally progressive mood that also found expression not only in the new constitution but also in state politics generally. Montana's two liberal Democratic senators, Mike Mansfield and Lee Metcalf, won re-election in 1970 and 1972 respectively and were joined in 1972 by a young, progressive Democrat, Tom Judge, as governor. Judge won re-election in 1976, and Treasure State Democrats prospered even more with the disgrace of the Republican Nixon administration amidst the Watergate scandal. By the late 1970s, following Mansfield's retirement and Metcalf's death in office, the Democrats had two new senators in the personages of two former congressmen, Max Baucus and John Melcher, and yet a new progressive western district representative, Pat Williams.

In this environmentalist-progressive climate, the legislature enacted the most noteworthy sequence of

The bison was nearly extinct in the first decade of the century when the American Bison Society collected 41 of them from private herds to stock the newly established National Bison Range at Moiese. As the bison population recovered, wildlife managers began to worry that the animals would overpopulate their range. They initiated fall roundups at the preserve to cull excess animals from the herd. These are sold at auction. *Photo by William Munoz*

With eye-catching stars and stripes, this old schoolhouse, 11 miles southeast of Lindsay in Dawson County, commemorates the centennial of Montana statehood. Montana was admitted to the Union as the 41st state in 1889, by proclamation of President Benjamin Harrison. *Photo by Michael Crummett*

laws the state had seen since the heyday of the New Deal. A sweeping Montana Environmental Policy Act of 1971 was followed between 1973 and 1975 by a Strip Mining and Reclamation Act, a Water Use Act, a Utility Siting Act, a Major Facility Siting Act, and the capstone enactment of them all, the Coal Tax Trust Fund Act, which passed in 1976. This epochal measure, which Governor Judge called "the most significant piece of legislation enacted in Montana in this century," set an unprecedented thirty percent severance tax on coal mined in Montana, the proceeds to be deposited in an interest-bearing fund for future generations living in a time when the coal would be gone but the social dislocations would remain.

Nothing so exemplified the rising fortunes of Montana and other western energy states as did this controversial coal severance tax. Immediately, a coalition of Midwestern and other regional utility and energy companies and governmental leaders filed a lawsuit against the Montana tax, arguing that it exploited their citizen-consumers and, more to the point, that it violated the interstate commerce clause of the U.S. Constitution. In July 1981, the U.S. Supreme Court allowed the tax to stand, and over the years the Coal Trust Fund has grown to contain more than half a billion dollars in its corpus. Although the courts may shrink the fund considerably due to Crow Indian litigation arguing that much of the revenues belong exclusively to that tribe, the coal severance tax and trust fund remain major issues today, since these revenues not only accumulate for the future but also help pay the General-Fund bills every year.

The decade from the early 1970s into the early 1980s marked not only a progressive but also a prosperous period. Having voted down a sales tax again in 1971, Montanans came to rely heavily upon taxing natural products instead, and for now it worked. The peak of the new prosperity came in the early 1980s, when booming tax yields led lawmakers to combine dangerously the strategies of both investing heavily in government services *and* offering popular tax breaks, especially in the form of "indexing" income taxes so that they would not rise with the heavy inflation of the time.

It probably could not have lasted, and in any event, it did not. The bust came with a break in energy prices in 1983, the result of unforeseen global conservation and the opening of new sources like the great oil fields in Alaska and the North Sea. Also by that time, unanticipated crop surpluses had returned, resulting in lower prices that soon climbed once again with droughts that reached truly disastrous proportions in several years, particularly 1988. Other problems compounded the situation, most notably the shutdown of the old Anaconda facilities at Butte, Anaconda, and Great Falls by the company's new owner, ARCO (Atlantic Richfield), from 1977 through 1983; major closures and layoffs by Burlington Northern; and the bankruptcy of the old Milwaukee Road.

Thus, through the mid- and late 1980s, the state found itself gripped in a true depression, along with the rest of the interior West. In fact, so severe was the depression in the rural northern and eastern reaches of the state that a national news magazine could speak of the region as an "American Outback." Emigration reached such dimensions that, for the entire decade of the 1980s, Montana grew by less than thirteen thousand net, from 786,690 to 799,065, a paltry growth rate that did not even keep up with the natural margin of births over deaths.

The sharp downturn in the economy created a thorny situation for government officials, who had grown accustomed to an easy prosperity based heavily upon taxing natural products. Popular and capable Wolf Point farmer Ted Schwinden, Judge's lieutenant governor, had unseated his former boss when Judge tried for a third term in 1980. After a pleasant first two years, Schwinden and the legislature, evenly balanced throughout the decade between Democrats and Republicans, found themselves in dire straits as a $100 million budget surplus in 1981 plummeted into deep deficits by mid-decade.

Montana, like the nation at large, moved appreciably to the right during the depressed 1980s. Looking ever more conservative, Governor Schwinden pressed for and got two series of budget cuts in 1986, and the closely contested legislature also got into the bad habit of offering tax breaks without finding replacement revenues, which predictably resulted in deepening deficits and cuts in already lean budgets and services. However, the more radical conservatives wanted even more than that and tried unsuccessfully to abolish property taxes outright. As it was, Constitutional Initiative 105, still in effect in 1998, capped property taxes and limited the abilities of local governments to deal with their problems.

Thus, when Montana set out to celebrate its centennial anniversary in 1989, it did so in a rather threadbare condition. Alone among the four Northwest states that had entered the Union in 1889, the Treasure State refused to spend any money on the celebration, choosing only to raise private funds. The state closed the depression decade on a conservative note in other ways, too. In the election of 1988, the Democrats lost the governorship for the first time in a quarter of a century to Havre businessman Stan Stephens. Conrad Burns took away the Senate seat of John Melcher and became only the second Republican sent to the Senate by Montanans since popular elections began three-quarters of a century earlier.

The Evolution of Community and Culture: 1900–1997

As earlier noted, the new century dawned upon a new-born state that could still, in many if not most respects, be termed a true frontier. The farmers' frontier, that greatest of land-takings and always the frontier that eclipsed all earlier ones, had not yet unfolded. When this final frontier closed, in the cataclysm of drought and depression of 1919 to 1922, the modern order was born.

The tiny populace of the early twentieth century, heavily concentrated in the mining-smelting-lumber towns of the southwest, was overwhelmingly Caucasian, heavily immigrant compared to today, and notably male and youthful in makeup—typical of frontier societies. Of course, here as elsewhere, the immigrants have long since assimilated, leaving behind many remembrances and bonds, like the Ancient Order of Hibernians at Butte and Anaconda, the Sons of Norway along the Hi-Line, and the annual Festival of Nations at Red Lodge. As for the youthful bent of those days gone by, it has long since given way to an aging society, most pronounced in the towns and hamlets. Our youth have gone elsewhere in search of opportunity, leaving behind the elderly, who often seem to turn up as longest-married couples on Paul Harvey's radio vignettes.

As for racial composition, things have changed little since 1900, to the great joy of racist groups like the Militia of Montana, who see the Northern Rockies as the last, best haven of blue-eyed, blond Nordics. Barely two thousand blacks inhabited Montana in 1990, and there were only 12,167 Hispanics; the latter were centered in Billings, where they clustered after being recruited as fieldworkers by sugar-beet growers. Of course, the primary non-Caucasian element is now, just as then, the Native Americans.

Montana's Indians faced the new century with only the bleakest of prospects, remembering recent defeats and the end of the old nomadic ways. They were isolated on seven reservations and largely forgotten. Their twentieth-century journey has been one of chaotic federal policies, from the New Deal emphasis upon preserving tribal ways and governance to the 1950s strategy of "termination" of the reservations.

Lack of economic opportunity and cultural uprooting had led to severe social problems, including high rates of unemployment, alcohol and drug abuse, and suicide; but the tribes have also acculturated and, at the same time, produced a genuine renaissance of their own cultures. This renaissance can be seen in economic development, including A&S Industries at Fork Peck, a pen and pencil manufacturing firm on the Blackfeet Reservation, and the Salish-Kootenai takeover of mighty Kerr Dam from Montana Power. Even more so, it is evident in the new tribal colleges, in Indian efforts to build their own gaming industries, and in cultural manifestations such as the Museum of the Plains Indian at Browning and the large annual fair staged by the Crows. Today, Montana's fast-growing Indian population stands at more than fifty thousand—more than six percent of the entire populace.

The most striking social development in Montana lies in what has not happened—that is, a rate of growth that has been far less than that of the nation at large. Montana has not been a growth state from a national perspective, although many of its western sisters, such as California, Nevada, Arizona, and Utah, have been. Rather, its slow growth has paralleled the experience of northern plains neighbors like Wyoming and the Dakotas. The primary reason has been agricultural-rural depopulation, most notably the decline in Montana farm-ranch employment from 82,000 in 1920 to roughly 31,000 by the 1990s. Of course, small-town populations have dwindled accordingly and sometimes spectacularly. For example, between 1960 and 1990, the population of Chinook on the Hi-Line fell from 2,326 to 1,512, while that of White Sulphur Springs in central Montana fell from 1,519 to 963. Sixteen Treasure State counties actually lost population during the first half of the 1990s, almost all of them in the east.

This loss of rural population mirrors a general trend in rural America, and so does its counterpart, the slow but steady growth of Montana's small cities. The 1990 census found an urban majority of 52.6 percent, a fact that seems incongruous to many people given Montana's most striking feature—endless expanses of open and forbidding ground. But the truth is that the Treasure State's vitality lies in its small cities, which are best viewed in four tiers.

In the top tier are three metropolitan areas with populations of fifty thousand or more. These include flagship Billings, with a metropolitan area of about 115,000 people and a sphere of influence that includes east-central Montana and reaches well into northern Wyoming. Traditionally a farm-marketing and energy production center, Billings has recently diversified its economy, especially toward health care and transportation. Great Falls

serves as a regional hub for north-central Montana; its looming grain storage facilities and the large Malmstrom Air Force missile base on the east edge of town symbolize the driving engines of its economy. Strategically situated Missoula serves as the hub of the western, mountainous region of the state, its economy heavily geared toward wood products, recreation, transportation, and higher education.

In the next tier are four more cities with populations ranging from 25,000 to 35,000: Bozeman, Butte, Helena, and Kalispell. These small cities resemble their larger sisters on a lesser scale. Each commands a sizable subregion; each houses substantial print and electronic media, as well as medical, service, and shopping facilities. Butte, Kalispell, and especially Bozeman—like Billings and Missoula—are magnets for Montana's small but growing high-tech and high-service industries.

Beneath this tier lies another of yet smaller cities with populations in the five thousand to ten thousand range, including fast-growing Lewistown, hard-hit

In 1942, as defense spending increased in response to U.S. entry into World War II, the federal government established a large Army Air Corps base on the outskirts of Great Falls. Known today as Malmstrom Air Force Base, it has so far survived a post–Cold War cutback in the number of U.S. military bases and remains a vital economic force in Cascade County.
Photo by Stuart S. White

Alpenglow highlights the snowy summits of the Whitefish
Range and, beyond them, the peaks of Glacier National Park.
Photo by Chuck Haney

Students from the small ranching community of Two Dot enjoy a momentary diversion from the tedium of schoolwork circa 1917. Montana has long been legendary for its plethora of school districts, many of them very small.
Photo courtesy of the Montana Historical Society

Havre, and others like Miles City, Glendive, Sidney, Whitefish, Livingston, and Hamilton. At the broad base of the community pyramid lie dozens of small towns that form the rural backbone of the state.

Over the course of the twentieth century, this far-flung state not surprisingly has developed far-flung systems of both elementary-secondary and higher education in which the priority has obviously been more upon geographic access than upon investing in quality. This is especially true of kindergarten through high school education, which in Montana has long been legendary for its plethora of school districts, many of them very small and some even of the old-fashioned "one-room" variety. On the eve of World War II, the state supported a mind-boggling 2,100 school districts, roughly one for each 260 people! As of the mid-1990s, it still had about 480 districts, a number that equals or exceeds the number in far larger states. To the surprise of many, these small schools do quite well in preparing their graduates to compete in college and in the workplace.

Montana's system of public colleges and universities also grew up after 1893 as a dispersed, multi-unit organization. The legislature initially located a comprehensive university at Missoula, a land-grant college at Bozeman, a normal college at Dillon, and a mining-technology campus at Butte. During the 1920s, two new normal schools opened their doors at Billings and Havre. Then, three regional community colleges arose, first with local and then state support, followed by five vocational-technical campuses in various cities. Actually, such a dispersed, multi-campus system is the rule rather than the exception in the West; and all of the campuses except for the community colleges, increasingly more developed although still severely underfunded, were consolidated by the Board of Regents in 1994. The University of Montana at Missoula assumed administration of schools in the western region, while Montana State University-Bozeman assumed administration in the east-central region.

One of the most remarkable and edifying aspects of Montana's twentieth-century history has been its cultural achievements, which are quite exceptional, especially in view of its sparse population. Take, for instance, the prestige of major cultural institutions of international renown, such as the Montana Historical Society at Helena and the C. M. Russell Museum at Great Falls, both famed for their Russell collections, and the Museum of the Rockies at Montana State University in Bozeman, noted especially for its paleontology and planetarium programs. There are numerous others of regional and even broader distinction, among them the Western Heritage Center and Yellowstone Art Museum Centers in Billings, Northern Lights Institute in Missoula, and the World Museum of Mining in Butte.

In the arts and literature, the Treasure State has won a truly impressive measure of renown over the past century, a tribute both to the appeal of the place aesthetically and physically and to the creative people living in and attracted to it. Of course, the man who made his name synonymous with art here was Charles M. Russell, who already had a well-established reputation by the dawn of the century and who was famous by the time he died in the mid-1920s. Russell's beautiful paintings, sketches, and sculptures majestically captured the pristine frontier environment and its Indian and pioneer peoples. Every March, his hometown of Great Falls hosts one of the world's premier art auctions in his name. Naturally, he also spawned a host of imitators, some of whom, like Edgar Paxson of Butte and Missoula and Russell's friend Olaf Seltzer of Great Falls, also rose to eminence themselves.

The artistic heirs of Russell and Seltzer are still very popular here today, witness the ubiquitous works of Gary Carter or Jack Hines or the fine sculptures of Bob Scriver. What surprises many observers is the impressive outpouring of nontraditional, modern, and impressionistic art the state has meanwhile produced, a good representation of which can be seen in the Yellowstone Art Center's Montana Collection. Excellent examples of such work are the modernist landscape paintings of the late Isabelle Johnson of Absarokee, the large steel sculptures of James Reineking of Billings, the fine horse sculptures of Deborah Butterfield of Bozeman, the widely acclaimed pastel landscapes of Russell Chatham of Livingston, and the expansive fabric art of Dana Boussard of Arlee.

During the early years of the century, writers like James Willard Schultz and Frank Bird Linderman gained a measure of fame, particularly for their writing about Indians. But the great harvest of regional writing came with the second half of the century, much of it under the stimulus of the exceptional creative-writing program founded at the University of Montana by H. G. Merriam. In addition to Dorothy Johnson, popular historian Joseph Kinsey Howard, and poet Richard Hugo, the outstanding writers of this generation included A. B. Guthrie, Jr., and Norman Maclean. Guthrie's *The Big Sky* (1947), a study of the fur trade, is one of the best historical novels ever written; and the lead story in Maclean's *A River Runs Through It* (1976) is one of the most hauntingly beautiful in all American literature.

The 1980s and 1990s have witnessed an even greater profusion of regional literature. Among the best of these contemporary authors are the fine Indian novelist James Welch, regionalist William Kittredge, central Montana novelist Mary Clearman Blew, naturalist David Quammen, and Ivan Doig, whose poignant memoir *This House of Sky* (1979) launched him upon a remarkably productive career that has resulted most recently in *Bucking the Sun* (1996), which is set amidst the construction of Fork Peck Dam. Also deserving of special note are Thomas McGuane, the writer of screenplays, short stories, and particularly ribald novels like *Nothing But Blue Skies* (1992), and Richard Ford, who has claimed Missoula and Chinook as home and who won the 1996 Pulitzer Prize for his novel *Independence Day*. This is a remarkable record for such a small state.

THE 1990S

Montana entered the final decade of the twentieth century in a dichotomous situation. Peculiarly, at one and the same time, the economy strengthened but voter unrest waxed even stronger than before. With plentiful precipitation, the agricultural economy rebounded; and contrary to anticipation, the wood-products industry remained relatively strong. Meanwhile, the tourist business continued to grow impressively, and so did retail trade and services which, along with a strong construction boom, accounted for almost three-fourths of the new jobs rapidly proliferating in the economy by mid-decade.

By the summer of 1994, the Treasure State boasted 431,600 jobs, the largest total in its history, and an unem-

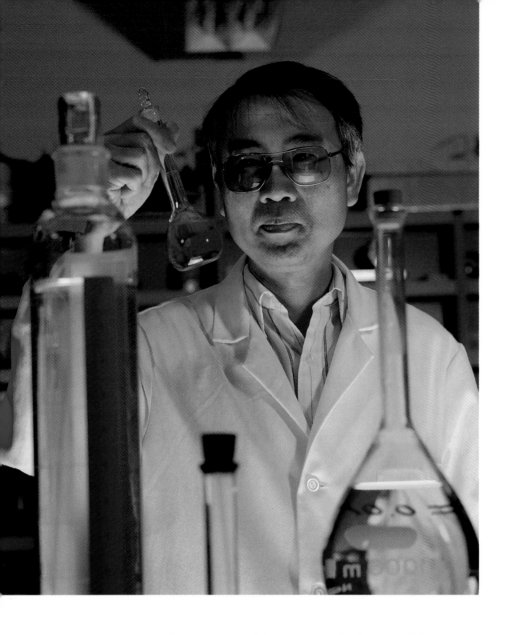

Dr. Hsing-Hsiung Huang, a scientist at Montana Tech in Butte, analyzes groundwater taken from the Berkeley Pit. Besides offering degrees in the technical sciences, Montana Tech is home to the state's Bureau of Mines and Geology.
Photo by John Reddy

ployment rate of four percent, the lowest in fifteen years. Butte scored well in drawing a new computer-chip material manufacturing firm, as did Great Falls in luring CUC International, a computing services company. In addition, a number of high-technology firms grew and thrived in the state, among them Ribi Immunochem at Hamilton, Semitool at Kalispell, and substantial clusters of such companies at Butte and especially at Bozeman, where laser-optic and other cutting-edge firms are linked to the science and engineering programs at Montana State University.

Admittedly, these impressive growth statistics also masked some troublesome trends. Here as elsewhere, many of the new service-sector jobs were low-end, even menial, in nature, including fast-food vending and janitorial work; and to those who had to take them after losing well-paying blue-collar jobs, the jolt to both family incomes and self-esteem could be truly severe. With an average 1994 annual income of $17,865, Montana ranked only forty-first among states, $4,000 below the national mean. But, in contrast to the severe loss of quality jobs in the 1980s, the 1990s truly marked a time of recovery and growth.

Politically, the fin-de-siècle decade saw a continuation of two pronounced trends of the 1980s: toward conservative Republicanism and toward populist anti-tax and anti-government utilization of the direct ballot. In the interesting election of 1992, Montana's two congressional districts were collapsed into one, as the state lost one congressman due to low population growth in the preceding decade. This forced its two congressmen, liberal Democrat Pat Williams and conservative Republican Ron Marlenee, to run against one another, and Williams narrowly won. Meanwhile, in the gubernatorial race, the moderate-conservative Republican Marc Racicot defeated liberal Democratic legislator Dorothy Bradley. Both candidates endorsed a sales tax, which residents would vote on in a June 1993 special election.

Predictably, when that election rolled around, the people once again buried the sales tax by a vote of three to one. But the plot thickened immeasurably when a coalition of tax protesters led by University of Montana law professor Rob Natelson and Ross Perot's United We Stand organization used the state's easy direct-ballot system to block a measure that would have raised income taxes to compensate for the lost sales tax. Then, in the 1994 election, the conservative trend reached new heights as Republican Senator Conrad Burns won re-election and as Republicans, many of them far-right freshmen, swept control of the legislature. The arch-conservatives tasted defeat, though, when Constitutional Initiatives 66 and 67, each of which would have severely limited the ability of legislatures and other public decision-making bodies to increase taxes and fees, even to deal with the effects of inflation, were defeated by the voters.

The legislature itself amply reflected the rising tide of conservatism and anti-government, anti-tax sentiment. A series of regular and special sessions from 1992 through 1994 slashed appropriations, especially to education, and grudgingly focused investments on the burgeoning costs of prisons, on Medicaid and welfare programs, and on dealing with the ballooning costs of the Workers' Compensation Fund. Then the 1995 session proved to be the most conservative in many years; despite a budget surplus, lawmakers slashed already lean budgets to facilitate nearly forty million dollars in promised tax breaks. In fact, the large Republican majorities in both houses, which included many far-right freshmen, sometimes clashed with their own, more moderate Republican governor.

The conservative tide continued to flow, perhaps a bit less strongly, into the 1996 campaign and election. While incumbent Governor Racicot rode his remarkable popularity to easy re-election and Democratic Senator Max Baucus won a tougher fight to keep his seat, Billings businessman Rick Hill captured for the Republicans the state's sole congressional seat, which veteran incumbent Pat Williams had earlier abandoned by retirement. Once again the Republicans, many of them on the far right, won control of both houses of the legislature. By the late 1990s, the prospect of further

budget cutting threatened to drag Montana into last place, or very near it, in many if not most measures of public program support in America.

This seeming anomaly—of budget cutting amidst relative prosperity—could be attributed simply to a growing rightward shift in the Treasure State. In 1996, for example, even as a large majority of states supported presidential candidate Bill Clinton, Montana joined the interior West in voting against him. But undoubtedly, the budget cutting is also the natural result of a badly unbalanced tax system. Anti-tax protestors, some of them clearly extremist and misusing data, wished to reduce income taxes and lower or even eliminate property taxes, while at the same time the majority refused to consider a sales tax. This situation has lead the state ever deeper into a cul-de-sac from which it can neither meet the needs of its citizens nor compete with other states, not to mention nations.

On the other hand, the 1990s found Montana riding higher than ever in the firmament of national and even global awareness. With each passing year, it seemed that the state was more romanticized and held up as a paragon not only of a vanishing "West" and of untrammeled nature, but also of a way of life fast slipping away, as captured by the frequently used descriptors "the last of what is best" and "the last best place." All of this can be seen in the big buy-up of choice lands by the wealthy from out-of-state, in the increasing use of "Montana" signatures in clothing and other trendy designs, in the popularity of writings by Montanans and about Montana, and especially in Hollywood's new preoccupation with the place. The many examples of the latter include such films as *A River Runs Through It*, *Far and Away*, and *The River Wild*. There are also frequent references to the place, such as the sounds of sheep being slaughtered in *The Silence of the Lambs*, the dying wish of a Soviet submarine commander to see it in *The Hunt for Red October*, and the movie-ending escape to it in *Short Circuit*.

With this fame, which Montanans enjoyed even as they often ridiculed it, suddenly came a large measure of

Mount Haggin, at 10,598 feet, is one of several peaks in the lofty Anaconda-Pintlar Wilderness to surpass 10,000 feet. This wilderness area southwest of Butte and Anaconda straddles 40 miles of the Continental Divide, encompassing alpine meadows and lakes and windswept, often snowcapped, ridges.
Photo by Michael Sample

notoriety as well, a stereotyped image of the state as a haven for extremists and nuts. Like all stereotypes, this one bore some measure of truth, since some truly radical organizations have been attracted to the state's wide open spaces and conservative milieu, and since some extremist politicians have even consorted with them. The most notorious are the Militia of Montana in the west and the Freemen in the east, both rooted in earlier organizations and both preoccupied with perceived foreign and racial threats, irrational hatred and fear of the government, and arming themselves. During the first half of 1996, Montanans suddenly found themselves the focus of twin lead stories on the evening television news, what with the Freemen standoff of federal agents near Jordan coinciding with the astounding news that the alleged "Unabomber" terrorist happened to be one of their fellow citizens at Lincoln.

Just as Montana's claim to be "the last best place" is hardly unique or uncontested, the extremist label, too, is hardly appropriate, although other actions of the state have encouraged such stereotyping. Among these were the madcap effort of some legislators in 1995 to treat homosexuals as if they were convicted felons and the state's notorious refusal to enumerate a highway speed limit, both of which attracted a torrent of ridicule. The truth is that the Treasure State has continued to move toward the right end of the American political spectrum, but it also remains well within the confines of that spectrum.

The real truth about Montana, as it approaches the close of this eventful century, is that no simple description of it is adequate. It still remains a natural-products state, especially an agricultural state, and seems likely to remain so long into the future; but its economy has markedly diversified, especially in a few urban locales, and it has moved much more markedly into full integration with the world economic order. In contrast to the frenzied growth of the early twentieth century, or the emigration of the 1920s, or the depression of the 1980s, the end of the century in Montana is characterized by relative prosperity and moderate growth. Montana has matured and stabilized.

Socially and demographically, the state likewise defies easy or simple analysis. Larger communities such as Butte and Anaconda and smaller cities like Glendive and Cut Bank have been hard hit, and the general trend of rural depopulation and urban growth still continues. In general, Western Montana grows while the eastern prairies continue to lose population. While the Treasure State is cultivating more quality jobs, the flight of those in their prime toward areas of greater opportunity continues; and in contrast to the first decades of the century, it remains a state of the young and old, with a relatively small young-adult and middle-aged populace.

For all the changes the twentieth century has wrought upon the Treasure State, the constants of its history are more compelling than are the vacillations. Montana remains a small state, a slow-growth state, a natural-products state, a "quality of life" state, a state on the margin rather than at the center of national life; and generally speaking, that seems to be the way most of her people want it to be. The great challenge facing Montanans with the dawn of the twenty-first century is how to maintain and build the socioeconomic substance of that vaunted quality of life by supporting the good jobs and stable communities that are required to make it possible.

The Eye of the Needle, a natural landmark about 50 miles downstream from Fort Benton, impressed travelers on the Missouri River for centuries until vandals destroyed it in the spring of 1997. A citizens group has since suggested rebuilding the arch on its original site, but the Bureau of Land Management wants to construct a replica in Fort Benton.
Photo by Chuck Haney

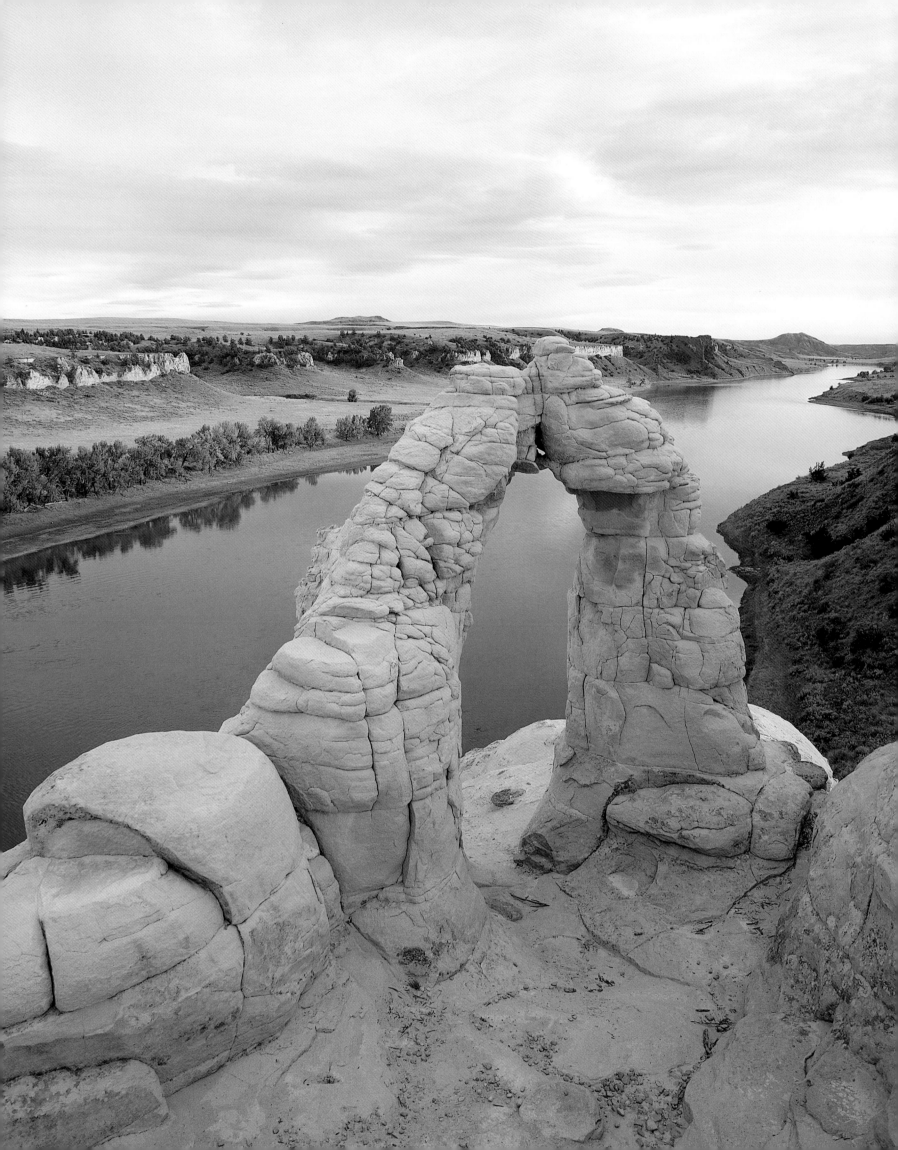

BIG ENOUGH FOR MAGPIES

WILD MONTANA IN THE TWENTIETH CENTURY

Here's an impossible task with which to amuse and bedevil yourself during the long, lonely drive from Lewistown to Malta, or as you endure afternoon rush-minute at a stoplight in uptown Butte: Choose a single animal to serve as token of the natural world in this state during the twentieth century. No fair consulting Montana Wildlife, *the glossy and informative picture book by Robert C. Gildart. No peeking at back issues of* Montana Outdoors.

If your mind turns to the bison, the bighorn, the moose, the grizzly, the Hereford, the gray wolf, or the westslope cutthroat, you can certainly offer a plausible case. Each of those creatures has its moments of resonant significance in the modern history of our shared place. If you lean toward the rainbow trout, the brown trout, Merriam's turkey, or the ring-necked pheasant, you might want to recall that none of them is an aboriginal native—but of course neither is the Hereford, nor the horse, nor the White man and woman. (Then again, it's also worth recalling that *everybody* hereabouts belongs to what, within some time scale or another, is an immigrant lineage, whether his ancestors arrived one hundred years ago via Ellis Island or fifteen thousand years ago via ocean-going canoe.) If you opt for the western meadowlark, our unexceptional but official state bird, my advice is to loosen up and let your mind fly in wider arcs. And if you say *Tyrannosaurus rex* (an indigenous Montana species, true enough) or the duckbill dinosaur, it's a

symptom that you've seen too many replays of *Jurassic Park*. Turn off your VCR and go outside.

How about the coyote, that most despised and resourceful of survivors? Or the grayling, that most beautiful and gentle of cold-river fish? Both are reasonable candidates, yes. But I'd offer another. My own choice for totemic animal, to represent the natural world as we Montanans have known it and acted upon it during this century, is the magpie.

The black-billed species is the one among us, *Pica pica* in scientific nomenclature, native to every Montana county. Unlike the Canada goose, unlike the white pelican, unlike the tourist, it doesn't escape southward in winter. This big flashy black-and-white bird, with its long tail and its bluish iridescent highlights, is here to stay. It's abundant, familiar, bold, opportunistic, disreputable, complicated, smart, and too often taken for granted. Taxonomically speaking, it's a corvid, closely related to those other bright and crafty devils, the ravens and crows. Personally speaking, I've

BY DAVID QUAMMEN

Opposite: Elegant in black and white, the magpie, according to writer David Quammen, is "abundant, familiar, bold, opportunistic, disreputable, complicated, smart, and too often taken for granted"—the perfect creature to serve "as a token of the natural world in this state during the 20th century."
Photo by Michael Sample

Above: Montana's Sun River Canyon is home to one of the largest native herds of Rocky Mountain bighorn sheep in the nation. The ram's horns, easily its most impressive feature, are truly horns; they are not shed each year like the antlers of elk or deer. Annual growth rings make it possible to determine the animal's age. *Photo by Michael Sample*

Opposite: Montana is one of the last stomping grounds of the powerful and majestic grizzly, which was named the official state animal in 1983. Once a plentiful inhabitant of the plains, the grizzly dwindled in numbers as its habitat shrank until, in 1973, it was declared a federally threatened species. As a result of this protected status, the grizzly population has begun to rebound to the point that some now argue for its declassification. Today, more than 900 grizzlies call Montana home. *Photo by Daniel J. Cox*

been biased in its favor ever since an afternoon near the confluence of the Clark Fork and Bitterroot Rivers, twentysome years ago, when I encountered an extraordinarily trusting magpie that would perch on my arm and eat grasshoppers out of my hand. Then it followed me back to my truck, but at the last minute declined to get in. Had that bird been reared and half-tamed by someone else, I've always wondered, and then abandoned to its own devices on Blue Mountain? I'll never know. The character of *Pica pica*, like its coloring, entails some shimmery subtleties beyond the piebald simplicity that shows to first glance.

Furthermore, its situation in Montana has changed drastically during this century, and that change reflects larger changes of public attitude, understanding, and purpose. To appreciate those changes and the magpie's position among them, we need to consider first a few facts, events, and historical trends.

The state of Montana comprises 147,046 square miles of landscape beneath exactly 147,046 square miles of sky—though civic pride and folkloric convention require us to note that the latter sometimes seems even bigger. About fifteen hundred square miles of that area is water surface, meaning lakes and rivers, and roughly forty thousand square miles stands in forest. There's also a vast area of prairie—so vast that a glance in any direction from the town of Ingomar, say, at sunrise on a clear day in autumn, can open your head like a decongestant. One of the first and most difficult feats of imaginative governance in our history was to recognize that this landscape, though huge, though bounteous in flora and fauna, is not infinite.

That recognition was registered back in 1864, when the first territorial legislature passed "An Act in Relation to Trout Fishing," mandating the use of rods and lines only, prohibiting seines, poisons, or nets. The gold boom had just begun, and the region was aswarm with hard-working, meat-hungry miners. Responding fast to the seller's market, commercial operators had started supplying mass quantities of fish and game to the placer camps. Responding almost as fast, the legislators moved to impose some restraints, so that individual citizens would still have their own chances for dinner and sport. A later bill, giving equivalent protection to moose, elk, both species of deer, bighorn, Rocky Mountain goat, and a few other mammals, became law in 1872.

It's no accident that these two early bills were sponsored by James and Granville Stuart, the brothers who played key roles not just in settling Montana but in defining it as an exceptional place. But such statutory protection (unsupported by effective enforcement) wasn't enough, especially after a company back East developed a way to make leather from buffalo robes. Commercial hunting for meat and hides continued; the slaughter of buffalo in particular became hysterical after Custer's defeat, as part of that infamous campaign to destroy the Indian peoples and their cultures. What was probably the last wild bison in Montana was killed near Billings in 1888. As the century neared its close, the state looked like an abattoir.

One measure of how badly market hunters had depleted game was the total closure of moose hunting in 1893, not to be reopened for fifty-two years. Other species stood likely to follow the moose and the bison to the brink of eradication. "In the late 80's and early 90's the markets featured elk and venison steaks, bear roasts, wild ducks and geese, swans, grouse," according to an outdoor columnist and historian named John Willard, writing forty years ago. "The prices were high and market hunters were glad to supply what the trade demanded." The people who stood to lose most—or at least, most immediately—from this meat rush were those for whom hunting and fishing were important but noncommercial pastimes. That's why the conservation movement in Montana drew its earliest energy and focus from the jealous, well-founded concerns of sportsmen.

Local sportsmen's clubs were the first evidence of this movement. In 1877 the Helena Rifle Club became the first sporting club in the territory, with Granville Stuart among its founding members. The Deer Lodge Rod and Gun Club followed in 1880, and then similar groups in Bozeman, Billings, and Butte. These clubs

petitioned the territorial legislature for a "Game and Fish Detective" to provide some enforcement. Their petition failed, but after statehood the idea took form as a Board of Game and Fish Commissioners (created in 1895) and then a State Game and Fish Warden (appointed in 1901). So the century's turning coincided with a milestone of conservation: Someone had finally been empowered to enforce the laws and regulations.

The first state warden was William F. Scott, a sober-looking young man with a handlebar mustache, from

Previous page: Two moose wade the Falls River in Yellowstone National Park. The largest member of the deer family (bulls can weigh more than 1,000 pounds), the moose makes its home along streams, lakes, and marshes in mountainous Western Montana. Its diet consists primarily of aquatic plants, willows, and grasses. *Photo by Michael Sample*

Left: After its near-extermination in Montana in the early 1900s, the wolf made a dramatic comeback near the close of the century, both by expanding its range across the Canadian border into the state's northern reaches and through a dramatic and controversial reintroduction program in Yellowstone. National Park. *Photo by Daniel J. Cox*

Opposite: A bull elk and his harem congregate at Mammoth Hot Springs in Yellowstone National Park. Many of the elk that summer in Yellowstone spend their winters just outside the park at lower elevations in Montana. *Photo by Jeff Foott*

Deer Lodge. In his second biennial report, after four years of work, he declared that "the slaughter has been stopped and killing in violation of the law reduced to a minimum." Moose and caribou were already doing better, thanks to their no-kill-whatsoever status. Elk were again plentiful. Deer were everywhere. He suggested some changes in the timing of bird seasons, for the sake of grouse, prairie chickens, and—significantly—pheasants. So we know from William F. Scott himself that the exotic pheasant species *Phasianus colchicus*, native to Asia and first released in Montana sometime in the late nineteenth century, had by 1904 become an object of solicitous management.

Two other signal events in the old century should be noted before we leave it. In 1879 a bounty on mountain lions was established. Four years later, the territorial legislators passed a law extending bounties to bears, wolves, and coyotes.

The wolf bounty was a dollar each, and the hunter was allowed also to sell the pelt for whatever he could get. During the law's first full year, bounties were paid on 5,450 wolves, 1,774 coyotes, 565 bears, and 146 lions. This 1883 bounty law had been enacted in response to concerns of stockgrowers, not of sportsmen, during what one historian has called the "cowboy legislature," suggesting that it was notably more rancher-friendly than most. But in the early decades of the century those two categories of people, stockgrowers and sportsmen, would converge on a shared attitude about predatory animals—until, still later, they would again diverge.

This brings us to a matter of language and of the implicit judgments sometimes enshrined within words. *Game* and *fish* were terms carrying a sense of the value accorded to "good" wild animals, animals that supplied food and sport. *Predator*, on the other hand, was in those days an invidious term, not a neutral description of an

"Old Trapper John," seen here relaxing at his cabin west of Dillon circa 1910, took full advantage of Montana's abundance of fur-bearing mammals during the first decades of the 20th century. Obviously, he profited, too, from the bounties paid on predators. *Photo courtesy of the Montana Historical Society*

ecological role; it applied to "bad" wild animals that sometimes killed livestock and routinely killed game. Fish and game were protected so that they might flourish and multiply, or at least sustain their populations against a calibrated human take. Predators were not merely unprotected but bountied so that they might be severely reduced, maybe even eradicated; they could be shot, trapped, poisoned at liberty, and the more so the better. Any creature that didn't qualify as game or a game fish or a predator fell into a hazy, indeterminate status with which lawmakers and other practical-minded people weren't concerned. The word *wildlife*, in turn-of-the-century Montana, was seldom heard.

And that's how things stood for roughly the next fifty years. Some academic scientists (such as Dr. Morton J. Elrod, an intriguing figure, professor of biology at Missoula and director of the biological station on Flathead Lake, who not only served as chairman of the Game and Fish Commission in 1900 but also, around the same time, published a book titled *The Butterflies of Montana*) were attuned to wildlife in a broader sense. And there were citizens, going back as far as Granville Stuart, who admired songbirds for their own sake. But public stewardship of the state's fauna and flora consisted almost solely of fish and game management and forestry (a whole different subject, though with some similar historical trends, involving changes in thinking about fire management and non-timber resources). Both were practiced to the best of the abilities and to the limits in scope of the earnest, diligent people who made careers of them.

With fish and game management, the goal was simple: maximize the supply of "good" animals available for

hunters and fishermen. The means were various but fairly simple also: fish hatcheries, producing millions of small trout (mostly non-native species) and grayling to be dumped into rivers and lakes; game preserves, in which elk, deer, bear, sheep, and other species could find refuge, thereby enhancing their reproductive success and sending them spilling back out (so it was hoped) to propagate the surrounding landscape; recurrent introductions of non-native game animals, such as the pheasant, the Hungarian partridge, and the chukar; transplanting of native game animals from one part of the state to another; and predator control. This was essentially the five-point program of fish and game management in Montana during the first half of the twentieth century.

The earliest hatchery had been built in Bozeman back in 1896, with another added in Anaconda a decade later, then still others. The first game preserves were established in 1911, one being the Snow Creek Game Preserve in Dawson County, intended primarily for antelope; the Sun River Game Preserve, eventually famed for its elk in particular, came into being in 1913.

Opposite: In 1988, forest fires roared out of control, burning 900,000 acres in Yellowstone National Park and 1.3 million acres in the Greater Yellowstone region. A combination of scant precipitation and plenty of fuel in the forests made for tinder-box conditions across the Northern Rockies that year. *Photo by Jeff & Alexa Henry*

Above: A bull bison crosses the road in the midst of firefighters and fire trucks battling the destructive Yellowstone fires of 1988. Though most of the wild animals in Yellowstone easily outran the flames, some were trapped and killed by sudden firestorms. In all, 254 large park mammals, mostly elk, died in the fires. *Photo by Jeff & Alexa Henry*

Below: Mountain goats are a thrilling sight for visitors to Glacier National Park. Louis Hill, son of railroad magnate James J. Hill and a major promoter of the park's tourism potential, adopted the animal as an enduring symbol for Hill's Great Northern Railway. It has also come to symbolize the park, which was established in 1910. *Photo by Michael Sample*

Above: A proud angler displays a 17-pound bull trout taken from the South Fork Flathead River. In 1963, state lawmakers passed one of the first stream preservation laws in the nation, then followed it with a series of laws designed to protect water quality and streambed integrity. As a result, Montana today can boast a wild-trout sport fishery of national significance. *Photo by Henry Thol, courtesy of the Montana Historical Society*

Opposite: Sunlight, snow, and shadow define the contours of Great Northern Mountain, on the east side of Hungry Horse Reservoir in northwestern Montana. *Photo by Michael Sample*

By 1935, at the peak of this strategy, there were forty-six game preserves across Montana. The earliest introductions of pheasants had not yielded thriving populations, according to Warden Scott, but the species was popular with hunters, so the stocking continued. Between 1909 and 1929, about seven thousand farm-raised pheasants were released. As for transplantations, the 1940s seems to have been their heyday; there was a transfer of mountain goats from Teton County to the Crazy Mountains in Sweet Grass County (1941), a transfer of bighorns from Teton County to the Gates of the Mountains area near Helena (1942), a transfer of mule deer from the bison range at Moiese to the Glendive badlands (1943), and a transfer of antelope from Broadwater County to Gallatin County (1946). Presumably it would have been much easier to truck the hunters from county to county instead of the game, but I suppose that misses the point.

Finally, predator control. The prevailing notion about this enterprise was expressed in the biennial report of the Fish and Game Commission (as it was called by then) for 1923–1924: "There is no better way to propagate game animals or game birds than by destroying the predatory animals and predatory birds that live upon them." Guided by such false certitude, the commission had set aside five hundred dollars from license fees as prize money for whichever rod and gun clubs destroyed the most predators in 1924. The published tally shows that sportsmen had proudly claimed credit for killing 6 lynx, 6 badgers, 25 kingfishers, 169 woodchucks, 211 great horned owls, 217 weasels, 783 hawks, and 23,287 gophers. They had also destroyed 12,927 magpies and 18,076 magpie eggs. I take this to be the low point in the sporting history of Montana.

Later, when magpies were saddled with an actual bounty, the going rate was ten cents per dead bird. Although the species may have qualified for despised-predator status on various grounds, its most notorious form of predation was practiced—rarely? often? nobody knew—against the eggs and the nestlings of ring-necked pheasants. Natural-history studies had documented that magpies feed on insects (especially grasshoppers in late summer and fall), rodents, carrion, and wild fruit, but those innocent if not redeeming traits tended to be overlooked in the heat of loathing. They also eat grain, which might have made them a minor annoyance to farmers. And there was concern (not necessarily unfounded) among ranchers that magpies, as well as ravens and crows, might occasionally peck out the eyes of newborn calves.

These other grounds for animus against *Pica pica* are small details that figure within a larger truth—that sportsmen weren't the only practitioners of, nor the only clients for, predator control in general. Because stockgrowers also had a stake, a cooperative relationship had been established among the state Livestock Commission, the Fish and Game Commission, and the federal Biological Survey (then part of the Department of Agriculture), using pooled funds to employ professional hunters and trappers. As reported in that same 1923–1924 biennial Fish and Game report, the professional trappers in 1924 had killed 12 mountain lions, 68 badgers, 73 wolves, 111 bobcats, 488 porcupines, and 4,080 coyotes. Evidently the professionals didn't trouble themselves with magpies, or else they just didn't bother to keep count.

We need to remember that all this predator-killing in Montana was no crude, anomalous holdover of frontier severity. Apart from the livestock-protection aspect, it was game management as best understood and most conscientiously practiced throughout much of America at that time. Even the National Park Service embraced it, killing wolves, lions, coyotes, bobcats, foxes, otters, mink, and pelicans (for the sake of trout) in Yellowstone and other parks. Even the iconic conservationist Aldo Leopold, in 1933, devoted a chapter of his book *Game Management* (a teaching text written for professional game managers, quite different from his posthumously published *A Sand County Almanac*, by which the general public knows him) to predator control, treating it as a complex but indispensable tool of the trade.

During the 1950s, though, conventional wisdom changed, as the game-management profession in Montana and elsewhere became informed by the science of ecology. Predation was a fascinating subject, a major focus of ecological research, and some ecologists had documented that the relationship between any given predator species and the population size of a given prey species was far more complicated than previously thought. Two leaders in that area were the Craighead twins, Frank and John. In 1956 they published a book about avian predator-prey relations, titled *Hawks, Owls and Wildlife*. It was based on several years' worth of strenuous field studies (including a lot of tree-climbing) in southeastern Michigan. "Predation is one of nature's normal, effective, and continually operating mechanisms for regulating wildlife populations," the Craigheads wrote. "Man, in managing wildlife, both desirable and undesirable, not only must take account of this function, but must understand the mechanics of it and as far as possible aid nature's efficient regulation to operate smoothly." They distinguished between a controlling effect (such as predation) that might crop off some portion of a prey population and, on the other hand, a set of less obvious factors (food supply, weather fluctuations, habitat) that might set the prey population's ultimate limits. Their point: More dead predators don't necessarily mean more living game.

"It would be well if the sportsman no longer thought of the number of Ring-necked Pheasants taken by a Horned Owl or the Bob-white consumed by a red fox as

Above: Each year, a mule deer buck sheds its antlers and grows a set of new ones. Mule deer are the most common species of deer in Montana. They can be found in virtually every type of habitat in all parts of the state. *Photo by Donald M. Jones*

Below: The great, or common, egret was close to extinction in 1900 because its magnificent plumes were popularly used to make women's hats. Its population rebounded only after the passage of international conservation laws and a ban on imports. Today, the bird faces yet another threat: its habitat is dwindling as wetlands are drained to make way for development.
Photo by Michael Sample

Opposite: Like many red foxes, these pups make their home in an open field or meadow not far from the cover of forest. Despite its name, the red fox is not always red. It can be silver, black, or marked with a dark cross across its back, but it can always be identified by its white-tipped tail.
Photo by Donald M. Jones

an indication of whether predation should be tolerated or predators controlled," they advised. Likewise with the number of pheasant eggs consumed by a magpie, they might have added. One of the two brothers, John, would soon be directing a study of exactly that question.

By this time the word *wildlife*, the notion of academic training in wildlife management skills, and the science of ecology had all arrived in Montana. So had John Craighead. The state's first degree in a discipline called wildlife technology had been granted at the University of Montana in 1939. Nine years later, a wildlife management curriculum had been established at Montana State College in Bozeman, with help from the Fish and Game Department. Back again in Missoula, a Cooperative Wildlife Research Unit had been established in 1950 by the university, the Fish and Game Department, the U.S. Fish and Wildlife Service, and something called the Wildlife Management Institute, based in Washington, D.C. By 1956, Craighead was the unit's leader.

That year, he guided a graduate student named Robert L. Brown into the first phase of a multi-year, multi-researcher study of the population ecology of magpies and pheasants in a small but representative valley in Western Montana.

The study site was along Burnt Fork Creek, two miles above its junction with the Bitterroot River, east of Stevensville. It was a tiny area, just 6.3 square miles of pasture and grain fields and hay, bordered on the north and south by high benches, on the east by a sagebrush flat. Alder and birch, hawthorn and willow and wild rose fringed the stream channels and irrigation ditches. With its combination of water, grassland, and cover, the site constituted fair pheasant habitat and excellent nesting-ground for magpies. Small as it was, that 6.3 square miles was big enough to support 348 nesting pairs of magpies during the first year of Brown's study.

During the second year, he found almost exactly the same number: 351 nesting pairs. The notable thing about this result is that, despite having produced 2,314 eggs, despite having fledged 1,225 young from those eggs, the magpie population had increased hardly at all. Yet there was no systematic control program in effect. The number had been held stable, Brown concluded, by natural mortality. Lesson: It wasn't easy to be a magpie in Montana.

Three other graduate students followed Brown's tracks through the Burnt Fork site within the next half-dozen years, each under John Craighead's supervision. Gerry C. Atwell studied reproduction and mortality among the ring-necked pheasants, gauging the extent to which their population size was affected by magpie predation. Patrick L. O'Halloran conducted his own experimental program of magpie control, investigating how that might affect the pheasant population size and reproductive rate. He "removed" (that is, trapped and killed) 556 magpies, which was enough to cut the annual

Above: A cunning predator, the mountain lion moves as silently as snowfall through the Montana backcountry. Mountain lions are ordinarily secretive and wary of human beings. But as humans have encroached more and more on lion habitat, encounters between cats and people have increased. *Photo by Daniel J. Cox*

Opposite: Biologists with Montana Fish, Wildlife & Parks conduct research on the rare fluvial grayling on the Big Hole River, one of the state's most famous wild-trout fishing rivers. The upper Big Hole is believed to be the only large river in the contiguous United States where grayling can be caught with regularity. *Photo by Jeff & Alexa Henry*

average number of nesting pairs by half. Then in 1963, drawing on the three earlier studies as well as his own two years of fieldwork, Robert L. Ruff wrote a master's thesis analyzing the question of whether magpie control at Burnt Fork had produced any significant benefit to the population of pheasants.

He concluded that the answer was no.

Although magpies did prey on pheasant eggs, Ruff found that skunks were a far more consequential enemy. Hay mowing also destroyed a sizable number of nests. The bottom line of Ruff's study was that—population ecology being what it is, an intricate tangle of factors—exterminating hundreds of magpies in the Burnt Fork area had virtually no effect, so far as pheasants were concerned, on the bottom line.

The Fish and Game Department was absorbing this new wisdom, partly through hiring young scientists trained by people like John Craighead. The first of the Burnt Fork investigators, Robert L. Brown, joined the department as a predator biologist soon after graduation. He even published a little information bulletin, under the department's imprint, titled "Magpie Ups and Downs," which described his own research by way of explaining why, in 1958, the Fish and Game Commission had rescinded its longtime offer of matching funds to sportsmen's clubs for paying bounties on crows and magpies.

That was no isolated event. In 1962 the bounty on mountain lions was dropped, and eight years later *Felis concolor* was classified a game animal—giving it the protection of a valued population in exchange for the travail of being hunted for sport, a bargain under which it seems to have thrived. By 1972, throughout America, attitudes toward predatory animals had changed, among both professionals and the public. They had changed so much, in fact, that a heroic act of conservation polity was performed that year by President Richard Nixon, of all people, when he signed Executive Order 11643, prohibiting the use of any chemical toxicants (such as strychnine, cyanide, or 1080) for killing predators on federal lands. Back here in Montana, the change showed in an official policy statement published by the Fish and Game Department. It was drafted by Jim Posewitz, a wildlife manager of the new sort, who would eventually spend thirty years within the department and become revered by many people as its wisest head on the subjects of conservation, professional independence from political pressures, and hunter ethics. Alluding to the Burnt Fork quartet and other studies, Posewitz wrote: "The preponderance of evidence indicates that predators have an acceptable and proper place within all animal populations; they are not only tolerable but, very likely, essential members of any animal community." Yes, Posewitz added, the Fish and Game Department did recognize the legitimacy of some concern among stockgrowers about predators, but that concern wasn't shared on behalf of wildlife. The department had come to appreciate that predators, like prey animals, are wildlife.

This change, enunciated by Posewitz twenty-five years ago, hasn't been the only one. Hatchery trucks no longer dump fishpond trout into Montana rivers already containing resident trout populations that would have been better off left alone. The game preserves, the transplanting of big mammals, the farm-rearing and releasing of pheasants and partridges have all been de-emphasized or abandoned. Sixty years after the wolf bounty was repealed because it had accomplished its purpose—total eradication—the wolf has recolonized Montana. The word *game* itself has disappeared from the name of the management body, now eloquently transformed into the Department of Fish, Wildlife and Parks. Habitat is presently recognized as the single most crucial issue for both fish and other forms of wildlife. Preserve habitat, improve habitat, restore habitat wherever possible, and the native creatures will flourish; otherwise, not. Preserving fish habitat means keeping sufficient water in the rivers and keeping bulldozers and chemical contaminants out. Preserving habitat for terrestrial animals means preventing Montana's forest and prairie wildlands from being further shredded and diced and degraded by careless resource extraction and land conversion.

To find ways in which we Montanans can live within our landscape and among our wildlife—rather than scraping away the landscape and subduing the wildlife to serve our needs and whims—is a tricky and arduous task, now occupying a number of private groups as well as a handful of public agencies. The shape of the threat has changed too. Market hunting is no longer a dire problem—unless you count market hunting for land. Among

Above: The oblique rays of day's end gild the Pryor Mountains in south-central Montana. *Photo by Michael Sample*

Opposite: A bull elk gorges on lush grasses and forbs to build up the fat reserves it will need to survive the rut and the tough Montana winter that will inevitably follow.
Photo by Michael Sample

the leading causes of habitat loss in the state nowadays, and arguably just as damaging as bad logging or bad mining practices, is subdivision. It's a dark irony of Montana's shining reputation that so much riparian habitat and winter range is being arrogated by people—some of them longtime residents who cherish the landscape deeply, some of them dilettantish sojourners who find it infatuating—for whom a twenty-acre home site in the countryside is preferable to a quarter-acre lot in town. Well, the arithmetic doesn't work. When everyone escapes to the wilds, the wilds become suburbia. There are some genuinely Thoreauvian souls among us, but we can't all be Henry David at Walden.

Not long ago I had a conversation with John Craighead that touched on this point. In his eighties now, he was retired from the university but still living in Missoula. I'd reached him by phone to ask a few questions about the Burnt Fork study, which in its odd, tiny, marginal way might be considered one of the definitive events in the modern history of Montana. We talked for a few minutes about magpies, about predators generally, about changes in attitudes toward predators among sportsmen and, to a lesser extent, among ranchers. Then I asked him about the Burnt Fork area today.

The magpie population seems to be way down, he said. Can't be sure why, because nobody has done a systematic study there in recent years. Also, the landscape itself has changed. Burnt Fork used to be pretty quiet, pretty rural, but you see a lot of homes up there now. "More and more, it's getting to be a subdivision," Dr. Craighead said.

Casting back into memory, he mentioned a day in 1953 when he'd taken his son goat hunting in the Bitterroots. Walking out after dark, they had come to an overlook and, gazing across the entire Bitterroot Valley, had seen very few lights. "The valley was essentially black at night. Well, if you fly over that now at night, it's all lit up. It's like flying over the eastern seaboard." As for the little drainage east of Stevensville, where 6.3 acres of hawthorn and alder and meadow had once harbored seven hundred nesting magpies, he said: "I think it's just a matter of time before the Burnt Fork would be called a subdivision. It's one of the things that concerns me a lot."

Size has always been an important part of Montana's extraordinary character, and size is no less crucial today. The state border still encompasses 147,046 acres, but some dimensions seem to have shrunk—dimensions of wildness, of tranquility, of time remaining before damage is irreparable. On the other hand, some things seem larger. We have greater diversity of talent and ideas. We have greater knowledge about how the natural world

functions, and maybe a little more patience in discussing with one another how to use it, enjoy it, care for it. We have more history behind us.

What we need now is largeness of imagination and of heart. We have sufficient space, if we choose to believe we do, for bison and elk and grayling and antelope and ranchers and farmers and town folk and grizzlies and coyotes. We have sufficient space even for wolves. And if the sky hanging over this state is as big as we like to think it is, then surely it's big enough for magpies.

"OH-P;SHE-DU WOK-PAH"
(MUDDY WATERS)

Montana Indians in the Twentieth Century

As Montana Indian tribes entered the twentieth century, they already had witnessed the destruction of the buffalo and the diminishment of their reserved lands. Their traditional way of life was gone, and the White population outnumbered theirs. The total population of the state in 1890 was 142,924, with an Indian population of 11,206, or 7.8 percent. By 1910, the state population had climbed to 376,053, while the Indian population had dropped to 10,745, or 2.9 percent.[1] As the end of the twentieth century nears, the 47,679 Indians on Montana's seven reservations represent the state's fastest growing ethnic group (5.9 percent of the total state population).

Indian population figures are affected by mixed-blood marriages and by tribal and federal definitions. When White settlers first began arriving in Montana and the West, most tribal members were full-blooded Indians, although there were a few mixed marriages between members of different tribes. Today, for the purpose of dispensing benefits, the federal government defines a Native American as someone who has at least a quarter Indian blood and who is an enrolled member of a federally recognized tribe. Most tribes require that an individual have a quarter tribal blood to be a member of that tribe. As a result of the federal definition, the number of enrollable Indians has decreased greatly, because the number of full-blooded Indians has decreased greatly.

The issue of the next century will be: Are tribes going to define themselves based on the federal definition, or are they going to use some other criterion to sustain their bloodlines? Right now, an Indian can enroll in only one tribe and can count, for federal purposes, only the blood quantum of that tribe. But what if the individual is half Crow and half Cheyenne? If he chooses to enroll in the Cheyenne tribe, does it make sense to consider him half-Indian instead of whole?

Indians in Montana today already face an uncertain future due to general trends established at the beginning of the century, trends that have characterized the relationship between Indian and White communities in the state ever since. The initial federal policy regarding

BY JEANNE OYAWIN EDER

Opposite: A Chippewa-Cree sun dance lodge on the Rocky Boy's Reservation catches the first light of day. The Cree and Chippewa were pushed into Montana from Canada and North Dakota in the 1870s. They were "landless" until the federal government finally gave them part of old Fort Assiniboine as a reservation in 1916. *Photo by Michael Crummett*

Above: Dressed in their best to attend a celebration in Eureka in 1910, members of the Kootenai tribe pause for a moment to pose for a photographer. *Photo courtesy of the Tobacco Valley Historical Museum*

Opposite: Northern Cheyenne elder Mary Looks Behind Lame Woman poses in 1993 in front of the log cabin at Busby in which she grew up. In the Northern Cheyenne culture, elders are accorded great respect because of their wisdom and their knowledge of tribal customs and stories.
Photo by Michael Crummett

Indians was to take everything the Indians owned and force them to assimilate into the White culture. The taking of Indian land and resources was the first attempt to force Indian people to acculturate, and that continues today with attempts to take away Indian hunting, fishing, and water rights.

The taking of Indian water rights began in 1927, after a series of floods damaged land along the Missouri River. Congress directed the U.S. Army Corps of Engineers to research ways to avoid future flooding. The resulting study, published in 1933, recommended the construction of a dam and reservoir at Fort Peck, Montana. The corps did not consult with the local Sioux tribes about the plan, and the Bureau of Indian Affairs did not alert the tribes to the potential drawbacks, pri-

marily the permanent destruction of rich bottomlands, until 1947.[2]

An explanation of some of the federal and state policies that have impacted life on Montana reservations will give some insight into how the Indian has fared in the twentieth century and may fare in the twenty-first.

EARLY POLICIES AND THEIR IMPACTS ON INDIANS

Until 1830, the American Indian nations were treated as sovereign entities, with all the rights to self-government that belonged to any nation with defined boundaries and populations. This included the right to negotiate with foreign powers.

Then, in 1832, the U.S. Supreme Court heard the case of *Worcester v Georgia*, one of three cases that have become the basis for determining issues of sovereignty in the field of Indian law. In this case, the state of Georgia passed a law requiring non-Indian residents of Cherokee County to secure a state license if they wanted to trade with the Cherokees. Samuel Worcester and several other non-Indian missionaries were arrested for violating this law. In its decision, the Supreme Court ruled that Indian nations were domestic and dependent nations under the protection of the U.S. government. Consequently, the

Opposite: Surrounded by symbols of both Catholicism and his native religion, The Boy, a Gros Ventre elder, celebrates the 50th anniversary of St. Paul's Mission at Hays. Jesuits founded the mission in 1886 to spread their teachings to the Gros Ventre tribe. The original building burned in the 1930s and was rebuilt of stone. *Photo by the Helmbrecht Studio, courtesy of the Montana Historical Society*

Above: Sporting traditional dresses, members of the girls' basketball team at the Fort Shaw Indian School line up for a group portrait, circa 1903. A government industrial academy for the Blackfeet, the Fort Shaw school—and others like it—sought to ruthlessly break up "tribal customs, manners, and barbarous usages" and to indoctrinate students in the White man's ways. *Photo by G. M. Eddies, courtesy of the Montana Historical Society*

federal government had a fiduciary responsibility to protect the rights of Indian nations, even though the tribes could be immune from some federal laws.[3]

The term *sovereignty* itself has proved problematic for Indian nations and state and federal governments. Throughout history, Indian people have dealt with foreign governments via treaties—legal documents between sovereign nations. Thus, they view their sovereignty as absolute. Federal and state governments, on the other hand, have chosen to adopt the U.S. Supreme Court's interpretation of sovereignty, which states that tribes are semi-sovereign and the federal government has a fiduciary responsibility to protect their rights.[4]

THE DAWES ALLOTMENT ACT OF 1887

The Dawes Act had a devastating impact on the reservations in Montana. The general provision of the act was to grant 160 acres of reservation land to each Indian head of family; 80 acres to single Indian people over the age of eighteen and orphans under eighteen; and 40 acres to single people under the age of eighteen. The federal government was to hold title to the land in trust for twenty-five years. This meant that the land could not be taxed or used as collateral. Indians had four years to select their individual allotments. If they failed to do so, the federal government would select their land for them. Each allottee would automatically receive U.S. citizenship.[5]

One thing that continues to anger many Indian people on the reservations is that the secretary of the Interior allowed non-Indians to buy the excess, non-allotted land. The money earned from such sales was supposed to be held in trust by the Interior Department and appropriated for the education, welfare, and civilization of Indians. Nonetheless, many Indians resented the loss of that land.[6]

The Dawes Act was often used to benefit non-Indians at the expense of Indians. On the Flathead Reservation, for example, the tribes were forced to sell their land at below-market prices. This forced tribal members into a lower economic class than their non-

Opposite: At her camp north of Arlee, folk artist Agnes Vanderberg (1901–1989) taught many Montanans, both Indian and White, the traditions of her Salish culture. Vanderberg was honored with the Governor's Award for the Arts in 1985. *Photo by Michael Crummett*

Below: A Salish-Kootenai baby naps on a beautifully beaded cradle board, circa 1910. *Photo courtesy of the Montana Historical Society*

Indian neighbors. According to a 1971 ruling by the U.S. Court of Claims, the land the tribes sold to homesteaders, the State of Montana, and the National Bison Range was worth $7.4 million in 1912. The tribes were paid only $1.8 million, or twenty-four cents on the dollar. In the 1970s, the tribes were finally paid the balance.[7]

Many Indians believe the Dawes Act was simply a new way for Whites to take Indian land. As Peter Beaverhead, a Salish elder put it, "They chased us away from our own land, our homes. The White man told us, 'This is to be your Indian land, your reservation. It is to be your homeland.' They surveyed eighty acres each for us. . . . There were many acres left over, and they found a way so that we sold the land. The White man bought the land and crowded us out."[8]

INDIAN CITIZENSHIP, 1924

Following World War I, Congress granted blanket citizenship to all Indian people as a reward for the high percentage of Native Americans who had voluntarily enlisted in the armed forces. Prior to the war, roughly two-thirds of Indian people had become citizens, either by treaty or by special statute, such as the Dawes Act. Thus, unlike other minority groups in the United States, Indian people today actually have dual citizenship. They are citizens of their own semi-sovereign tribes, and they are citizens of the United States.[9]

The Depression years had similar impacts on both Whites and Indians living in Montana. The exodus of Whites from farming was mirrored among Indians. Nearly all Indian farmers quit farming during the Depression and went to work instead for the Works Progress Administration, the Civilian Conservation Corps, and other New Deal programs.[10]

THE INDIAN REORGANIZATION ACT OF 1934

According to author Francis Paul Prucha, the assimilationist ideas of the nineteenth century were a failure, and a group of reformists under the New Deal formulated a new policy to assimilate Indians in the twentieth century. Known as the Indian Reorganization Act of 1934, this new policy was "one that sought protection, preservation, and strengthening of Indian ways in art, religion, and social organization."[11]

Under this policy, each tribe could design and adopt a tribal constitution with the approval of the secretary of the Interior. Such a constitution could not be changed without the approval of Congress. In addition, the tribes could develop and incorporate a system for financial credit that included the utilization of a revolving credit fund from which only incorporated tribes could borrow. This credit fund was an attempt to solve a problem created by the Dawes Act: Because trust land could not be used as collateral, Indian farmers and ranchers could not use it to secure loans they needed to buy seed and equipment.

The Reorganization Act superseded the Dawes Allotment Act and extended the trust period for Indian lands indefinitely. It also called upon the Bureau of Indian Affairs (BIA) to give Indians a preference in hiring within the agency.

Tribes were allowed to choose whether to be governed by the Indian Reorganization Act. In Montana, two tribes rejected the policy: the Crows and the Fort Peck Assiniboine/Sioux. The effects of that decision have plagued these two tribes throughout the twentieth century.[12] For example, in 1961, the secretary of the Interior revoked the Fort Peck tribe's constitution, saying that it was not in the tribe's best interest. The tribe continues to

operate under the constitution nonetheless. The Crows, despite pressure from the federal government to adopt a constitution, continue to govern themselves through a general council, a form of pure democracy. All men and women eighteen years old or older are members of the tribal council, which meets quarterly. Under this form of government, a quorum of one hundred tribal members can change government policy and leadership every few months, if they choose. Today the Crow tribe comes under constant scrutiny by the federal government, and one wonders if their rejection of the Indian Reorganization Act plays a part in that scrutiny.[13]

WORLD WAR II

Montana Indian tribes contributed heavily to the war effort beyond just the enlistment of "warriors." For example, the Crow tribe voted to place all its resources, including minerals, oil, and coal, at the disposal of President Franklin Roosevelt for the duration of the war.[14] During their military service, Indian "warriors" were exposed to the world outside their reservations. Some chose to stay in the cities, and many policymakers saw this as an opportunity to keep Indians in an urban setting and, in doing so, assimilate them.

Following the war, policymakers argued that the best Indian leaders in the country had left the reservations for urban areas and had worked side-by-side with non-Indians in support of the war effort. Therefore, this would be a prime time for complete assimilation. The policymakers also contended that Indians would be among the first to be affected by the postwar rise in unemployment and that they would return to the reservations with no jobs awaiting them. Some Indian veterans would take advantage of the GI Bill, leaving the reservations to pursue their education. Other policymakers argued that Indians needed to be freed from the oppression of the BIA. Thus, certain congressional groups began to push for termination of the federal trust relationship between Indians and the U.S. government. Tribes were to be "terminated" in three phases. If those in the first phase seemed to fare well, then the other two

Opposite: On the Crow Reservation, the women of the Moccasin family model their elk-teeth dresses, which have been passed down through the family for generations. The Crows are noted for their strong ties to tribal traditions.
Photo by Michael Crummett

Above: The tops of tepees catch the last light at Crow Fair, held each August at Crow Agency. Crow Fair is believed to be the largest Native American gathering in the nation, drawing as many as 40,000 participants and spectators.
Photo by Michael Crummett

phases would be implemented. In Montana, the Flathead Reservation was marked for termination in the first phase.[15]

In 1951, the federal government implemented a relocation program and opened urban centers for Indians in Chicago, Cleveland, Dallas, Denver, Los Angeles, San Jose, and Washington, D.C. The University of Montana served as a training center to provide Indian families with urban living experiences before they moved to larger cities. According to S. Lyman Tyler,

Opposite: This haunting sculpture stands in the Lodge Pole and Tipi Village at Browning on the Blackfeet Reservation, which sprawls across 1.5 million acres of prairie and foothills just east of Glacier National Park. *Photo by Donnie Sexton / Travel Montana*

Above: Blackfeet elder George Kicking Woman conducts a pipe ceremony on the grounds of the C. M. Russell Museum in Great Falls during a Native American encampment that the museum sponsors each summer. *Photo by Stuart S. White*

Opposite: During a Blackfeet mid-winter fair in the 1920s, tribal members gather in the Browning High School auditorium to hear a visiting lecturer. The Blackfeet tribe is one of the largest in the state, with an enrolled membership in 1990 of about 9,000 people. *Photo courtesy of the Montana Historical Society*

Left: Blackfeet elder Mary Ground (1882–1990) witnessed extraordinary changes during her 107 years of life, from the near-extinction of the buffalo to the exploration of space and the advent of computers. Known as Grass Woman among her people, she had 14 children and 475 grandchildren and worked for the Great Northern Railway, greeting visitors to Glacier National Park. *Photo by Michael Crummett*

Below: At North American Indian Days in Browning, the setting sun silhouettes a row of tepees. Held the second week of July, the popular powwow features drumming, dancing, and traditional games. Native Americans come from all over the West to compete. *Photo by Chuck Haney*

author of *A History of Indian Policy*, employment opportunities and the relocation policy of the BIA were incentive enough to create a new trend among Indians. He estimated that forty percent of Indians left their reservations during the war, two-thirds of them without BIA assistance. Some Indian people have called the relocation program a "self-termination" project. Today, urban Indian centers provide services and programs for Indians who leave the reservation to find employment.[16]

In 1953, Congress passed House Concurrent Resolution 108, also called the Termination Policy. This policy, along with the individual laws that implement it, was designed to bring about an end to the federal trust relationship in three phases. The reservation land of those tribes designated for termination in the first phase was appraised and sold to the highest bidder. State legislatures and county boards assumed authority over these tribes' education, adoptions, alcoholism, land use, and other social concerns. Public Law 280 gave states concurrent jurisdiction on Indian reservations over civil and criminal matters.[17] In Montana, the Flathead Reservation accepted Public Law 280, and that has remained a concern even today. In fact, the tribe would like to rescind its decision to accept state jurisdiction.

Two other laws were passed in 1953 to end discriminatory practices against Indians. The first of these was Public Law 281, which allowed Indians to purchase firearms, and the other was Public Law 277, which concerned the sale of liquor to Indians. Under the latter, tribes were allowed to decide for themselves whether they would allow taverns on their reservations. Some chose to be "wet" reservations and others chose to be "dry." In Montana, the Crow, Northern Cheyenne, Fort Belknap, and Rocky Boy's Reservations decided to prohibit taverns, while the Flathead, Blackfeet, and Fort Peck Reservations opted to allow them.[18]

Despite legislated policies, many Indian people today move back and forth between their reservations and urban areas. They see the reservation as "home" even though they may have to leave it to gain employment. They see the cities as places to visit, get jobs, and go shopping, but they prefer to stay near their ancestral lands. Historian K. Ross Toole wrote in 1959: "The reservations, although called 'open-air ghettoes' by a recent critic of Montana's reservations, still provide the Indian with a sense of belonging and security he cannot find elsewhere. The majority do not like to leave them for long."[19]

Barely another twenty years went by before policymakers again changed their minds. The termination policy did not get beyond phase one because terminated tribes fared poorly. They have spent the rest of the century trying to return to trust status. Charles F. Wilkinson may have said it best in his book *American Indians, Time and the Law*: "Indian tribes possess a right to change and grow; they are not frozen in time. Indian tribes are permanent entities in the American political system."[20]

THE INDIANS SELF-DETERMINATION AND EDUCATION ASSISTANCE ACT OF 1975

The purpose of this law was "to promote maximum Indian participation in the Government and education of the Indian people; to provide for full participation of Indian tribes in programs and services conducted by the Federal Government for Indians and to encourage the development of the human resources of the Indian people; to establish a program of assistance to upgrade Indian education; to support the right of Indian citizens to control their own education activities; and for other purposes."[21]

In July 1970, President Richard Nixon told Congress: "Both as a matter of justice and as a matter of enlightened social policy, we must act on the basis of what Indians themselves have long been telling us. The time has come to break decisively with the past and to create the conditions for a new era in which the Indian future is determined by Indian acts and Indian decisions."[22]

Several debates took place over the adoption of this "self-determination" policy. Lucy Covington, first vice president of the Northwest Affiliated Tribes, stated:

> *[W]e have not had a voice in policy decisions affecting our destiny. . . . This must not happen again. . . . The money must be tribally controlled. Indian schools belong in Indian*

communities. If the old way of sending Indian students out of the Indian communities had been successful, we would be educated by now. . . . [T]here has been a lack of implementing programs by local, State and Federal governments for the advancement of educational opportunities for Indians. Education is a valuable tool. . . . [A] concerted effort has been made by this country to keep this tool out of the hands of the Indians. . . . It is against this background that we support this bill. . . . [23]

Some Indian people have referred to this policy as "self-termination." It pits smaller tribes against larger tribes in competing for the same dollars. In many ways it has become a true example of survival of the fittest. There are those tribes that can and will usurp the best of the opportunities available. And yet, once again policy-makers have chosen to emphasize the drawbacks of this policy. It has been twenty years since this policy was put on the books, and now voices calling for termination are rising to the forefront. Montana newspapers are filled with articles purporting mismanagement of tribal funds and federal dollars and accusing tribal leaders of ineptness and the BIA of corruption. The result will be another policy against Indian efforts.

LATE TWENTIETH-CENTURY POLICIES

The last two decades of the twentieth century have seen struggles between Indians and non-Indians in Montana regarding the issues of sovereignty and natural-resource use. This has been a time of negotiation, misunderstanding, success, and failure.

In an opinion issued June 13, 1986, U.S. District Judge Edward Rafeedie ruled in *Windy Boy et al v Big Horn County* that the county's at-large voting system violated the 1973 Voting Rights Act. The challenge involved the method used to elect county commissioners and school board members. Big Horn County is larger than Connecticut; its population at the time of the lawsuit was 52.1 percent White and 46.2 percent Indian, yet no Indian had ever been elected to the three-member board of commissioners. The district court recognized that the at-large voting system tended to minimize the voting strength of the Indian population. This case was just one example of discriminatory treatment of Indians in Montana in the twentieth century. Indian people are ever watchful for such discrimination.

On a more positive note, the State of Montana and the Assiniboine and Sioux tribes of the Fort Peck Indian Reservation entered into a Water Compact Agreement

Opposite: Almira Jackson, an Assiniboine artisan famous for her star quilts, poses with a stunning example of her craft. Indian women—particularly the Sioux and Assiniboine of the Fort Peck and Fort Belknap Reservations—began making star quilts in the early 1900s after learning the craft from female missionaries. Today, such quilts are considered one of the most honorable and prestigious gifts a family can give or receive. *Photo by Michael Crummett*

Right: On an outing in the early 1920s, Boy Scouts from the Fort Belknap Agency School display the characteristic exuberance of youth. The 645,000-acre Fort Belknap Reservation is home to the Gros Ventre and Assiniboine tribes. *Photo courtesy of the Montana Historical Society*

Crow children are indoctrinated in the ways of the White culture at a boarding school at Crow Agency. In an effort to force assimilation, Indian boarding schools required students to cut their hair and abandon their native dress and language.
Photo courtesy of the Peter Yegen Museum

Above: Nature splashes color over the dun-colored foothills of the National Bison Range near Moiese. The Mission Range makes a spectacular backdrop for the 18,500-acre wildlife preserve, which was established in 1908 on land fomerly owned by the Confederated Salish and Kootenai Tribes. *Photo by Michael Sample*

Opposite: In 1991, at a ceremony in Pryor marking the 50th anniversary of the revival of the sun dance among the Crow tribe, Crow spiritual leader Heywood Big Day prays for world peace, healing power, strength, and vision. Plains tribes consider the sun dance a supremely sacred religious rite of purification and renewal, but near the end of the 19th century, the federal government banned the "heathen" ritual in an effort to "civilize" them. Not until the 1930s did the government acknowledge the value of preserving Indian culture. *Photo by Michael Crummett*

session of House and Senate. The following represents a small portion of his speech:

> *Too many times our hopes are always up when a new government comes in, but we always find ourselves back in the same predicament that we are always in.*
>
> *It has become very complicated to live in this country, especially by the Indian people, because of the never-ending process, and unless you are within the political realm, you will never have the opportunity to be up front where these decisions and laws are made. The Indian people are never within the place where the recognition is.*
>
> *We often talk about the unity and dialogue, working together on government to government basis, but we still see that separation takes place. The laws I have referred to too often are applied against the Indian people to never advance themselves in this society.* [25]

on May 15, 1985. This agreement was the first of its kind and represented willingness on the part of both parties to negotiate a reasonable solution to a controversial issue. The basic reason for the compact was to determine the rights of the Assiniboine and Sioux tribes "to water on, under, adjacent to, or otherwise appurtenant to the Reservations, to settle existing disputes and remove causes of future controversy between the Tribes and the state and between Indians of the Fort Peck Reservation and other persons concerning waters of the Missouri River, its tributaries, and ground water. . . ." [24]

On March 11, 1993, Earl Old Person, chairman of the Blackfeet Nation, presented the first State of Indian Nations address to a joint session of the Montana Legislature. While Indians had previously testified before each of the legislative bodies, Old Person was the first Indian leader ever to be invited to address a joint

By the end of the twentieth century, most Indian elders will have passed on and left to their grandchildren the task of remembering their stories and traditions. The words of Earl Old Person are ones to remember as we approach the twenty-first century. Indian people have seen the loss of land, buffalo, and a traditional way of life. Now they work for recognition as proud and noble people.

Opposite top: Crow rancher Bill Yellowtail made an unsuccessful bid for Montana's single seat in the U.S. House of Representatives in 1996, after representing Bighorn County as a state senator for almost a decade. *Photo by Michael Crummett*

Opposite bottom: Blackfeet of all ages prepare for a sun dance ceremony—the most sacred Blackfeet ritual—on Little Badger Creek in June 1941. Traditionally held in early summer when the prairies are at their greenest, the sun dance requires three days of rigorous preparation, including fasting and ritual sweats, before the participants erect the medicine lodge that honors the sun. *Photo by Roland H. Willcomb, courtesy of the Montana Historical Society*

Below: Mrs. George Star and Mrs. Yellow Kidney, members of the Blackfeet tribe, share a light, some gossip, and a tranquil moment in March 1949. *Photo by T. J. Hileman, courtesy of the Montana Historical Society*

Right: Wolf Plume and Calf Robe, members of the Blackfeet tribe, weave baskets at Heart Butte Round Hall in 1933. *Photo courtesy of the Montana Historical Society*

ALLOYED MONTANA

ETHNIC COMPONENTS OF A TWENTIETH-CENTURY PEOPLE

Montana's twentieth-century population has been an alloy of lighter and darker skins, of oriental and occidental cultures, of Christian and non-Christian faiths, and of two dozen or more languages. A metallic metaphor is appropriate, for it was mineral mining and smelting that had so much to do with attracting such a polyglot population to the state. In places such as Butte, Red Lodge, Philipsburg, Anaconda, and Great Falls, ethnicity marked every aspect of life, from parish and congregation to saloon and political club and during holidays and festivals. And as in modern metallurgy, where sophisticated alloys suggest high technique and progressive science, the people of Montana often congratulated themselves on their engaging diversity and social intelligence, even believing that occasional conflict among groups built a well-tempered community.

The image of an alloyed Montana, one that identifies and celebrates the ores contributed to a blended composite, more accurately portrays the state than the oft-repeated characterization of the American commonwealth as a "melting pot." That stewlike description, which both wished and demanded conformity, never accurately reflected the place of ethnicity in the national story, and it fails as well with Montana. Modern scholars define ethnicity in a pluralistic society as group identity based on a shared language, cultural affinity, and sense of common heritage. More familiarly, the term connotes traditional foods and dress, cultural ceremonies, and idiomatic—even creolized—language. Ethnicity is unmistakable in distinctive community rituals such as the Croatian Mesopost prelenten drama or the Chinese New Year cele-

bration and in food such as Cornish pasties and Slavic *povititza*. In the American culture, ethnicity is really two things that push and pull on one another. It is a conservative retention of meaningful cultural relationships, primarily among family, extended family, and religious communities. It is also a dynamic and distinctive contribution to the larger culture, especially in the workplace, political arena, and community hall. In twentieth-century Montana, the dynamic side has generally dwarfed the conservative side.

From our vantage point at the end of the century, when just over 1.5 percent of the nearly 800,000 people living in Montana are foreign-born, the state looks remarkably homogeneous, a paler and less variegated place than it was nine decades ago. Finding such homogeneity in

BY WILLIAM L. LANG

Opposite: A Chinese merchant poses outside his store in Virginia City at the dawn of the century. In 1900, more than 1,700 Chinese made their homes in Montana, primarily in Butte, Helena, and Great Falls; the 1990 census counted only 655 Chinese Montanans. *Photo courtesy of the Montana Historical Society*

Above: A pair of Chinese drivers show off their new taxicab, one of the first in Havre, in 1917. Many of Havre's Chinese residents came to the town to work as section hands on the Great Northern Railway. By 1920, fewer than 50 Chinese remained in the Hi-Line community. *Photo courtesy of the Al Lucke collection, Montana Historical Society*

Opposite top: The raucous St. Patrick's Day parade in Butte, which attracts fun lovers from all corners of the state, honors the Irish heritage of many Mining City residents. Butte's rich ethnic mix also includes the Welsh, Cornish, Serbs, Finns, Italians, Scots, Swedes, Norwegians, Chinese, and Jews. *Photo by John Reddy*

Opposite bottom: In their cozy homestead near Coalridge in 1909, John Haaven whips up a meal while brother Henry reads about "Montana's Bonanza Crops." The sodbusters who flocked to the state during the great homestead boom came primarily from Scandinavia, Germany, and the Midwestern states. *Photo by Henry Syverud, courtesy of the Montana Historical Society*

1910, when one in four Montanans was foreign-born, would have been difficult. In Silver Bow, Deer Lodge, and Granite Counties, where ethnic communities made up a sizable portion of the population, more than half of the residents claimed at least one foreign-born parent. Ethnic diversity stood cheek and jowl in the smoking cities that powered those counties. In the decade before the Great War, Butte and Anaconda had clearly designated neighborhoods for each group. People lived in districts with self-proclaimed identities, where they frequented saloons that rang with their language and where they worshiped and buried their dead at different parishes and congregations. These near-isolate populations stood with and against each other in work and play as they built and rebuilt the social structure of the greatest metal-mining district in North America. In a place such as Butte, where work was split between above-ground and below-ground operations, ethnicity penetrated the employment line, the union hall, and social life. Even as late as mid-century, a "mixed marriage" in Butte referred to a wedding outside of one's ethnic and religious group.

Decade by decade during this century, the ethnic mix in Montana has changed. Overall, the proportion of ethnics has declined. With a smaller percentage of non-Whites in the population, Montana has become much less diverse. But during the early years, Montana drew people from around the world like a magnet. The immigrants, whether from other North American communities or directly from European or Asian countries, created a dynamic and booming place. By 1909, three transcontinental railroads crossed Montana, making it faster and cheaper to move to Big Sky Country and more necessary for railroad investors to encourage more and more immigrants to feed their lines. Thousands came on the Northern Pacific, Great Northern, and Milwaukee Road, especially during the boomer land rush before World War I, when crop yields and prices made Montana a high-profile agricultural destination. Dutch, Danes, Norwegians, Scandinavians, Croatians, and Slovenians followed other European immigrants to

farming communities that promised more than the immigrants could hope for at home.

West of Bozeman, in the rolling countryside of the Gallatin Valley, today's traveler drives through one of those immigrant-attracting propositions. Drawn to the Gallatin just before the dawn of the century, Dutch farmers established Amsterdam, Churchill, and Manhattan as Dutch-Reformed communities dedicated to living out their religious dogma and growing grain for the New York and Brooklyn Malting Company. By the 1930s, the Dutch-Reformed community had splintered its religious core into rival denominations, but the Americanized Hollanders retained an essential ethnic cohesion that extended its influence to nearby towns. Like other groups who came to Montana for both cultural and economic reasons, the Dutch succeeded as farmers while they ultimately failed to create a religious enclave safe from intrusion. In no small measure, they became Montanans at the expense of an idealized community.

Montana attracted other immigrants who also sought space to create a cultural and religious sanctuary from modernity. At Dagmar in the northeast corner of the state, early in the century, Danish Lutherans established a farming colony that centered on a conservative church tradition. In southeastern Montana, Norwegian Lutherans tried to create similar communities. These and other homestead settlements, born of the enthusiasm that brought so many settlers to Montana before 1920, succeeded as long as good times kept a critical mass of religious adherents in the area. More radical religious communities came as well, each pursuing religious freedom and economic opportunity. The histories of the Mennonite Gemeinde, Old Order Amish, and Hutterite groups that came to the state during the late nineteenth century demonstrate the power of Montana as an imagined

and religiously sanctified place. Among the Anabaptist Protestants who came, the Hutterites have been the most successful. By the late 1970s, nearly two dozen Hutterite colonies farmed large acreages in the Missouri and Musselshell Valleys. The oldest communistic society in the world, Hutterites live in colonies apart from other Montana communities, holding all real property in common, ordering their lives on a strict religious mode, and practicing consumption austerity. Still, they live fully within Montana's cultural life and trade with impressive success with the outside capitalistic world.

The Hutterites live distinctive lives, yet they share their German language with thousands of other ethnic Montanans. Other than English, German has been spoken by more Montanans than any other language in the twentieth century. From 1910 to 1950, Germans and German-speaking populations constituted the largest ethnic group in Montana, with Norwegians and Swedes closest in numbers. But during the two world wars, especially during World War I, Germans came in for heavy criticism and an anger that often boiled to dangerous levels. Under specious regulations promulgated by the quasi-official Montana Council of Defense in 1917, speaking the German language brought legal and vigilante judicial proceedings. Superpatriots burned German books in Lewistown. The patriotic furor led pacifistic and German-speaking Mennonites to flee to Canada.

To an extent that can hardly be imagined today, ethnicity became a political label during World War I. In Butte, where Irish lived and worked alongside Cornish and Welsh fellow immigrants, no friend of the British forces could be considered a friend of Ireland. This often led superpatriots to lump Sinn Fein members with German sympathizers and the radically pacifist Industrial Workers of the World, an organization with significant Irish and Finnish membership. The Finns had long been at the forefront of socialist and pacifistic labor organizing, while a conspicuous and active portion of Butte's Irish had boastfully supported the Irish cause before and after that country's revolutionary Easter Rising of 1916. Before the political-cultural conflicts abated in 1920, the Montana National Guard occupied Butte six times, ostensibly to enforce order.

Among the most patriotic immigrant groups during the divisive World War I period were Croatians, Slovenians, and Serbs. The 1920 Montana census lists nearly ten thousand Slavic people from Yugoslavia and Austro-Hungarian regions. Often derisively called "hunkies," the Slavs worked across Montana, in coal mines in Yellowstone and Rosebud Counties, in smelters in Cascade and Deer Lodge Counties, and as stonemasons and farmers in Judith Basin and Fergus Counties. Among the most remarkable of these workers were the Croatian stonemasons who literally built Lewistown and erected structures in Red Lodge and other towns on the lower Yellowstone River. Their own fear of prejudicial treatment during World War I in part prompted their patriotic reaction, as they energetically embraced the nationality of their new country.

Prejudice and suspicion had a much more devastating impact on other ethnic groups in Montana during the twentieth century. Color and race, as elsewhere in the nation, drew a tight boundary around populations that were not White, not Christian, and not European. African Americans who came to Montana after the Civil War settled principally in booming mining and railroad towns. Some came directly from slavery with their White owners calling them "servants." Others came as free individuals, either as manumitted by the Thirteenth Amendment or as never enslaved people. Helena, Anaconda, Butte, and Great Falls had the largest Black communities during the first three decades of the century, but African Americans also lived in White Sulphur Springs, Billings, Livingston, and Missoula. In Helena, their numbers topped four hundred in 1910, and they comprised 3.4 percent of the population, the highest concentration of African Americans in any Montana city during the twentieth century.

Blacks worked in a broad range of occupations in Montana cities, but most labored in service trades and jobs, from draymen to house servants. A high percentage of Black women worked outside the home, and in Helena and Anaconda they owned real property and businesses. African Americans organized their communities around the Baptist and African Methodist Episcopal Zion churches and around women's clubs, which were organized into a statewide confederation that held meetings until mid-century. For example, in 1953, the Pleasant Hour Club in Helena held its thirty-second annual meeting, with two dozen women in attendance. But by 1960, the African-American population had declined in real numbers in Helena, Butte, and Anaconda and in percentage throughout the state. Fewer and fewer families could trace their heritage to late-nine-

teenth-century frontier settlers. The 1990 census lists 2,381 Blacks, a figure that compares favorably to the 1,834 enumerated in the 1910 census; but these migrants were different from those who had been lured to Montana for mining, railroad work, freighting, and service labor at the beginning of the century. Post–World War II African-American migration to Montana brought primarily armed forces personnel, students, and business people.

The diminishment of ethnic populations in Montana during the century is more than simply a decrease in raw census numbers or relative size. It is both a change in populations, as communities have become more and more homogeneous, and a restructuring of populations, as different ethnic groups have brought new experiences

Opposite top: Mrs. Susie Hofer and her granddaughters visit relatives at the Turner Hutterite Colony in Blaine County. Montana is home to more than 40 Hutterite colonies and more than 3,000 Hutterites. *Photo by Michael Crummett*

Opposite bottom: Josh Waldner harvests cabbages at the Fairhaven Hutterite Colony near Great Falls. Like the Amish and Mennonites, Hutterites are Anabaptists who live communally and follow traditions that date from the Protestant Reformation of the 16th century. *Photo by Steve Shirley*

Below: In 1913, German-Russian immigrants gather for a church picnic in Eastern Montana. The following year, with the outbreak of World War I, many people of German ancestry would become the victims of prejudice and suspicion as patriotism among Montanans rose to a fever pitch. Some would be hounded and forced to demonstrate their loyalty, while others would be openly terrorized. Most German immigrants were loyal to their new nation, though many opposed involvement in the war against the Fatherland. *Photo by Evelyn J. Cameron, courtesy of the Montana Historical Society*

to add to the Montana alloy. In the 1990 census, for example, Hispanics were easily the largest ethnic group, with 20,536 residents living in the state. Also prominent were foreign-born from the Philippines, Korea, Vietnam, Laos, and Malaysia. Foreign languages are still spoken on Montana's streets in the late twentieth century, but they are much different from those spoken during the 1920s, just as the food cooked, religious traditions observed, and arts pursued are different.

The changing dimensions of Montana's ethnic populations have often been the result of national and even international trends—sometimes the legacy of economic change, sometimes of war. After World War I, for example, most African Americans who had arrived during the 1880s and 1890s left Montana. As nativist politics and poor economic conditions made staying in Big Sky Country more difficult during the 1920s, Blacks migrated east and west out of the state. Jewish Montanans, who had been prominent in mercantile trades in Butte, Anaconda, Helena, Billings, and Great Falls since the 1860s, also left during the 1920s and 1930s and for generally the same reasons that Blacks left. In both cases, families often moved to

relocate with or near extended families in the Midwest or Pacific Coast regions. Those same regions siphoned off more ethnic Montanans during World War II, when wartime factories begged for workers and paid high wages to lure them.

World War II dramatically changed Montana and the American West. Wartime investments in factories, large shifts of population, and increased demands on mineral, timber, and agricultural production fundamentally restructured the region. Among the most disturbing wartime policies was the identification of Japanese Americans as a dangerous population that deserved political incarceration. Although the Japanese population in Montana had dropped by more than half between 1900 and 1940 to under a thousand people, the state's interior location made it conducive for an internment camp. During the war, the government labeled Japanese and Italians (seamen who had been shipboard in American ports in December 1941) as "dangerous" or as dislocated and alien. Cast into this politicized category, interned Japanese and Italians lived side by side at Fort Missoula during most of the war years. Most of the Japanese had come to Montana during the late nineteenth century as railroad workers. Preponderantly men, they had worked for the Northern Pacific, Great Northern, and Union Pacific lines, mostly as maintenance crew members. They had lived in railroad division-point towns, such as Missoula and Dillon, but had increasingly either left Montana for other employment or been replaced by other workers. The 1900 census had listed 2,441 Japanese in the state. By 1950, census enumerators counted only 524 Japanese Montanans, and by 1990 the census listed just 829.

Japanese suffered racial prejudice that had long been directed at all Asiatic people. They had to endure characterization as a suspicious people who were non-Christian and proponents of strange religious and cultural practices. It was the Chinese, however, who took the most abuse. Partly as a legacy of nineteenth-century anger directed at them because of their industry, success, and insularity, the Chinese had a difficult time translating their economic acumen into social acceptance. Part of the difficulty was the lack of Chinese women and the absence of families. In 1900, only 39 of 1,739 Chinese in Montana were women. The nearly all-male Chinese work force also came in for attack because of the powerful clan organizations that ordered their economic and social lives. It gave them an appearance of secrecy, collusion, and corruption. With these stereotypes as justification, Whites inflicted anti-Chinese laws, inflamed the populace with nativist rhetoric, and promulgated racist legal decisions that severely compromised Montana's Chinese community. Despite these conditions, a sizable number of Chinese resisted the pressure to move; and in Butte, Helena, and Great Falls, where the largest number of Chinese lived, many held on up to and after mid-century as owners of businesses, some as second- or third-generation Montana families. Nonetheless, the Chinese population in Montana decreased from 1,739 in 1900 to 209 in 1950. In 1990, only 655 Chinese lived in the state.

The decline in Chinese population reflected another factor that contributed to the composition of the ethnic alloy in the Big Sky State. Some immigrants had no intention of making Montana—or America—their permanent homes but had come to acquire wealth before returning to their native lands. Some continued an active correspondence with families in their home countries, and it was not uncommon for immigrants to return home for visits and bring additional family members to Montana. Always the primary lure was economic. For French-speaking Basques, sheep-tending on Montana's

Opposite top: Croatian immigrants Vinko Kalafatic and Mrs. Joseph Pipinch make a little music during a picnic at a countryman's ranch on Ruby Gulch. Like many Croatians in the Lewistown area, Kalafatic was a stonemason. Besides the accordion, he played mandolin and windpipe at Croatian dances in the vicinity.
Photo courtesy of the Montana Historical Society

Opposite bottom: The baseball team representing Rocker, just outside Butte, poses for a group portrait. Blacks have never comprised a very large segment of Montana's population. In 1910, fewer than 2,000 African Americans lived in the state, primarily in Helena, Anaconda, Butte, and Great Falls. By 1990, their population had grown to only about 2,300. *Photo courtesy of the Butte–Silver Bow Public Archives*

Above: Seen here with his accompanist J. Rosamund Johnson in 1927, Taylor Gordon of White Sulphur Springs (right) became a world-renowned spiritual singer and wrote the vivid memoir *Born to Be*, an important document of the Harlem Renaissance.
Photo courtesy of the Montana Historical Society

Left: Mao and Pao Moua, owners of the Iron Wok restaurant in Missoula, are members of Montana's significant Hmong community. Many Hmong refugees from the mountain country along the Laos-Vietnam border settled in the Missoula area following the Vietnam War. *Photo by Michael Crummett*

Left: More than 600 men of Japanese heritage were interned at Fort Missoula during World War II, along with 1,200 Italian POWs and Italian nationals. An executive order issued within months of Pearl Harbor prohibited people of Japanese descent from living on the West Coast. As a result, more than 120,000 people, many of them loyal citizens of the United States, were forced to leave their homes. Most spent the duration of the war in internment camps. *Photo courtesy of the K. Ross Toole Archives of the University of Montana-Missoula (84-297)*

Below: In the first decade of the 20th century, Billy Kee, a Chinese immigrant, grew wealthy running the post office, hotel, and store in Lombard, a community in the Gallatin Valley. Here, Kee poses with his family for a formal portrait. *Photo courtesy of the Gallatin County Historical Society*

Opposite: On May 19, 1909, 4 miles west of Garrison Junction, workers prepare to drive the last spike for the Pacific Coast extension of the Chicago, Milwaukee & St. Paul Railroad. Many men came to Montana from Asia during the late 19th century, hoping to get jobs with the railroad gangs. *Photo courtesy of the Montana Historical Society*

high plains provided a start. Later, ranching offered a solid basis to attract even more immigration. Families followed families, and northeastern Montana became a destination for Basques, much like other settlements in Nevada, Idaho, and Oregon. For all immigrants, whether from Asia or Europe, better wages and broader entrepreneurial opportunities beckoned from Montana.

For Irish, Finnish, and Slavic metal-ore and coal miners and for smelter workers in Butte, Anaconda, Great Falls, and East Helena, the work continued until after World War II, when the industry began a rapid decline that brought closure or minimal operations by the 1980s. Fewer jobs meant that fewer sons and daughters remained with their families. By the 1970s, Butte's heyday as a wide-open mining camp was long gone, and its more recent ethnic history steadily eroded. Open-pit mining during the 1950s and its expansion during the 1970s ate away at Butte's eastern neighborhoods, completely eliminating the Italian Meaderville section, while the city expanded south away from the hill onto the flats. The once-thriving ethnic neighborhoods on the hill became bare remnants of an earlier and dynamic era.

As Butte and the rest of Montana became less and less heterogeneous, the preservation of ethnic heritage became popular and even thrives as a tourist draw. Today, no ethnic celebration in the state is more successful than Red Lodge's Festival of Nations, an expansive and multi-event remembrance of that coal-mining area's

rich heritage. The Festival of Nations has become an annual opportunity to remember and relive a time when Red Lodge and other mining towns were polyglot. But while the festival memorializes an earlier ethnic diversity, new immigrant groups have brought additional ethnic traditions to Montana since World War II.

Among the fluctuations in Montana's ethnic populations, there is no sharper discontinuity than the increase in Hispanic settlement, especially since World War II. In 1930, the census listed only 214 Hispanics in Montana, most of them living in Billings, where sugar refiners employed them as field workers. According to the most recent census, however, more than twenty thousand Hispanic and Mexican people live in the state. This dramatic increase came in three waves. Beginning in 1921, the sugar-beet industry attracted seasonal workers from Mexico, and some began "wintering over" in Montana. Then, during World War II, the U.S. government con-

tracted with Mexico to provide thousands of agricultural workers in the American West to replace field help drained off in the war effort—the so-called *bracero* program. Finally, the seasonal migration of workers from Mexico and Texas to labor in irrigated agriculture has included year-round residency since the 1960s. The Latino community has flourished in Montana, especially in Billings, where the majority of new migrants live. The community's strong church and social organizations are not unlike the cultural groups that created a critical mass for African Americans in Helena and Butte many decades earlier.

What is most significant in the recent influx of new immigrants—whether from Mexico, Southeast Asia, or Eastern Europe—is the contribution they make to the state's culture and the reminder they provide that much of twentieth-century Montana was built by immigrants. The state is not just better for this ethnic alloying, but it

is also unthinkable without it. Modern Montana is the product of its ethnic past, and to forget that salient fact is also to mistake Montana's future, even during this era of extreme homogeneity. Even more importantly, to misunderstand Montana's ethnic heritage or to repeat some of its racist and discriminatory practices is to diminish the state's potential as a dynamic and creative society.

As in metallurgy, Montana has relied on its alloyed ethnic composition to resist corrosion and to provide flexible strength. Ignoring this critical component in Montana's history and in its contemporary society is analogous to relying on one metal for all uses. The recent appearance of a new nativism and anti-government politics that often inflame prejudice against minority populations threatens to melt the Montana alloy, to destroy the century-crafted composition, to make it too brittle or too vulnerable to withstand future obstacles. Montana's ethnically alloyed culture has served its people well and is strong enough to structurally frame up the next century.

On the south side of Billings, Jose Arredondo passes a mural celebrating Latin American culture. Hispanic farm workers first came to the Billings area in the 1920s to work in the sugar-beet fields. Today, more than 20,000 Latin Americans make their homes in Montana. *Photo by Michael Crummett*

ALICE SISTY IN HER FAMOUS ROMAN JUMP
OVER AUTO (@ HOUGLEDAY)

VOTES AND VIOLETS

MONTANA WOMEN IN THE TWENTIETH CENTURY

In the late 1890s, Madeleine Blair, a prostitute trying to get out of Butte, found that no madam in Chicago would send her a train ticket because they thought that "the girls in the West, especially in Montana, become tough after they have been here a short time." Madeleine was not new to the underworld, but never had she seen such naked vice as she did on the streets of Butte. If women like Madeleine found early Montana a daunting place, middle-class matrons, such as Lizzie Chester Fisk, were even more dismayed. Surveying the sordid landscape of the urban West and the disreputable suitors attracted to her daughter, Lizzie complained to her mother back in Connecticut, "I wish any woman who imagines it easier to bring up a family of children in the west than at the east might have her lot cast in Helena for a time."

At the birth of the twentieth century, the state of Montana was only eleven years old and predominately male—women and girls comprised a mere thirty-eight percent of the fledgling population. Most non-Indian women lived in the western part of the state, in mining and lumber towns and on ranches and farms. In the 1910s, the homestead boom flooded the eastern plains with families from all over the United States and Europe, greatly increasing the number of female residents. For the rest of the twentieth century, women along with men would migrate to and from the Treasure State, following the boom-and-bust cycle of Montana's economy.

The one constant in the lives of the majority of Montana women was work. Whether living on hard-scrabble homesteads, in rowdy mining cities, in hastily built railroad towns, or on one of the new Indian reservations, women in early Montana faced a challenging landscape and a society that ranked them as second-class citizens. Making a living and making a livable world occupied the bulk of their time.

Until 1940, the most common occupation for Montana women who worked for wages was domestic service. In the East, women worked in textile mills, shoe factories, and at other kinds of light manufacturing. But Montana's economy, based on the extraction of natural resources, provided few factory jobs for women. In Butte, long the state's largest city, the only factory that employed women was one that made macaroni. Women

BY MARY MURPHY

Opposite: Astride two horses, Alice Sisty performs her "famous" Roman jump at the Bozeman Round-Up, circa 1935.
Photo courtesy of the Gallatin County Historical Society

Opposite: The "Spinning Marvels" perform wondrous
feats on roller skates at the 1958 Marias Fair in Shelby.
Photo by Jack Gilluly, courtesy of the Montana Historical Society

Above: Hard-working nurses take a break in their spartan quarters at the Sidney hospital in 1915. At the outset of the century,
nursing was one of only a handful of careers open to respectable
women. By century's end, women had proved themselves in a
full spectrum of career fields. *Photo courtesy of the Montana
Historical Society*

Above: Mrs. Max Big Man of the Crow tribe was, according to Montana author Joseph Kinsey Howard, an "excellent bead-worker." Here, she proudly poses with her beadwork and her family. *Photo courtesy of the Montana Historical Society*

Opposite: Sisters Inez and Ora Belle Greene serenade family and friends at their home on Greene Lake in northwestern Montana, circa 1912. *Photo courtesy of Vivian Purdy*

cooked and cleaned for their own families, as well as in hotels, boarding houses, and cafes for the single men who wrested from the earth its natural wealth.

A few women engaged in unusual occupations. A Madame Godefroy taught fencing in Butte at the dawn of the century; the Reverend Hazel Earle, judged one of the leaders of her profession, was a trance medium and spiritualist. Fannie Sperry Steele, born and raised on a ranch outside Helena, became the "Ladies' Bucking Horse Champion of the World" at the first Calgary Stampede in 1912, went on to compete in rodeos across the nation, and eventually ran a dude ranch with her husband. Mary MacLane's scandalous diary of her teenage years in Butte, *The Story of Mary MacLane*, published in 1902, prompted reviewers to advise taking away her paper and pen and administering a spanking. Her royalties allowed her to take New York by storm.

But for most women, rural and urban, their days cycled through a litany of chores. One homesteading wife described her typical routine: "You'd go to bed about eleven-thirty, twelve o'clock, you'd get up at four, and you go out and help harness the horses, you milked the cows, get breakfast, strain your milk and put it away. Wash up your dishes, feed your chickens and slop the pigs. If there was any time left, you could start your washing."

Another woman recalled that the only time she sat down during the day was to nurse her babies. Evelyn Cameron, a British-born gentlewoman who settled near Terry with her husband Ewen, chronicled life on the eastern plains with her camera and pen. She documented the influx of hopeful dry-land farmers in the 1910s and the work of immigrants like the young German-Russian women who plowed from daylight to dark, sacked and hauled grain, and rode bareback across the prairies.

In the 1920s, a new wave of rural immigrants arrived in Montana: Mexicans and Mexican Americans recruited by the Great Western and Holly Sugar Companies to cultivate and harvest sugar beets. The new migrants came and worked as families and lived in company housing built by the sugar companies near their factories. Sugar-beet production was not mechanized until the 1950s; until then, men and women planted, hoed, thinned, weeded, harvested, and topped the beets by hand.

Even with their loads of backbreaking labor, some farm women found time to parlay their agricultural skills into money-making enterprises and to add beauty to the artifacts of everyday life. Butter and egg money is well known as the coin that paid many farmers' bills, but some women were more ambitious entrepreneurs. One farm wife used money she earned milking cows to file mining claims in the Cabinet Mountains and "occasionally hired a neighbor to baby-sit while she went off prospecting." Another woman earned enough cash selling turkeys to put a down payment on the family's first car. Esther Rivera remembered that, in addition to making quilts and clothes, her mother found time to embroider every pillowcase the family owned.

Women's days were filled with labor, but still they made time to appreciate Montana, seeing beauty in the very land that froze and blistered them. Pearl Price Robertson and her husband spent eleven years on a homestead in the Judith Basin before drought and

grasshoppers drove them to the Flathead Valley. Pearl knew the prairie. She "feared its relentlessness, its silence, and its sameness" even as she "loved the tawny spread of its sun-drenched ridges, its shimmering waves of desert air, the terrific sweep of the untrammeled wind, burning stars in a midnight sky." Mary MacLane called Butte sordid and beastly, but still "full of romance and poetry and the wideness of the West."

It is through the work of people such as Pearl Price Robertson and Mary MacLane that we have come to know Montana. Women who narrated, wrote, painted, and photographed the land they worked and the people with whom they lived helped compose what Montana means to us today. We gain some notion of the buffalo days by reading about the life of the Crow woman Pretty Shield as she told it to author Frank Linderman. We can empathize with the double discrimination faced by mixed bloods through the words of novelist Mourning Dove. The struggle to appreciate Montana for what it is and at the same time seek to turn it into what we want is captured in the poetry of Grace Stone Coates and Gwendolen Haste, the prose of Dorothy Johnson and Mildred Walker, the paintings of Fra Dana and Elizabeth Lochrie. The legacy of their work is found in the contemporary labors of writers and artists such as Mary Clearman Blew, Deirdre McNamer, Annick Smith,

Above: A pair of farm girls shock wheat in the Gallatin Valley. For many homestead women, life was a litany of seemingly endless chores, with little time out for pleasure or leisure pursuits. *Photo by Albert Schlechten, courtesy of the Montana Historical Society*

Opposite: A rancher's wife in 1939 employs that indispensable invention, the telephone. For many years, rural phones were on party lines, which allowed shameless eavesdroppers to keep up with the latest neighborhood gossip. *Photo courtesy of the Montana State University Archives*

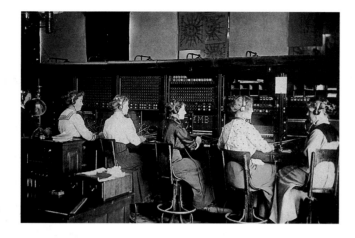

Above: Telephone operators in Bozeman maintain the lines of communication. The first Telephone Operators' Union in the nation was founded in Butte in 1902. *Photo courtesy of the Gallatin County Historical Society*

Opposite: In 1938, members of the Happy Hour Club in Plentywood don symbols of their Western heritage. Throughout the century, Montana women formed all sorts of organizations in their search for female companionship, intellectual stimulation, and spiritual sustenance. *Photo courtesy of the Montana Historical Society*

Debra Earling, Deborah Butterfield, Gennie DeWeese, and Jaune Quick-to-See Smith.

Throughout Montana's past and into its present, despite long days and evenings spent farming, writing, cleaning, or teaching, Montana women have involved themselves in local community affairs and local politics. Farm women joined such groups as the Non-Partisan League and the Farmers' Union, hoping that solidarity with others in similar situations would give them the power to improve the economic and social position of their families. Urban women who labored as laundresses, waitresses, cooks, sales clerks, bookkeepers, and telephone operators founded and joined labor unions to better their working conditions. In the 1880s, when one boss swore at a waitress who refused to perform an inappropriate task, she hit him in the nose with a syrup pitcher and then threw a plate in his face for good measure. By the early twentieth century, such direct action was less necessary. Women were able to resolve grievances through the Women's Protective Union, the Laundry Workers' Union, the Clerks' Union, various teachers' unions, and the first Telephone Operators' Union in the country, founded in Butte in 1902.

Farm and labor organizations were not the only or even the most common organizations that women joined. In virtually every Montana community, women formed church societies, cultural clubs, ethnic organizations, and ladies' auxiliaries for their own pleasure and edification, as well as to provide community social services. Great Falls women had their Shakespeare Club, whose summer performance of *A Midsummer Night's Dream* inspired a whimsical sketch by Charlie Russell. Missoulians echoed the Shakespearean theme with their As You Like It Club. Kalispell women faced a dilemma at the dawn of the century: their women's club, known for its interest in contemporary issues, would become hopelessly out-of-date if it kept its original name, the Nineteenth Century Club. Stevensville, Red Lodge, Bozeman, Billings, and Laurel all had literary societies, and Butte had dozens of organizations, ranging from the Homer Club, founded to study ancient Greek culture, to

Above: The Buttrey's Store in Havre hosts a show of the finest women's fashions of 1917. Despite their distance from the fashion centers of the world, Montana women kept up with the latest trends by poring over mail-order catalogs and women's magazines and copying the styles they saw there.
Photo courtesy of the Al Lucke collection, Montana Historical Society

Opposite: In 1917, delegates gather in Havre for the annual convention of the Women's Christian Temperance Union. The WCTU, together with the Anti-Saloon League, led the fight for prohibition of alcoholic beverages in Montana. In 1918, they succeeded in their aim, taking Montana "dry" two years before the rest of the nation. *Photo courtesy of the Al Lucke collection, Montana Historical Society*

the Circle of Serbian Sisters, which served the Serbian immigrants of the Mining City.

Thanks to the three transcontinental railroads that traversed the state, Montana women easily kept up with national trends. They subscribed to an array of magazines that apprised them of cultural and political issues. They bought the latest fashions through mail-order catalogs. In turn, some attempted to modernize the nation's women. In 1919, Belle Fliegelman Winestine, who had campaigned on street corners for equal suffrage, designed six maternity dresses for her pregnancy. Maternity clothes were nonexistent at the time. As she recalled, "You just wore your ordinary clothes until you got very conspicuous and then you didn't go out in public for about four months, except perhaps at night when nobody would see you." She decided to share her innovation with other women and submitted her patterns to the *Ladies' Home Journal.* But the nation was not ready for such novelty. Along with a printed rejection slip, Mrs. Winestine received a note from the editor, informing her that "The *Ladies' Home Journal* does not mention babies before they are born."

Montana's clubwomen did far more than read literature, practice decorative arts, and keep up with the latest fashions. Part of a national women's movement, they tackled the social problems of the day, especially when they felt that local and state governments were not. As Mary Meigs Atwater remembered, "The absurd state of politics was one of the reasons that—once I gave up bridge—I decided to go in for public work." Women's voluntary associations worked for pure-food laws and milk inspection; created public playgrounds, parks, and gardens; raised college scholarships for girls; and founded many of the state's public libraries. Women in cities as diverse as Bozeman, Miles City, and Butte petitioned local governments to hire women police officers to work with juveniles and female offenders. None of the cities did so, although Butte eventually assigned a woman probation officer to patrol dance halls. In contemporary times, women's voluntary clubs continue their community work, staffing hotlines for farmers in crisis, helping equip

volunteer fire departments, and establishing shelters for battered women.

Women's major political campaign in the twentieth century targeted the right to vote. Montanans first debated equal suffrage during the 1889 constitutional convention but declined to include it in the original state constitution. In several subsequent lawmaking sessions, the state legislature defeated proposed constitutional amendments for women's suffrage. Revitalized by a series of victories in other western states, Montana women launched a new campaign in the 1910s. With the assistance of Jeannette Rankin, a University of Montana graduate who had worked as a social worker and suffrage organizer in New York, Washington, California, and many other states, Montana women won the vote in 1914, six years before the Nineteenth Amendment

Opposite: Montana holds the distinction of sending the first woman to Congress, in 1917. In her inaugural vote as a member of the House of Representatives, Jeannette Rankin drew a storm of criticism by voting against U.S. entry into World War I. She devoted much of her life to the cause of peace and worked equally hard for suffrage and other women's issues.
Photo courtesy of the Montana Historical Society

Above: Entrants in the first Miss Montana contest, held in 1933, line up for a group portrait in front of a plane belonging to the contest sponsor, Northwest Airlines. The winner, Marie Braida, impressed judges with her virtuosity on the accordion.
Photo courtesy of the Peter Yegen Museum

granted all American women that privilege. Capitalizing on the momentum of that triumph, Montana women sent Rankin to the U.S. House of Representatives in 1917; she was the first woman to serve in Congress.

Jeannette Rankin is best known for her staunch pacifism. In her first vote in Congress, she joined fifty-five of her colleagues in opposing U.S. entry into World War I, rising from her seat to state, "I want to stand by my country, but I cannot vote for war. I vote no." Re-elected to the House in 1940, she cast the lone vote against declaring war with Japan in 1941. What is less often remembered about Rankin is her political work on behalf of women. She helped spur the government to enforce the eight-hour day for female federal workers. Alarmed by high rates of infant mortality in the United States, and particularly in the rural West, she designed the first federal measure to provide funding for instruction in maternal and infant care and hygiene. Her dedication to peace lasted her lifetime. In 1968, at age eighty-eight, she

marched at the head of a phalanx of nearly five thousand women protesting U.S. involvement in Vietnam.

The early decades of the twentieth century witnessed Montana women's efforts to improve their status and opportunities in the workplace and in the political arena. In the 1920s and 1930s, they and their families were hard-pressed to hang on to their livelihoods. The depression and drought that hit the state at the end of World War I ushered in two decades of economic hard times, in which women struggled to hold together their families, homes, and farms. Not until World War II did economic prosperity return and new opportunities for Montana women emerge.

In the 1940s, thousands of men and women left the state to serve in the armed forces and to work at lucrative jobs in the aircraft and shipbuilding industries of the West Coast. Those women who stayed home faced new challenges. Some had taken over men's jobs during World War I, driving trucks and streetcars, running elevators, and working on the railroads. In the mid-1940s, women stepped into industrial jobs at the copper smelter in Anaconda and the refinery in Great Falls. Reluctantly, the Anaconda Company and the unions agreed that the solution to the labor shortage was to hire women. But women's contracts stipulated that they would be hired only "for the period of the manpower shortage or the duration of the war, which ever shall be the shortest period of time."

Opposite top: Skye Fuller wears protective clothing and a smoke filter mask while fighting the wildfires that ravaged the state in 1988. *Photo by Jeff & Alexa Henry*

Opposite bottom: A Harlowton mother, Faye Talmadge, shows off her pride and joy. In 1900, only 38 percent of Montana's population was female. A decade later, the homestead boom brought thousands of women and girls into the state, narrowing the gender gap. *Photo courtesy of the Montana Historical Society*

Left: This woman railroader works for the Central Montana Railroad, a grain growers' cooperative near Denton. *Photo by John Reddy*

Below: A construction worker spikes logs together to build a log house in the Paradise Valley. Women have long played a role in the building of Montana—both literally and figuratively. *Photo by Jeff & Alexa Henry*

Eventually, over ninety women worked in traditional men's jobs in the Anaconda smelter. This was far from equal opportunity, however. The women had to be "Anaconda residents, wives of smelter workers in the service or former workers recently deceased or disabled, and primary breadwinners with children or parents to support." Placed in unskilled, entry-level jobs, the women still earned on average more than twice what they had made in their previous work, such as waitressing. Their on-the-job transformation carried over into life off the job as well. Breaking long-standing taboos against respectable women frequenting bars, female smelter workers began stopping off after work at Third Street taverns to see "what it was that the men enjoyed so much." Some made a habit of drinking a few beers, talking about work, and shooting pool before heading home to cook dinner for their families.

The smelter women were laid off early in 1946 as men returned from the war. Despite their short-lived

sojourn, the experience of satisfying work and good wages had long-lasting effects. It changed their ideas of what women were capable of, and it changed the way they raised their daughters. In the 1970s, young women took advantage of equal-opportunity legislation to get permanent jobs at the smelter.

Montana women in the postwar years have mirrored the roles of other American women. Increasingly, they have sought higher education, better economic opportunities, and increased political power. Although Montana women earn college degrees at the same rate as women across the nation, more Montana girls graduate from high school than the national average. Greater access to education and job training throughout the century has dramatically increased women's participation in the labor force. In 1900, when 14.5 percent of Montana women worked for wages, they comprised only 8.5 percent of Montana's employed workers. By 1995, more than 56 percent of the state's women were employed, constituting

46.8 percent of Montana's labor force. However, although women are no longer shunted almost exclusively into service jobs, Montana's economy still provides limited occupational opportunities for them. The largest numbers of Montana's female employees work in technical and administrative support and sales. Professionals—a category dominated by teachers—form the second largest group, and service workers make up the third.

Women have made visible inroads into governing Montana. When territorial representatives met to draft the original state constitution, no women participated. But nearly one-fifth of the delegates who drafted the new state constitution in 1972 were female. Emma Ingalls and Maggie Smith Hathaway were the first women elected to the Montana Legislature, in 1916; by 1995, the legislature was nearly one-quarter female. Women do not yet sit in the catbird seat of political power—Dorothy Bradley lost the 1992 gubernatorial election by the slimmest of margins—but they are present in virtually every branch of local and state government. Times have changed considerably since 1911, when Jeannette Rankin was allowed to speak to the Montana Legislature only by special invitation. To mark and perhaps mock that occasion, male legislators each contributed fifty cents for bouquets of violets to deck the chambers. Rankin appreciated the gesture, but nosegays of violets did not satisfy her.

In the years since Rankin's call for political equality, Montana women have extended their domain beyond the confines of kitchen and parlor. Now comprising half of the state population, women leave their mark in every corner of Montana's public and private life. Alberta Bair was a prime example of one woman who changed Montana's face. Born in 1895, her life spanned nearly the full course of the twentieth century. Before she died in 1993, Alberta had tasted and relished all that Montana had to offer. But she ensured that she returned to the state the means for others to share her pleasures. Alberta's father, Charles Bair, made his fortune in Montana; with that fortune, Alberta endowed clinics, hospitals, museums, colleges, symphonies, and theaters across the state. Her attention and money supported the public's health, education, and arts. Today, Lizzie Chester Fisk and Madeleine Blair would find Helena and Butte considerably less daunting than they did one hundred years ago—in great part due to the efforts of women like Alberta Bair, whose time, labor, and money have sculpted Montana's physical and social landscape.

Full social and economic equality still eludes Montana women, and they themselves are divided by class, culture, and political persuasion. Still, there is no doubt that they will carry Alberta Bair's exuberance and Jeannette Rankin's sense of justice into the twenty-first century.

Opposite: Democrat Dorothy Bradley challenged Marc Racicot in the gubernatorial race of 1992 and came very close to being elected Montana's first female governor. Montanans elected another woman, Republican Judy Martz, as lieutenant governor four years later. *Photo by Stuart S. White*

Below: Judge Gail Stewart, the first woman to preside over Billings City Court, served in that capacity from 1990 to 1998. *Photo by Michael Crummett*

EARTH, THE ESSENCE

MONTANA AGRICULTURE IN THE TWENTIETH CENTURY

Montana's essence is steeped in its land. The land is at the core of its being; it is the elemental force of its inhabitants, indigenous or immigrant. The geological smorgasbord that crisscrosses the map finds its singular expression in the fields around Plentywood and the high mountain valleys at Wisdom, in the grasslands at Alzada and the alpine meadows near Yaak.

No story of Montana can be told without acknowledging its climate and seasonal weather patterns, including the unexpected storms that alter or destroy lives and livelihoods. Those same storms replenish the lifeblood of the soil. Montana's high plains, arid prairies, and mountainous valleys are worth absolutely nothing without water—timely, sustaining water. And it is water that has vitalized Montana agriculture in the twentieth century. Water, or its absence, has been the determining factor for farmers and ranchers as they have struggled—and continue to struggle—to reap grain and grass from the land. At the same time, governmental land-use and fiscal policy has ebbed and flowed with nature's climatic assaults, often against all reason, leading to the absurdity of congressional attempts to "guarantee" the weather during the agricultural price crisis of the 1980s. The timely arrival of adequate moisture to slake the land's thirst was and is the only guarantee of existence in the territory that is Montana.

It was the search for a Northwest Passage, a waterway leading to the Pacific Ocean, that brought the first White men to the land now known by its Spanish name, Montana.

In the early eighteenth century, French explorers Louis-Joseph and François de la Verendrye were on such a quest when they pushed west and south from the Mandan villages on the Missouri River in what is now North Dakota and into the region that would become Montana. They were the first of a trickle, then a wave, of explorers, adventurers, and exploiters who would invade the wilderness to harvest its raw treasures, exposing the wealth of the land to the world. Trappers and hunters were followed by miners and sawyers, who spawned the merchants, farmers, and livestock producers they needed to sustain them. Railroad barons and financiers followed quickly to consolidate and control distribution of the bounty that was harvested with backbreaking labor. From its inception, Montana has been, and continues to be, a resource colony for the world. Beaver hats and buffalo coats gave way to gold, silver, and lumber. In turn,

BY JIM GRANSBERY

Opposite: As the Sweetgrass Hills slumber in the distance, sunrise gilds a wheat field near Chester. *Photo by John Lambing*

Opposite: A stunning rainbow arches over a beaverslide haystacker in Western Montana's Big Hole, the "Valley of 10,000 Haystacks." Two Big Hole ranchers developed and patented the beaverslide in the first decade of the century. Much faster than previous methods, the new stacker created tightly packed haystacks impervious to wind.
Photo by Chuck Haney

Above: Boxcars await a load of grain in Fairfield, a small farming community on the edge of Montana's Golden Triangle. Montana is the nation's third largest wheat producer, and the Golden Triangle—the region bounded by Great Falls, Havre, and Cut Bank—produces about half of the state's wheat. The Fairfield area also produces a significant barley crop.
Photo by Chuck Haney

wheat and beef became the currency of exchange, the chattel of collateral for bankers and land brokers. Today, the intelligence and talent of Montana youth are exported to the corners of country and globe.

The desire of early railroad tycoons to ship grain to the West Coast for trade in the Orient is realized today in the export of Montana wheat to Japan, Taiwan, and Korea. As much as seventy percent of the annual yield goes to feed the populous nations of the Far East. Agricultural science and technology, developed at Montana's land-grant college and Agricultural Experiment Station, feed the country and produce favorable trade balances through the overseas sale of food and fiber.

The history of Montana agriculture in the twentieth century is the story of men and women laboring against the elements to make a living for themselves and their children. The challenge is no less daunting at the end of the century than it was at the beginning. Although some variables have changed, the recurring impediments to success resemble the retrograde epicycles of Ptolemaic astronomy. Nonetheless, Montanans have repeatedly toiled and triumphed, each generation renewing its covenant to the essence of their being: the Land.

It is the "hidden" stories that explain the present.

Often the ignored or unacknowledged facts of the past provide the building blocks, the "truths," necessary for understanding the present. A combination of acts and events in the last half of the nineteenth century led to the boom and bust of twentieth-century American agriculture. The Jeffersonian ideal of a nation of self-sufficient producers found support in the conscious and unconscious motivations of a president and a Congress in the midst of the country's greatest crisis, the Civil War. The foundation stones for modern agriculture were quarried and chiseled haphazardly, squared and plumbed at disparate sites, but by the beginning of the 1900s, they were mortared together, forming the basis on which American farmers and ranchers would provide food for the country and eventually the world.

Despite infighting, Republicans in the 1862 Congress managed to produce an impressive body of legislation. They passed the original Homestead Act, chartered a transcontinental railroad, established a system of land-grant colleges, and created the Department of Agriculture, all while dealing with the weighty issues surrounding the Civil War.

The Homestead Act of 1862 offered 160 acres of the

Left: Christine Finkelson stands in the doorway of her homestead, circa 1910. Austere by contemporary standards but well appointed in its day, the Finkelson homestead was located near Sidney in Eastern Montana. *Photo courtesy of the Montana Historical Society*

Opposite: With elaborate designs crafted from the various agricultural products of Montana, the state advertised its bounty at a Land Show sponsored in 1911 by the Northwestern Development League at St. Paul, Minnesota. *Photo courtesy of the Montana Historical Society*

Opposite: Suitably outfitted in spurs and chaps, a rodeo cowboy waits his turn to prove himself in the arena.
Photo by Joanne M. Berghold

Above: A determined cowgirl tosses her lariat. Derived from the day-to-day tasks of early cowboys, rodeo has become the quintessential Western sport. *Photo by David R. Stoecklein*

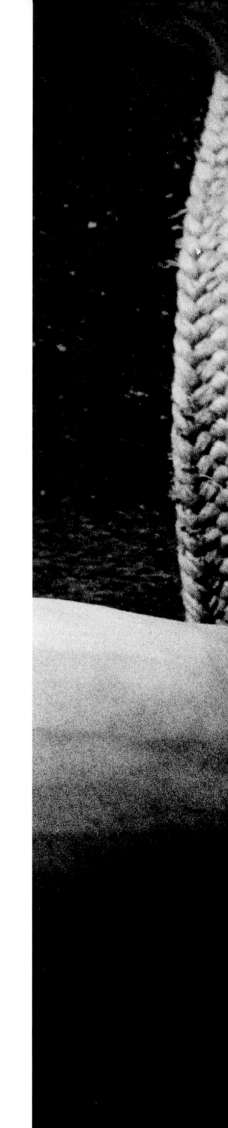

Above: A bull rider loses his seat and plunges into a sea of mud at a rodeo in Browning. Every summer, more than 50 sanctioned National Rodeo Association and Pro National Rodeo Association events are held across Montana, along with dozens of ranch rodeos, old-timer rodeos, youth rodeos, and team roping contests. *Photo by Stuart S. White*

Opposite: A bareback rider gets a good grip on his rigging as he waits to leave the chute. *Photo by Joanne M. Berghold*

public domain to any man or woman who was the head of a family and who was an American citizen, or who at least had filed intentions of becoming one. To gain title, the settler had to reside on the land for five years and pay a nominal registration fee. This original Homestead Act was of slight consequence in Montana, which had not yet joined the Union. The acreage it provided was not enough to support a family in a region where water was not readily available, and few farmers applied. But Congress was compliant. It passed the Desert Land Act in 1877, making 640-acre sections available for $1.25 an acre if the buyer "proved up" in three years and irrigated part of the plot. The Desert Land Act was used widely in Montana but mostly by unscrupulous ranchers who wanted access to prime grazing lands. In 1909, Congress enacted the Enlarged Homestead Act, which offered 320 acres per person. Immigrants began to flow onto the

northern Great Plains, aided and abetted by railroad promoters.

"It was the railroads that put us [Montana farmers] into business," asserted Robert G. Dunbar, a former professor emeritus of history at Montana State University in Bozeman during a 1986 interview. "The Great Northern and Northern Pacific made possible the large-scale production of wheat and cattle. It was this expansion of markets plus the Homestead Acts that put us into business."

The Northern Pacific Railroad, under the leadership of Frederick Billings, pushed west from Bismarck, North Dakota, in 1879. By 1881, crews were laying track along the Yellowstone River, and that same year the Union Pacific entered Montana from the south and established a railhead in the copper-mining city of Butte. In 1887, Jim Hill pushed his Great Northern Railway across the Hi-Line and into Great Falls, linking up with the

Montana Central Railroad. This opened the way to the markets of the Midwest and East Coast. A fourth rail link would be constructed in 1906. The Chicago, Milwaukee, St. Paul & Pacific—the "Milwaukee Road"—linked Montana with the West Coast.

Montana agriculture got another boost in 1887. That year, Congress passed the Agricultural Experiment Station Act, which led to the development of new varieties of wheat, barley, and oats. In 1914, the Extension Service was created to disseminate the scientific breakthroughs discovered at the experiment stations.

Two more episodes would help form the foundation of modern agriculture in Montana: the "Hard Winter" of 1886–1887 and the failure of officials to listen to a one-armed prophet crying in the arid wilderness.

The winter of 1886–1887 was a critical point in Montana history. It marked the beginning of the end of the open range and left thousands of bloated cattle carcasses in its wake. It made cowboys cry, and not just because of the knife-cold wind.

A combination of drought, low cattle prices, overgrazing, and hunger-weakened cattle set the stage for the disaster that began in November 1886. Heavy snow

began to fall that month, followed by a brief chinook in January. Then a long, severe cold spell encased the scant forage in ice. When chinook winds finally cleared the snow and ice in March, thousands of carcasses littered the ground—an estimated 362,000 head of cattle had died of starvation and cold. Granville Stuart, a prominent Montana cattleman at the time, wrote: "A business that had been fascinating to me before, suddenly became distasteful. I wanted no more of it. I never wanted to own again an animal that I could not feed and shelter."

One of the most famous and enduring vestiges of that Hard Winter was a small postcard painted in watercolor by Charlie Russell. It showed a gaunt steer with bowed legs and lowered head surrounded by hungry

Opposite: This irrigation flume brought much-needed water to thirsty fields near Billings during the droughts that haunted the first decades of the century. Today, more than a quarter of the cropland in Montana is irrigated; the rest is farmed using dryland methods. *Photo courtesy of the Western Heritage Center*

Above: Black Angus cattle line up for mealtime on a snowy day. The Hard Winter of 1886–1887, in which thousands of cattle died of starvation because their forage was encased in ice, convinced Montana ranchers of the need to provide their stock with supplemental winter feedings. *Photo by Jim Wylder*

Opposite top: In almost any season, hanging your clothes out to dry in Montana can be risky business. *Photo by Stuart S. White*

Opposite bottom: Railroad tracks veer toward a grain elevator at Acton, not far from Billings. *Photo by Michael Sample*

Above: The spectacular "big sky" for which Montana is famous outlines a lone rider at sundown. *Photo by Scott Spiker*

Above: Steam threshers revolutionized the wheat harvest in the first years of the century. These rigs were photographed in 1913, probably in Hill County. In 1915, Montana farmers would produce a record 60 million bushels of wheat, encouraging a flood of homesteaders to cast their lot here.
Photo courtesy of the Al Lucke collection, Montana Historical Society

Opposite: The wheat harvest grew increasingly mechanized as the century progressed. This photograph was taken in 1966. Wheat has long been Montana's most valuable agricultural commodity. In 1910, the harvest was valued at $8 million; today it accounts for close to $700 million in cash receipts.
Photo by Jack Gilluly, courtesy of the Montana Historical Society

wolves. Russell sent the postcard to a cattle owner in Helena who had inquired about the condition of his animals. Under the picture, the cowboy artist wrote, "Last of Five Thousand."

That deadly winter represented the apex of open-range ranching, and the practice rapidly declined thereafter. Speculators went bankrupt, and smaller ranches, where hay was produced for winter feed, became the norm. Even large outfits began providing forage for their stock. But hay meadows require water, and controlled sources of water were few.

Flood irrigation began in the United States in 1847, when the first group of Mormon pioneers to reach Utah diverted water from City Creek near present-day Salt Lake City. But it was not until 1902 that Congress passed the National Reclamation Act, which authorized the U.S. government to plan and construct irrigation projects, with water users repaying the cost over a period of years. At the end of the twentieth century, taxpayers still are paying directly and indirectly for this legislation.

In the four decades between passage of the Homestead Act and the Reclamation Act, the dire predictions of Major John Wesley Powell were realized. Despite the loss of his right arm at Shiloh in 1862, Powell went on to explore the Colorado River and the

Intermountain West. In 1878, he concluded in his "Report on the Lands of the Arid Region of the United States" that an unirrigated farm of 160 acres could not support a homesteading family, while, with water, eighty acres would suffice. He noted, too, that 160 acres was not enough on which to graze livestock and proposed grazing tracts of 2,560 acres. And he recommended that water rights be attached to the land in streamside units so that every homestead would have access to water. He proposed that the government finance and build irrigation projects and encourage the creation of cooperative irrigation districts to build dams and ditches to control and distribute the water. His advice was ignored; the report collected dust.

As the twentieth century dawned, the foundation for an agrarian revolution was in place. Land was available, railroads ran through it, and science and technology were poised to overcome the aridity of the climate. New water projects would make the "desert" bloom.

And they did—for a while.

"In the first sixteen years of the twentieth century, Montana's grasslands yielded an annual average of more than 25 bushels of wheat to the plowed acre. In 1919, the yield was 2.4 bushels." That was the effect of drought described by legendary Montana journalist-historian Joseph Kinsey Howard in *Montana: High, Wide, and Handsome*.

It was a script that would repeat itself several times throughout the 1900s: wet years, abundant crops; dry years, disaster. Boom and bust is a three-word short course in Montana's economic history, and it has not been limited to agriculture. With gritty determination, Montana farmers and ranchers have endured cycles of surplus, scarcity, and wild price fluctuations that have often contradicted the law—or in the cynical words of former *Billings Gazette* farm writer Charlie Femling, "the lie"—of supply and demand. Their determination was born of the grit in their teeth as plow was put to prairie, as "drouth" and wind parched the plains.

In the early nineteenth century, farmers had skipped over the plains—the Great American Desert—as they

Opposite top: Proud farmers near Sidney show off the sizable fruits of their labor. The railroads used images like this one, depicting a bumper crop, to lure thousands of homesteaders to Montana in the early 1900s. *Photo courtesy of the MonDak Heritage Center*

Opposite bottom: A derelict ladder dangles from a granary west of Bozeman. *Photo by Tom Murphy*

Above: Nearly three million cattle roam the range in Montana today, including these in the lush Flathead Valley. In fact, cows outnumber human residents by more than three to one. *Photo by Jeff & Alexa Henry*

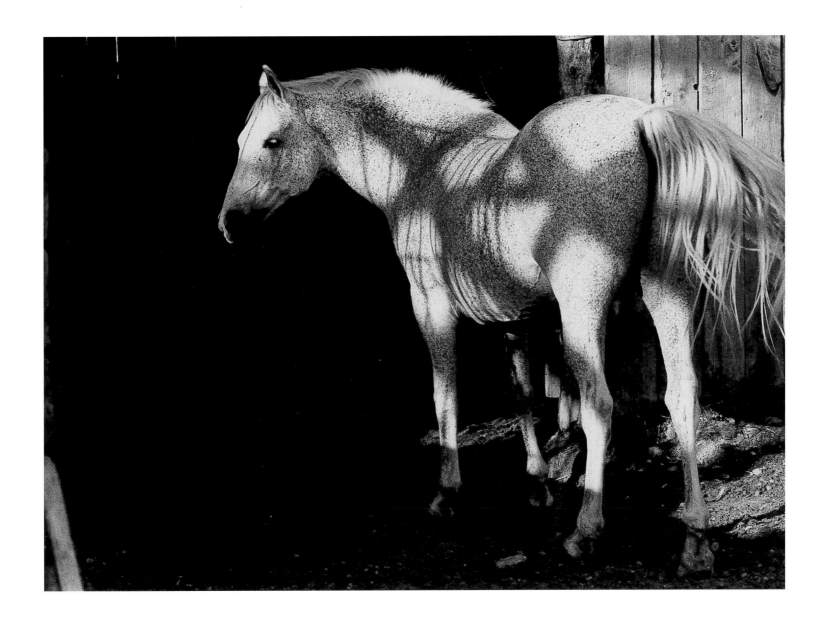

Opposite: Virginia and Harold Sprague pose with their dog,
Stubs, on their spread in Rosebud County, one of the top 10
livestock-producing counties in the state.
Photo by Michael Crummett

Above: The sun turns an ordinary barnyard animal into a
striking work of abstract art. *Photo by Joanne M. Berghold*

farming. Enticed by new farming theories, a disingenuous public-relations campaign, and favorable rail rates, thousands of would-be farmers flocked to the "promised land" via the iron roads. Historians note that, for as little as $22.50, a homesteader could ship his family and all his worldly possessions from St. Paul to Montana. The wave of new farmers began arriving in 1908–1909 and crested in 1910. It slackened in the next couple of years and then rose again until 1918. The population of the state climbed from 243,329 in 1900 to 376,053 in 1910. During the same period, the number of farms doubled from 13,370 to 26,214. A state promotional bulletin in 1918 pegged the population at 769,590, but the figure was probably inflated. The 1990 census counted just over 799,000 Montanans.

Although the longest river system in the country runs through Montana, large-scale irrigation was slow to develop. In the first decade of the twentieth century, the Huntley Project brought irrigation to sugar-beet fields along the Yellowstone River near Billings. But most homesteaders had to rely on dry-land farming methods devised by Hardy Webster Campbell. These focused on conserving what little moisture there was by reducing runoff and evaporation and by increasing absorption and retention. Campbell emphasized packing the subsoil so that it would absorb water from deep underground. He suggested using a dust mulch to protect against evaporation.

Agricultural scientists at the Experiment Station in Bozeman were not enthusiastic supporters of Campbell's methods. Instead, they developed drought-resistant grain varieties and encouraged farmers to diversify and raise livestock. They also developed strip farming, which remains the most popular dry-land technique at the end of the twentieth century.

The land-rush promoters of the early 1900s had an unlikely ally: the weather. The influx of homesteaders coincided with a period of ample moisture so that many believed they could expect a "normal" rainfall of sixteen inches a year. Such abundant moisture resulted in the "miracle year" of 1915, when forty-two million bushels

migrated west. They were eager to reach the fertile mountain valleys and the lush Pacific Coast. But at the dawn of the twentieth century, new laws, new machines, and a new breed of hucksters lured Midwesterners and Europeans to the "free land" on the Montana prairie. Historians Michael Malone, Richard Roeder, and William Lang contended that Montana should have been called the "Homestead State," because, between 1909 and 1923, settlers filed a record 114,620 claims on almost 25 million acres of land—more than in any other state. The sodbusters found the land wide open.

* * *

"I know Big Jim Hill, he's a good friend of mine.

"I ride on his railroad most all of the time."

That hobo ditty postdates the homestead era, but it was Hill's railroads that transported the flood of farmers to Montana. Everybody knew Jim Hill, who wanted everybody to move to Montana to take up dry-land

of wheat were harvested—almost four times the yield of 1910. Prices were high as the war in Europe created demand for U.S. wheat. But on the horizon, a dark cloud loomed, and it bore no rain. Its portent was ruin.

Who were the homesteaders, or "honyockers" (a slur formed from the corruption of a German phrase meaning "chicken chaser"), who bet their lives and livelihoods on the arid plains? Most were young, and most were the native-born descendents of British immigrants, although many of German and Norse heritage congregated in northeastern Montana. They came from all walks of life. Some were even single women who filed claims for themselves. Their lives were harsh, and their futures held no promise. As World War I ended, wheat prices collapsed and the rain disappeared. The next twenty years brought drought, wind, fire, gophers, locusts, and poverty. Government aid was scant. Nearly seventy years later, in 1988, history would repeat itself, as fire, drought, and grasshoppers destroyed Montana cropland. But this time, congressmen and presidential candidates would outbid one another in their efforts to save the farmers.

It has been said that economic statistics are the stories of peoples' lives without the tears. From 1919 to 1925, roughly two million acres passed out of production and eleven thousand farms were abandoned. Twenty thousand mortgages were foreclosed, and half of Montana's farmers lost their land. The average value of an acre of farmland dropped fifty percent.

The winter of 1982 would serve as a prologue for the late 1990s. It was the beginning of a fundamental shift in U.S. farm policy, developed during the Depression and maintained for sixty years, and it would culminate in the Freedom to Farm Bill, which Congress passed in 1996 and which put farmers into the free market. Leaders of the Montana Grain Growers Association invited their counterparts from other wheat-producing states to join them at Big Sky, Montana, for a closed-door discussion about low prices and surplus grain. The U.S. government's high loan price for wheat had become the de facto world price, and it encouraged farmers in the United States and every other grain-growing country to produce

Opposite: Proving the value of irrigation in Montana's semiarid climate, corn grew 10 feet high at Huntley Project in 1915. The Huntley Project was a federal irrigation development established east of Billings in the first decade of the century, before the widespread advent of dry-land farming.
Photo courtesy of the Montana Historical Society

Above: Sheep parade down the chute at shearing sheds near Great Falls, circa 1925. In 1910, there were almost six million sheep in Montana, making this the nation's premier wool-growing state. But with the close of the open range and the rise of sheep production elsewhere, Montana's sheep population dwindled to less than half a million by century's end.
Photo courtesy of the Montana Historical Society

Opposite: Ranch hands brand a calf during the spring roundup on the Top Hat Ranch near Two Dot, circa 1959. Witty Westerners have called brands the "heraldry of the range" and "pyroglyphics." In 1999, almost 76,000 different brands were registered with the state Department of Livestock.
Photo courtesy of the Montana Historical Society

Above: Homesteader George Nitz is up to his elbows in laundry in 1912. Many Montana homesteaders were bachelors, but the boom also brought large numbers of single women eager to file homestead claims. In some areas, as many as 20 percent of all claims were made by unmarried women.
Photo courtesy of the Montana Historical Society

Bales litter a hay field near Avon. Many of the valleys of south-western Montana—including the Beaverhead, Big Hole, Flint Creek, and Deer Lodge—are famous for their lush hay fields.
Photo by John Reddy

too much wheat. Because the market price was lower than the value of the loans they received, U.S. farmers were forfeiting the grain to the government, which was stuffing it into every empty bin it could find. Grain elevators sprouted just to store grain for the government, which paid more than thirty cents a bushel per year for the storage. Out of the Big Sky meeting came the idea that the loan rate had to be forced down to clear the surplus and allow farmers to earn their money in the marketplace. The government had to give the surplus away or sell it at reduced prices. The idea was not popular, but later that year the MGGA passed a resolution asking for a reduction in the loan rate. The National Association of Wheat Growers rejected the proposal, but it made its way into the 1985 Farm Bill.

Initially, the result was painful. Low wheat prices and drought slammed Montana producers in 1984 and 1985. The following year, the federal government gave U.S. farmers more than $26 billion in price-support payments for all program commodities, including Montana's major crops: wheat and barley. That was the high-water mark for government payments to farmers. It set the stage for the sharp reduction and eventual elimination of price supports, which had originated in Montana during the dark days of the Depression.

* * *

The 1920s were bleak. Half of Montana farmers lost their land, and half of the state's banks failed. Those who had the means fled the state for the West Coast. Some sixty thousand people sought a new life elsewhere. Despite some respite in the last couple years of the decade, when crops briefly rallied, the 1920s were a dress rehearsal for the difficult times to come.

The decade between 1929, when the stock market crashed, and 1939, when World War II began, was one of constant struggle against hot weather, dust storms, low commodity prices, and food surpluses. Wheat worth

$100 in 1920 brought only $19.23 in 1932. Beef cattle that sold for $9.10 per hundred pounds in 1929 went for $3.34 in 1934. Sheep prices also plummeted. The decade saw the loss of twelve percent of the state's farms, and the value of those that survived dropped by thirty-five percent. Americans, especially rural Americans, needed help, and the federal government stepped in to offer them a New Deal.

Beginning in the mid-1930s, Montana farmers and ranchers had a constant companion in the U.S. Department of Agriculture. At first it was a lifesaver, but when economic and climatic conditions improved, grumbling about government interference began to color the coffee klatches in rural towns and taverns.

Nonetheless, the New Deal was a good deal better than what Montana agriculture had endured since 1919. In the six years from 1933 through 1938, the federal government provided half a billion dollars to Montanans through direct expenditures and loans. The Rural Electrification Administration literally enlightened the countryside.

The major help for Depression-era farmers throughout the United States came from Montana, according to a history of the Agricultural Experiment Station and the Extension Service at Montana State University. The first Agricultural Assistance Act (1933) was written in the university's Ag Building (now Linfield Hall) around 1932 after agricultural economist M. L. Wilson spent time with some Gallatin County farmers. They told Wilson they would cut back on wheat production to reduce the surplus if other farmers in other states would do the same thing. This idea led to national farm programs that reduced acres planted in exchange for price supports.

Until the Farm Bill of 1996, which phases out government price supports by 2002, national farm policy consisted of tweaking the ideas generated at Linfield Hall more than sixty years earlier.

Economic conditions for ranchers paralleled those for farmers. Out of a need for more rangeland, a group of cattlemen in Rosebud and Custer Counties formed a

Opposite: In a scene reminiscent of the earliest years of the century, cowboys take a coffee break by the chuckwagon during a roundup. *Photo by Michael Sample*

Above: This prosperous farm near Great Falls underscores the importance of agriculture, and especially wheat growing, to Montana's economy. *Photo by Richard Mousel*

Opposite: A Montana blacksmith pounds out a horseshoe in the same way as generations of blacksmiths before him.
Photo by Jim Wylder

Above: The day's chores at last behind her, Mrs. Arnold Schiefelbein heads in from her barn near Whitefish.
Photo by Michael Crummett

Left: A cowgirl dresses to dazzle at Helena's Last Chance Stampede. Montana women have long distinguished themselves in the tough rodeo arena. In fact, in 1975, Red Lodge native Alice Greenough Orr became the first person inducted into the National Cowgirl Hall of Fame. She won four world saddle bronc championships in the 1930s and 1940s.
Photo by Donnie Sexton / Travel Montana

cooperative grazing district in 1928 and leased more than a hundred thousand acres of public and private land. The ranchers controlled the number of animals feeding on the range, and as a result the forage recovered from years of overgrazing. This Mizpah-Pumpkin Creek Grazing Association provided a national blueprint. In 1934, Congress passed the Taylor Grazing Act, which still governs the grazing of cattle and sheep by private livestock producers on public land. The value of that forage is a subject of contention at the end of the twentieth century.

As World War II got under way, Montana farmers and ranchers entered a period of prosperity created by adequate moisture and wartime demand. They reinvested their capital in land and new machinery, giving agriculture a new infrastructure and allowing it to remain the basis of the state's economy. In 1941, farmers reaped their best crops since 1927. The yields in 1942 were the best since World War I, and 1943 was the best year Montana farmers had ever seen, according to statistical records. Crop and livestock receipts that year were pegged at more than $300 million. Property values climbed as agriculturists reinvested their wealth and the consolidation of farm holdings accelerated. With the growth of technology and the continuation of scientific research, farmers and ranchers got the tools and incentive to produce quality food for the nation and export markets around the world.

Through the midriff of the century, Montana agriculture was transformed as scientists discovered new, more efficient methods of cultivation and breeding. Retired Montana State University soil physicist Hayden Ferguson has noted that scientific developments in the forties, fifties, sixties, and seventies led to "phenomenal" growth in plant and animal production. Publicly funded research at the Agricultural Experiment Station in Bozeman benefited the public by yielding higher-quality grains and meat.

Development of the Line 1 Hereford herd at Fort Keogh in Miles City showed that certain traits could be selected in bulls and passed to their progeny. The "indexing" of bulls through performance records

changed opinions on how to breed range cattle for the efficient production of beef. "In the 1950s through the 1970s, we learned to breed cows," Ferguson said.

Development of the spring-wheat variety Rescue, which has a solid stem, saved the spring-wheat industry from the ravages of the wheat stem sawfly. Research to develop a solid-stem winter wheat called Vanguard continues. The advent of the drought-resistant barley Campana allowed dry-land farmers to produce thirty bushels an acre. When under stress, the variety produces no leaves but large seeds. In the mid-1940s, Yogo, the first really winter-hardy wheat was released. The development of the deep-furrow seed drill allowed farmers in northern Montana's Golden Triangle to produce winter wheat in yields that surpassed spring wheats, Ferguson noted.

Opposite: Newly shorn ewes head en masse for the lambing corrals of the Matador Ranch in Phillips County. *Photo by Michael Crummett*

Below: Danielle Allen's prize-winning sheep nuzzles her ear at the Last Chance Stampede in Helena. Stock shows sponsored by 4-H give Montana young people invaluable experience in showing and selling the animals they raise themselves. The 4-H program is jointly sponsored by the counties, Montana State University, and the Cooperative Extension Service of the U.S. Department of Agriculture. *Photo by Donnie Sexton / Travel Montana*

COW BOYS AND SADDLE PONNIES IN CAMP ON THE RANGE.

Herbicides and sprayer prototypes gave farmers a weapon against unwanted, yield-reducing weeds. However, the major revolution in yields, according to Ferguson, came with the understanding of how plants use fertilizer most efficiently. That knowledge, coupled with new, hardy varieties of grain, doubled the number of bushels produced per acre over the fifty-year period from the late 1930s to the late 1980s.

Equipment changes, too, contributed greatly to increased production. In cultivation, power equals time-liness. Getting the field work completed in a timely manner gives crops time to mature. Research indicates that farmers lose a bushel per acre per day for every day after May 20 that planting is delayed. Powerful equipment helps to preempt those losses.

In the final quarter of the century, several boom/bust cycles have run their course: the seventies, eighties, and nineties have had their highs and lows for

farmers and ranchers. For Montanans, it is difficult to find the high in the eighties. While the rest of the country enjoyed the "prosperity" promulgated by the Reagan administration, every state whose base economy was built on energy and/or agriculture went into recession. Through the heartland of the plains states, from the Canadian border to the Mexican, it was a time of economic trial—and not just in the rural areas. Harsh droughts in 1984, 1985, and 1988 threw salt in the wounds.

Nevertheless, agriculture continues to be the primary source of income in Montana; tourism is a distant second. The state's crops and livestock have produced cash receipts of at least $2 billion each year since 1990. Its hard red wheats are world-renowned, and its feeder cattle are considered the best available. Its seed stock is shipped around the globe. As the number of farms and ranches has declined, the amount of crop and rangeland

Their saddle ponies picketed nearby, cowboys working for the XIT Ranch dig into a chuckwagon dinner, circa 1908. This camp was probably in northern Montana, near the Blackfeet Reservation. *Photo by G. V. Barker, courtesy of the Montana Historical Society*

has remained fairly constant at about sixty million acres. Montana's once mighty sheep industry, which produced 5.7 million head in 1903, has declined to a mere shadow of itself in the 1990s, with less than 400,000 head. Loss of the Wool Act in 1993, foreign competition in the wool and lamb markets, sustained losses to predators (mostly coyotes), and the loss of funding for lobbying and promotion has brought it to its knees.

As the twentieth century closes, Montana has hosted a new type of immigrant. Wealth generated in other states is being invested here. Sharp increases in population and land development in Flathead, Missoula, Ravalli, Gallatin, and Yellowstone Counties have forced prime farmland to give way to homes and septic tanks. Acreages in rural Montana are quite the rage in celebrity circles. Prices paid for pristine home sites on hay meadows and range are often greater than any income that could be earned by cultivating or grazing the land, thus eliminating food and fiber production at a time when world demand is growing.

* * *

On the banks of the Big Hole River south of Melrose, rancher Tom Cramer, his wife, and their extended family raise commercial cattle and hay. The water rights on the property were filed in 1875, and the ranch has belonged to only two families since its inception. Cramer's stepfather bought the ranch from the founding family in the early 1950s. The Cramers still hold a summer grazing permit for range in the Humbug Spires. They have weathered the ups and downs of Montana agriculture for almost half a century. The lush hay meadows, supplemented when a neighbor retired, have nourished stock cows and their feeder calves for almost 125 years.

The enterprise survives because the Cramers and thousands of others like them know that the real Montana lies in its land and its productivity. Ironically, they now understand the truth in the words of the Nez Perce dreamer, Toohoolhoolzote, who told General Oliver O. Howard: "I belong to the land out of which I came. The Earth is my mother."

Despite the 20th-century homestead boom and the advent of dry-land farming, large expanses of Montana prairie remain as pristine as they were in the days when great herds of buffalo roamed them. *Photo by John Lambing*

Above: Dwarfed by snowy Columbia Mountain, schoolchildren head home from Deer Park School, near Columbia Falls, on a spring day in 1948. By 1950, only 1,300 one- and two-room schools remained in Montana; only 20 years earlier, the state could claim more than 2,500 small rural schools. *Photo by Mel Ruder, courtesy of the Montana Historical Society*

Opposite top: At the 1953 Farm Bureau Hoedown in Bozeman, farm kids from all over Montana swing their partners in hopes of winning the top prize. *Photo courtesy of the Gallatin County Historical Society*

Opposite bottom: The joys of a rural childhood have changed little over the decades. This young farm girl near Billings mixes a generous batch of mud pies, circa 1908. Thousands of farm families had to abandon their homesteads during the disastrous 1920s, when severe drought made farming—and mud pies—nearly impossible. *Photo courtesy of the Drake Family and the Western Heritage Center*

THE DIVORCE THAT COULD NOT LAST

CITY AND COUNTRY IN THE TWENTIETH CENTURY

"The country produces that without which the city could not live; and did the city not exist, the produce of the country for all but family consumption would be valueless. Its outlet, its market is the town. There is thus a mutual interest between them, one sustaining the other, ministering and being ministered to."

Prairie Farmer, May 1849

When we think of the history of western cities, Chicago is probably not the first city to come to mind. But according to William Cronon, author of *Nature's Metropolis: Chicago and the Great West*, "in the most literal sense, from 1848 to the end of the nineteenth century, it was where the West began." Railroads emanating from that centrally located metropolis brought together East and West, city and country. A Chicago railroad analyst drew the picture clearly when he declared that eastern roads were built to Chicago and western roads from it.

The fecundity of the countryside was instrumental in the growth of Chicago's population and economy. The city served as a go-between, linking the settlements and natural resources of the Great West with the cities, factories, and commercial networks of the Northeast. Westerners recognized that Chicago was their most effective gateway to eastern markets, the mechanism that could transform their natural resources into capital.

Eastern capitalists saw the city as a nexus of transport and commerce focused on western supply and demand. Through the railroad, Chicago linked East with West, but it also did more; it reached out and organized the Great West. Through the development and transportation of the West's natural resources, Chicago linked and changed both country and city.

The central role of Chicago as an economic and social link is echoed on a smaller scale in the history of Montana towns and cities. The three largest cities in the state—Great Falls, Missoula, and Billings—all have utilized railroads as a key link to the countryside, and all three have seen the resources of the countryside as the stuff of their own prosperity.

Farmers growing corn, wheat, oats, and barley on the outskirts of Chicago saw that city as an obvious place from which to market their grain, especially since early fur traders had already established a navigable system of

BY DANIEL KEMMIS

Opposite: The downtown streets of Great Falls, Montana's second largest city, sparkle late at night. The community is known as the "Electric City" not because of its neon lights but because of the cheap electricity generated by a handful of dams on the Missouri River, which runs through town. *Photo by Jim Wylder*

waterways. Middle America, the "breadbasket," naturally turned to Chicago's growing transportation system to distribute its crops. As that transportation system reached farther and farther into the countryside, it finally stretched to the Great Falls of the Missouri.

The history of the city of Great Falls begins naturally with that cascade for which it was named, a waterfall described in 1805 by Meriwether Lewis as "this sublimely grand specticle [sic] . . . the grandest sight I ever beheld." That spectacular natural phenomenon became the nucleus of the city, but railroads reaching out from Chicago and grain moving back along their tracks were fundamental to the growth and identity of Great Falls.

Paris Gibson, who established the first important flour mill in Minneapolis, moved to Montana in 1879 looking for other water and power resources and found them at the Great Falls of the Missouri River. With his business partners, Gibson sketched out plans for an industrial city above the falls. Realizing that the success of the new town depended upon railroad connections, he solicited and won the support of James J. Hill, founder of the Great Northern Railway. In 1884, the Black Eagle Dam began providing a source of controlled water power, and by 1887 regular railroad service to the new town commenced, with eventual connections to Helena and Butte. The combination of abundant industrial water power and railroad transportation quickly resulted in a successful mercantile and industrial town, whose population by 1890 had reached 12,000.

Rail lines provided the connection between grain production in the country, milling operations in the city, and markets in the East. But it was the water flowing through the midst of the arable prairie that formed the real basis of Great Falls. This was the natural feature upon which Gibson and the other founders capitalized, both by producing electricity and by establishing flour mills throughout the new city. Great Falls prospered during the twentieth century in no small part because of its connection with the great Golden Triangle, some of the best wheat-producing land on the continent. The rail system served as carrier, the iron link to the earth—and to Chicago. But by the time the railroad reached this far west, the link of city to countryside was becoming a more complex matter than it once had been—more complex and, in a strange way, less visible, less palpable, easier to ignore. It may have begun with the grain itself, pouring into Chicago from as far away as the Golden Triangle.

With the development of the steam-powered grain elevator, grain became an abstract commodity rather than a specific food grown on a specific farm. The grain elevator meant that numerous farmers could mix and store their wheat together in huge quantities to await the next rail-car shipment. The individual farmer lost his tie to his own grain harvest, buyers lost their tie to individual farms, and the city markets lost their connection to the countryside altogether, as grain was bought and sold not in the field but through futures markets on speculative paper. The personal link was broken, as commodity replaced community and became simply business as usual.

Chicago had played out another version of the same story in the nineteenth century: its link to nature had evolved into something like the opposite. Nature in the form of northern forests was converted to capital as logs moved from countryside to city and then back to the countryside in the form of lumber shipped to prairie farmers via the railroads. "Ecology and economy had converged," said Cronon; "the city lay not only on the border between forest and grassland but also on the happy margin between supply and demand."

Previous spread: Incorporated in 1885, Missoula has become the third largest city in Montana after Billings and Great Falls. Since this photo was taken, circa 1930, it has sprawled into every corner of the fertile basin in which it is located, thriving in large part because of the wood-products industry and the presence of the University of Montana. *Photo by Herman Schnitzmeyer, courtesy of Kenneth & Betty Vincent*

Opposite: The Great Falls of the Missouri, which 19th-century explorer Meriwether Lewis described as "the grandest sight I ever beheld," dazzles sightseers at the beginning of the 20th century. The river has since been harnessed by a series of hydroelectric dams. *Photo courtesy of the Cascade County Historical Society*

Right: The elegant façade of Butte's famed Uptown Cafe, considered by many to be one of the best restaurants in Montana, matches the great food available within. In the 1980s and 1990s, fine restaurants sprang up all over Montana. Not only did they offer delicious meals inspired by the cuisine of many cultures, but they often featured Montana-grown ingredients, such as huckleberries, morel mushrooms, venison, trout, and lamb. *Photo by Donnie Sexton / Travel Montana*

But ironically—and prophetically in relation to Western Montana cities—Chicago's dominance in the lumber industry declined drastically by the end of the nineteenth century, due primarily to the exhaustive logging of the northern forests. Chicago was logging itself to death. Disregard of natural systems by urban capitalists resulted in the demise of the industry that had served both city and countryside. As a result, the fate of entire ecosystems, including the human communities within them, forever changed.

That self-defeating form of city-to-countryside connection was then exported to places such as Missoula, where nearby forests began supplying timber in abundance for railroad ties, mine supports in Butte, and eastern housing markets no longer able to rely upon Great Lakes timber. Missoula grew modestly before statehood because of its strategic location at the confluence of the Blackfoot, Bitterroot, and Clark Fork Rivers—and because it straddled the Mullan military road, which brought a steady stream of wagon trains through the valley. But the factors that firmly established Missoula's status as a city were the public university system and the railroad. The Northern Pacific reached Missoula in 1883, an event regarded as significant by local residents

Above: In addition to boasting a healthy stock of antiques, the Virgelle Mercantile, northeast of Fort Benton, rents canoes and offers fully outfitted trips to people eager to float the Wild and Scenic Missouri River. *Photo by Donnie Sexton / Travel Montana*

Opposite: St. Helena Cathedral is one of the finest examples of Gothic architecture in the nation and a beloved landmark of the capital city. Designed by Austrian-born architect Albert O. Von Herbulis, it was patterned after a cathedral in Vienna and cost more than $600,000 to build. It was dedicated on Christmas Day 1914, six years after the cornerstone was laid. *Photo by John Lambing*

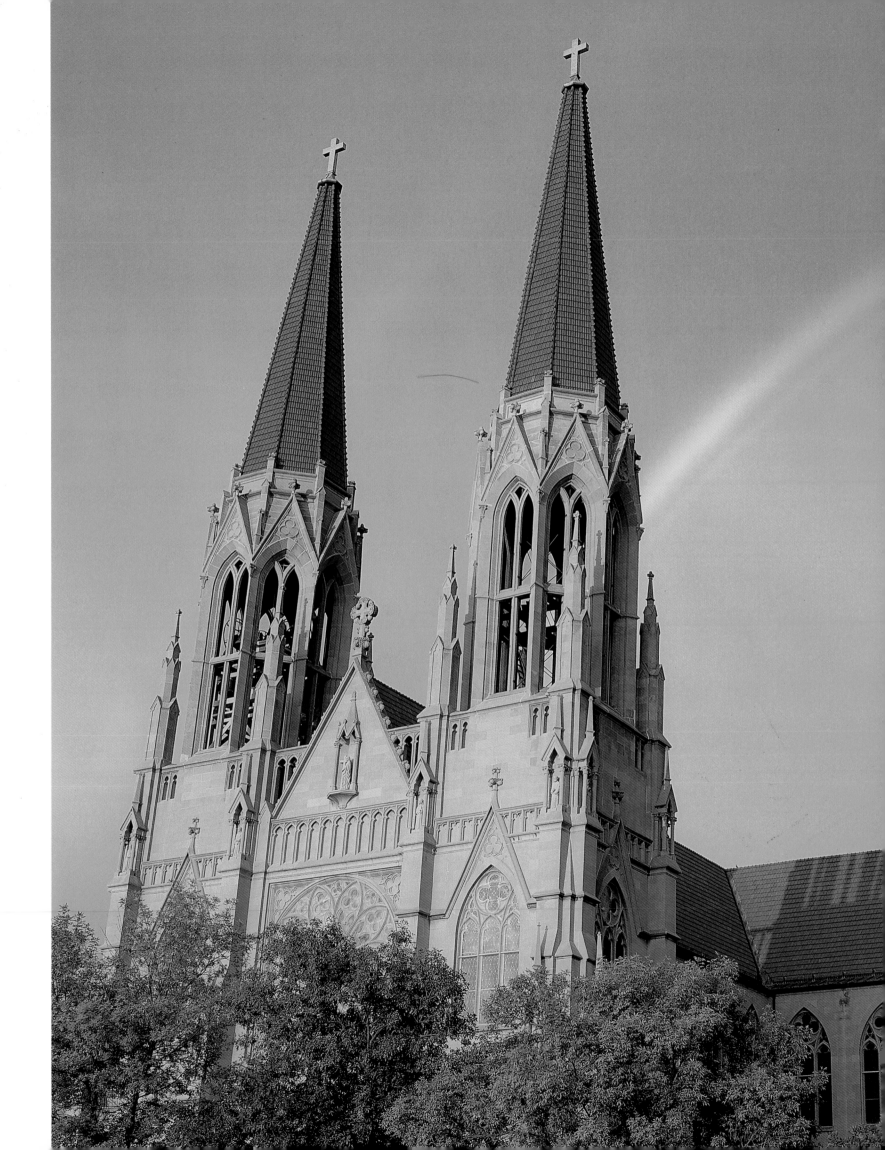

Above: The Yellowstone River overflows its banks in 1937, swamping the streets of downtown Billings. The farm, livestock, and petroleum industries have boosted Billings to primacy as Montana's largest city. *Photo courtesy of the Western Heritage Center*

Below right: Bozeman third graders are on their best behavior in their classroom at Longfellow School, circa 1905. Montana has long boasted a literacy rate far above the national average, in large part because of the state's commitment to public education. *Photo courtesy of the Gallatin County Historical Society*

Opposite: Located in the magnificent Mission Valley, the St. Ignatius Mission was the second Catholic mission established in Montana. Jesuit priests built a simple log chapel here in 1854 but replaced it with this imposing brick church in 1891. A set of striking murals depicting biblical scenes decorates the interior. *Photo by Michael Crummett*

because it served as an impetus for the development of retail shops and industry. After decades of relying on timber cutting and sawmill production as the base of its economy, Missoula at the end of the twentieth century, like Chicago at the end of the nineteenth, has seen the supply of timber drastically reduced because of over-cutting. Consequently, it has seen its market reduced because of increased competition from the South, as Chicago's northern hinterlands had lost out earlier to competition from Pacific Northwest forests.

Meanwhile, another Montana city grew out of the connection of a different commodity with the Chicago-centered rail system. Early in its history, Billings estab-lished a system of stockyards to stimulate the shipment of high-plains cattle back to eastern markets. Named for Frederick Billings, the president of the Northern Pacific Railroad, Billings was a classic railroad boom town, rising out of the bare prairie. With Chicago as a model, investors laid out the streets, avenues, and parks; engraved a map; and began selling whole blocks to absentee specu-lators by promising them a paradise of resources in the Yellowstone Valley and its tributaries. Like Chicago's own early speculators, Billings promoters gambled on an urban future, risking great sums on raw land they hoped would turn into a significant metropolis.

The new town, sponsored by the railroad, grew quickly as a result of concerted advertising in cities such as St. Paul, New York, and Chicago. By the spring of 1882, business lots near the railroad that had sold origi-nally for five hundred dollars were changing hands for much higher prices. Boosters made exaggerated claims that natural resources were God-given gifts to be appro-

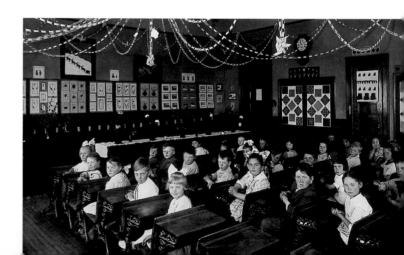

priated for the use of the future city. The pace of development in Billings increased when it was designated the seat of Yellowstone County. It got another boost when the stockyards were built and yet another when the Northern Pacific reached town in August 1882.

In 1883, approximately 20,000 cattle and 600,000 pounds of wool were shipped to eastern markets (that is, to Chicago) over the Northern Pacific. By 1884, cattle shipments had doubled. Resources meant little without a means of transportation, and the railroad became that means. Eventually, droughts, a disastrous fire, and competition from other frontier towns dampened the Billings boom, but by 1904 a second rail line, the Burlington, also served the city, and Billings continued to serve as a livestock shipping center for the eastern plains and the Front Range of the Rocky Mountains. Billings' dependency on and outreach to the countryside was evident, as its ability to offer railroad shipping access to ranchers served both the country's and the growing town's needs.

What we see repeatedly is that the early history of Montana cities centers on the foresight of a few men who recognized the combined possibilities of abundant natural resources and transportation access to a certain site and pursued those possibilities through to the establishment of a town. Always at the core of those possibilities was the way in which the activity of people in the surrounding countryside could be translated into town prosperity, and always that prosperity was understood as being mutually bound to the prospering of the relevant countryside.

Given that seemingly inescapable mutual dependence of city and countryside, it is surprising how little of the history of Montana in the twentieth century reflects that relationship. What is even more surprising is how often and with what determination rural and urban Montanans have distrusted and mistreated one another. Of course, we might find deep roots of that distrust and mistreatment in Jeffersonian dogma. Thomas Jefferson once wrote, "Those who labor in the earth are

the chosen people of God, if ever He had a chosen people, whose breasts He has made His peculiar deposit for substantial and genuine virtue." On the other hand, cities were to him the root of all evil and corruption.

Because farming and ranching have been so integral to Montana's political culture, this way of thinking about city and country was practically bred into the bones of the state. But as deeply as that Jeffersonian seed may have been planted, it would not have been enough to obscure so thoroughly the natural, mutual interdependence of city and country if it had not been exacerbated by the structure of government itself. By putting so much of our political energy into state and national governments, Americans in general and Westerners in particular have in a myriad of ways encouraged city and countryside to consider themselves independent of one another; encouraged them to use those larger forums to pursue the chimera of that independence; and worse, used them as battlegrounds upon which to do damage to one another.

It is perhaps not surprising to discover, then, that the severing of the crucial connection between city and countryside has been nowhere more evident than in the operation of the Montana Legislature. There, with

increasing intensity throughout the twentieth century, city and country have essentially treated each other like enemies. Almost never would rural legislators consider how the prospering, or at least the smooth functioning, of a city could contribute to the prosperity of its surrounding countryside. The reverse was equally true. Thomas Jefferson may not have been surprised, and he might well have concluded that the fault lay with the wrong-headedness of city dwellers and those who represent them.

But the great thing about Jefferson is that he was never simply one thing. If he was the greatest agrarian apologist in our history, he was also one of our greatest observers of history; he understood that humans and

Opposite: In March 1904, the Walkerville Fire Department holds its festive annual banquet at Butte's Utopian Mandolin Club. *Photo courtesy of the Montana Historical Society*

Above: A crowd teems through the streets of downtown Miles City during its Diamond Jubilee in May 1959. Miles City is a major trade center for farmers and ranchers, and in the heyday of the great cattle drives, it was the next-to-last stop for tens of thousands of Texas cattle destined for eastern markets. Hence its nickname: "Cow Capital of the West."
Photo courtesy of the Montana Historical Society

One of the subtle but powerful effects of globalization is that it is gradually weakening the effectiveness of those larger structures of government (states and nations) that we have relied upon so heavily throughout the pre-global, industrial era. The net result is that communities are increasingly on their own in a brutally competitive global environment. For some, this will be a traumatic experience. But others will discover in this challenge sources of strength that have nothing to do with how effectively they manage to pull strings in Helena or Washington, D.C., and everything to do with how well they remember that fundamental interconnectedness between city and countryside.

It is not uncommon now to hear people talking about "lifelong learning," "learning organizations," and "learning communities." There is good reason to believe that in the fiercely competitive new global economy, communities that see themselves as "learning communities," that try to be as responsive and adaptive as possible, will gain a competitive advantage over communities that in various ways shut themselves off, that fail to learn everything they can from their past and their working environment.

In these terms, the fate of Montana's cities and towns in the next century may well be determined. To speak of cities as adaptive organisms is already to speak of them in terms of natural systems; it is to suggest that the distinction we have made between nature and city may itself be a non-adaptive distinction. One question for the future, then, would be whether our cities are capable of learning their way back into a more natural, more organic relationship with their surroundings—both their wild surroundings and their rural surroundings. There is now every reason to believe that those cities that learn that lesson will prosper, while those that fail to learn it will fail.

What would it mean to begin learning (or relearning) that lesson? For one thing, it cannot be learned only inside the city limits; this is fundamentally a matter of co-evolution, of city and countryside either adapting together toward a more sustainable future or failing

their institutions must always be adaptively alert to what he so famously called "the course of human events." Things will not stand still, Jefferson argued, and the real test of a democratic people is the ability to recognize when the forms and structures we have inherited no longer serve us well.

The course of human events is now changing fundamentally the environment within which Montana cities operate. The globalization of the economy is a fact of life for every Montanan and every Montana city. It is often a brutal fact of life; we often wish it were not so, but if wishes were horses. . . .

encouraged to be good cities, which means that they should be given the scope, the authority, and the vital capacity to *be* a city, to operate as a city.

No ranch or farm can prosper unless it is allowed to operate under the principles that make a ranch or farm a thriving organism. Nothing less is true of cities. They cannot perform their natural synergizing, energizing role within a regional economy if they are not enabled to operate on the principles inherent in their organic form. At a minimum, that means they must receive the authority to govern the urban area as what it is: an area that has either already become a city or is in the process of becoming a city. Cities must be able to apply city-like land-use guidelines to urban areas. They must be allowed to require that everyone who chooses to live in the city (that is, in the area that walks like a city and talks like a city and looks like a city) behave as if they were in fact part of the city.

The founders of Montana's cities understood this. Just as they understood that the well-being of a city depends upon the prosperity of the countryside it serves, so they also understood that in order to serve that function, and to prosper in doing so, the city must approach that enterprise as a unitary force. So they planned cities and platted them with a clear recognition that you were either in the city or not in the city. In order for the city to thrive and prosper, everyone who was part of it had to

together to adapt. What that adaptation would involve at the simplest level is the recognition that, as Cronon so powerfully argued, the fate of city and countryside are fundamentally interwoven, that neither can possibly prosper without the other.

What that would require of cities is a deepening awareness that it is to their advantage to be good neighbors to the smaller towns that surround them, to look for ways to help those small towns prosper. What it would require of rural Montana is a recognition that cities are not intruders on the landscape; they are not enemies to be rebuffed or restrained. Instead, cities need to be

Opposite: Abandoned gas pumps in Monida recall better times. *Photo by Bob Allen*

Above: Downtown Philipsburg reflects its residents' desire to maintain the historical integrity of the community. Many of the Victorian storefronts are well preserved, and some even feature their original signage. In 1998, the Montana Tourism Advisory Council gave Philipsburg the first Tourism Community of the Year Award for its exceptional work in promoting and preserving its mining heritage. *Photo by Donnie Sexton / Travel Montana*

Right: Though drive-in theaters are a dying breed, the Prairie Drive In at Terry refuses to give up the ship. *Photo by Michael Sample*

Opposite: The community of Walkerville, on the outskirts of Butte, lights up and hunkers down for another long winter night. *Photo by John Reddy*

Above: A Lewistown retailer makes sure that the sidewalks, at least, are passable following a spring blizzard in April 1955. Cooke City, outside Yellowstone, holds the state record for the most snow in one winter—almost 35 feet in 1977–1978. In Montana, no month of the year is guaranteed to be snow-free. *Photo courtesy of the Montana Historical Society*

Right: This 27-foot-tall giant penguin, sculpted of concrete and steel by Ron Gustafson, is a symbol of Cut Bank's pride in being the "coldest spot in the nation." Actually, the coldest temperature ever officially recorded in the contiguous United States was minus 70 degrees F, measured in 1954 just west of Rogers Pass, more than 100 miles farther south. *Photo by Tom Ferris, courtesy of the Montana Historical Society*

and almost glorifying Montana grains and meats. Together, they profit from a growing cosmopolitan taste for more indigenous cuisine and on a growing theme in the state: "Made in Montana."

In the 1970s and 1980s, Missoula business interests looked for alternatives to the declining timber industry. They realized that, along with sawmills, the hospitals and the university played crucial economic roles, not least by extending their services out into the countryside. Writers and artists, too, began flocking to the area, attracted largely by its wild surroundings, and galleries and bookstores sprang up to support them. Bicyclists from around the nation and even the world were drawn to this bike-friendly town in the Rockies, and national bicycle organizations and businesses followed in their wake. Outdoor-recreation enthusiasts created further environmental awareness, which led national wildlife habitat-preservation groups such as the Rocky Mountain Elk Foundation and the Boone & Crockett Club to locate their headquarters in Missoula. So as it diversified its economy, this once timber-dependent town forged new, non-extractive relationships with the surrounding countryside.

Missoula has proved more resilient than many other sawmill-dependent towns in Western Montana. This is partially due to its expansion of retail and other service industries but also to a recognition that Missoula's long-range welfare would be better served by supporting the viability of the smaller towns around it than by growing at their expense. In fact, in the late 1990s, civic and business leaders in both Missoula and Billings seriously began to explore how their respective regional economies operated. By overlaying maps of newspaper distribution areas, hospital service territories, retail trade, and other activities, they began to get a sense of their organic connection to most of the Clark Fork Basin and Yellowstone Valley. In the case of Billings, that connection took no notice of the Wyoming border or county lines. When it was mapped, it showed a compelling picture of what Billings founders had known from the beginning: the well-being of the city was fundamentally

follow its rules, pay its taxes, and enjoy its benefits. Rural members of the territorial and later the state legislature seemed to understand the same thing; they created rules of incorporation that enabled cities to operate in this unitary, city-like way. But as the twentieth century progressed, those fundamental insights dimmed and finally almost vanished.

Almost . . . but not quite. Certainly by the end of the century the legislative misunderstanding of what it takes to be a city is as deep as it had ever been. On the other hand, changes in the economy, from the global scale on down, are slowly teaching Montana cities and their surroundings some of the sound old lessons about their interdependence. To take one small but instructive example, many Montana cities now boast their own microbreweries and take pride in the fact that they use Montana hops. These new breweries playfully reflect Montana landscapes, flora, and fauna with names like "Beargrass Pilsner," "Scape Goat," and "Moose Drool." Often, the state's railroad history is reflected as well; the Iron Horse Pub in Missoula brews a local beer in the old Northern Pacific depot.

In Kalispell, a new partnership called the Chef's Collaborative links rural agricultural producers and urban restaurateurs in a common enterprise emphasizing

connected to the vitality of the communities around it.

Butte has found yet another way to heal the relationship between the city and its surroundings. The city of Butte and the county of Silver Bow have consolidated their governments, making no distinction between the two. This cooperative form of government allows city and countryside to operate as a single unit. It also has allowed them to face together the seemingly disastrous consequences of the closure of the open-pit mine known as the Berkeley Pit, the mile-wide site of the world's greatest copper-mining operation. In the 1980s, the population of Butte dropped from 50,000 to 44,000, yet the city and county rebounded in the 1990s. Ironically, the new mainstay of the Butte economy is the massive federal and corporate investment in cleaning up the environmental devastation caused by a century of mining and milling. While some of the old and classic copper-era buildings in uptown Butte stand in disrepair, new residential areas spread south of town, the result of sophisticated high-technology businesses that are locating within Silver Bow County. The consolidation of city and county governments has given the area the ability to work cooperatively to rebound from the demise of the traditional resource-extraction economy. Much the same has happened in nearby Anaconda, where the consolidation of the city of Anaconda with the county of Deer Lodge has helped that community respond to the closing of the Anaconda smelter.

However, other Montana cities—Helena, Kalispell, and Bozeman among them—have taken a very different approach to their urban challenges. These cities maintain separate city and county governments, leaving urban and rural areas essentially on their own to deal with substantially uncontrolled urban sprawl. In Bozeman, elaborate new homes cluster around the city and sell for some of the highest prices in the state. The Gallatin Valley is experiencing what some call a "frenzied rate of growth," which could compromise the very quality of life, picturesque scenery, and recreational opportunities that are attracting so many to the Bozeman area. The same pattern has created uncontrolled urban sprawl in the Flathead and Helena Valleys. In both cases, county governments continually approve suburban subdivisions until they surround the incorporated cities, creating more and more urban problems with no corresponding urban government to control the growth or respond to its effects.

This lack of coordination between city and county governments, combined with the unwillingness of state government to give local governments effective growth-management tools, results in diffuse zoning and development regulations and a potpourri of prob-

Opposite: Montana Air National Guard jets, sporting a distinctive Montana logo on their tails, line up, ready for flight, at the MANG base on Gore Hill on the southwestern edge of Great Falls. *Photo by Stuart S. White*

Right: In Butte, historically a blue-collar city with a rough and ready reputation, this pink house and matching car seem a bit incongruous. *Photo by John Reddy*

Opposite top: Avid young readers patiently wait their turn to browse the selection in the Great Falls Public Library Bookmobile in 1956. *Photo courtesy of the Cascade County Historical Society*

Opposite bottom: Delighted onlookers watch as fireworks sizzle over the Midland Empire Fairgrounds in Billings during the 1940s. *Photo courtesy of the Western Heritage Center*

Above: Founded in 1891 along the main line of the Great Northern Railway, Kalispell was still a gritty transportation town when this photo was taken in 1902. Today, with a population of around 12,000, it serves as the metropolitan center of northwestern Montana. *Photo courtesy of Helen Schagel and the Tobacco Valley Historical Museum*

Left: Workmen measure the entryway arch of the Denver Block in Helena as they prepare to move it to a city park. The arch survived a fire in 1981 that destroyed the rest of the building. At its new location just off Last Chance Gulch, it has become a familiar city landmark. Fire ravaged downtown Helena often in the mid-19th century, prompting the city to build the fire tower known as the "Guardian of the Gulch," framed here by the arch. *Photo by Gene Fischer*

lems: subdivisions encroaching on flood plains and wildlife habitat and twenty-acre ranches (known locally as "rodeo ranchettes") dividing open spaces and depleting or polluting valuable water resources.

As we face the next century, then, we face also the need to change our political behavior and our political language. We need to stop talking about "rural America" or "rural Montana," "urban America" or "urban Montana," as if they were separate, distinct, adversarial entities and adopt a new form of political discourse that acknowledges that these abstract places don't exist at all. What do exist are real places, such as Missoula, Billings, Great Falls, Butte, Bozeman, Kalispell, Helena, and all

the rest, and regional economies for which Missoula, Billings, and the other cities serve as hubs.

Missoula does not exist in a vacuum; it has no meaning in a vacuum. It is not the city of roughly sixty thousand urbanites that has a chance of building sustainable prosperity in a global environment. It is the city and its two dozen or so surrounding towns whose long-term prosperity depends upon their ability to forge a cooperative economy. The same is true of every other Montana city. The great hope of twenty-first-century Montana is that our communities will be wise enough to learn from the lessons of history and adapt successfully to the ongoing course of human events.

In this panoramic view, photographed in 1921, the citizens of Absarokee line the streets of their town in Stillwater County. Small towns have always been the backbone of the state. In 1996, a little more than half of the incorporated communities in Montana had populations of fewer than 1,000.
Photo courtesy of the Montana Historical Society

NEXT-YEAR COUNTRY

COMMERCE AND INDUSTRY IN TWENTIETH-CENTURY MONTANA

"Montana never has had a stable economy; it never has had time to develop one." –Joseph Kinsey Howard

Much as a baseball player returns to second to "tag up" before advancing on a fly ball, the historian of the American West feels compelled to make contact with Frederick Jackson Turner before scampering down his topical base path. This practice frequently proves painfully artificial. However, to survey Montana's commerce and industry during the twentieth century, it makes sense to begin with Turner's momentous 1893 essay "The Significance of the Frontier in American History."

Turner's emphasis on "the end of the frontier" creates a natural watershed for this topic. In addition, his perspective places Montana in a regional context—where it belongs economically. For Montana never has operated as an isolated, autonomous economic unit. It has functioned always in complex regional, national, and even global contexts.

Further, the simultaneous Panic of 1893—the worst U.S. depression to that time—marks a convenient economic demarcation. Following this devastating event, Montana commerce and industry developed distinctive characteristics and patterns. Although some of these qualities later dissolved, others have survived for more than a century.

MONTANA'S BASIC ECONOMIC CHARACTERISTICS

At the base of any assessment of Montana's twentieth-century economy lies an amalgam of the state's distinctive characteristics. Both praised and damned by residents for more than 150 years, these peculiarities are fundamental to an understanding of Montana's economy—past, present, and future.

1. Montana is a hybrid straddling two distinct geophysical regions: the Great Plains and the Northern Rockies. Land remains the base of Montana's economy, whether through agriculture, lumbering, or tourism. The inclusion of two different environments within a

BY DAVE WALTER

Opposite: Gold miners congregate circa 1907 at a portal of the Bald Mountain mine, owned by Irish immigrant Thomas Cruse. A self-made millionaire, Cruse struck it rich at this and other mines in Marysville, near Helena. Cruse was a devout Catholic and contributed generously to the building of St. Helena Cathedral, including half the money needed to raise its majestic twin spires. *Photo by S. J. Culbertson, courtesy of the Montana Historical Society*

single political unit has produced a sometimes con-
tentious relationship between Eastern and Western
Montanans. Yet, if the state has one unifying characteristic, it is that this country is dry. Water remains its most
precious commodity.

2. Montana is a large state in which relatively few
people live. With an area of 147,046 square miles,
Montana is the fourth largest state in the Union. Yet its
population has remained small (see population table,
page 201). The *cities* of Birmingham, Honolulu, and
Austin each contain more people than the entire state of
Montana. Since about half of the state's population lives
in or near seven cities, the spaces surrounding these
urban islands seem even more empty. Most recently that
population has shifted, depleting the dry eastern plains
and river bottoms and surfeiting the western mountain
valleys.

Montana's light population (currently about 5.5 persons per square mile) offers only small local markets for
the state's products. In addition, the state lacks a dominant
"metropolis," one that could serve as an economic mecca
for the Montana "hinterland."[1] The combination of vast
distances and few taxpayers imposes real limitations on the
state's infrastructure.

3. Much of Montana's economy depends upon the
extraction of its natural resources. Reliance on materials
from Montana's "treasure chest"—from copper to timber to wheat to cattle to petroleum to coal—places these
industries (and their workers and support businesses) at
the mercy of national and international demands, market
prices, political decisions, and competitive labor forces.
As a result, decisions that affect the Montana economy
are most often made outside the state. This reliance on
natural resources has led to boom-and-bust cycles in specific industries.

4. Montana is isolated and far from populous markets for its natural resources. This distance adds transportation costs to exported materials. The transportation
systems themselves often are controlled from the same
out-of-state financial centers that serve as sources of capital for developing Montana industries.

Above: In Libby, Joel Nelson, a second-generation lumberjack,
is dwarfed by the timber he has helped to harvest. Throughout
the century, northwestern Montana has relied on the lumber
industry to provide jobs and fuel its economy.
Photo by Michael Crummett

Opposite: Mary McGovern stands in the doorway of her modest
dry goods store in Virginia City in the 1930s. Founded in 1863,
Virginia City was one of the first gold-mining camps in
Montana. It was designated a National Historic Landmark in
1961 and was later added to the National Register of Historic
Places. In 1997, the state legislature initiated efforts to buy the
community and preserve it as a state treasure.
Photo courtesy of the Montana Historical Society

5. The outside forces that affect Montana are so numerous and powerful that the state exhibits a "colonial economy." Montana businesses regularly have been susceptible to national business cycles, new technologies, shifting patterns of economic geography, competition in national and international markets, and changing government policies. Although such factors can benefit state businesses, they also can devastate them. In either case, key determinations about goods from Montana's natural-resource larder derive from outside the state in distant metropolises.

6. The federal government exerts a strong influence in Montana. Since 1864, when Congress created Montana Territory, federal actions have remained a significant factor in shaping the Montana economy. Although the federal government holds only 29.6 percent of the land in Montana, it has dictated development by various means: land grants to private companies, military subjugation of Native Americans, transportation subsidies, incentive mining and homesteading legislation, social programs, crop subsidies, military installations, research-and-development grants, dam construction, and timber-cutting policies.

Because Montana's economy has relied heavily on the extraction of natural resources, it remains in constant flux. The apparent commercial stability of the boom inevitably becomes the instability of the bust. Economists emphasize that Montana always has played a role in a national/international economic and financial network; historians refer to the state's "colonial economy."

As author Joseph Kinsey Howard aptly put it in his book *Montana: High, Wide, and Handsome*, "Montana, [a] subject colony, has been the end of the cracked whip."[2]

In sum, even a cursory look at Montana commerce and industry in the twentieth century reveals that the state simply has not been able to dictate its own course.

A Montana Economy in Transition: 1900–1930

After 1893, the link between the Montana economy and the land became firmly entrenched. As with other western states, that pattern rested heavily upon conflicting federal land policies and upon transcontinental railroad lines.

Since the creation of Yellowstone National Park in 1872, the federal government has pursued conflicting policies for western lands. On the one hand, it has reserved land from future private ownership, creating a federal responsibility for preserving and managing these public holdings.[3] On the other hand, it has asserted the rights of private individuals to claim and develop western lands, as with the Mining Law of 1872. The tension between these two policies has extended through the twentieth century on myriad fronts. For example, the

potentially divisive "Sagebrush Rebellion" of the late 1970s depended upon this contradiction.[4]

The significance of transcontinental railroad lines to a state as remote as Montana cannot be overemphasized. Between 1883 and 1893, Montana's "treasure chest" of natural resources was linked feasibly and economically to industrial centers and populous markets. That relationship of Montana hinterland to distant financial metropolis has survived through the twentieth century—and some observers assert that it has even intensified. Transportation access—first by rail and later by highway and nominally by air—has tied Montana commerce and industry to regional, national, and international economies.

Once it was connected to the nation by rail lines, Montana joined the Industrial Revolution. Into the state

Opposite top: The Chili King Lunch Room, doing business in Dillon in 1902, caters to customers with a taste for the hot and spicy. *Photo courtesy of the Montana Historical Society*

Opposite bottom: By early in the century, every Montana town of any size boasted its own photography studio. Here, a Deer Lodge woman dressed in her finest poses for a portrait at the Hartley Photography Studio, circa 1930.
Photo courtesy of the Montana Historical Society

Above: Window dressing can be an effective way to advertise one's wares. In 1952, Kaufman's of Great Falls, one of the state's oldest and most elegant men's clothiers, entices passersby with its natty selection. *Photo by Robert Anderson, courtesy of the Montana Historical Society*

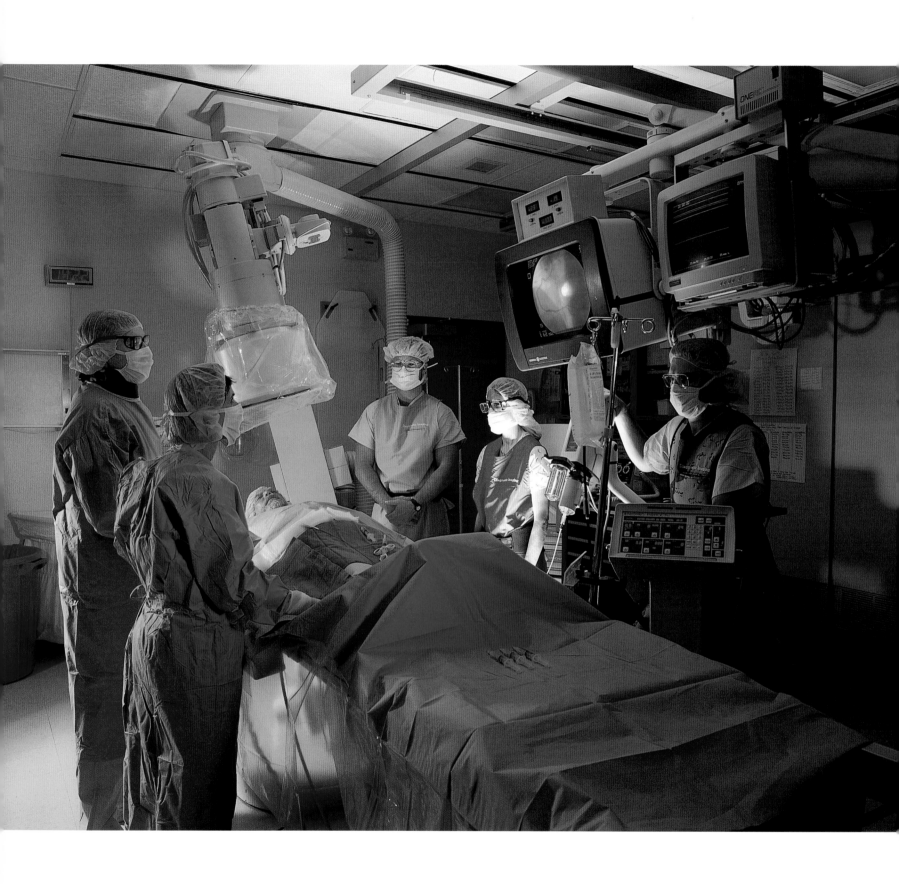

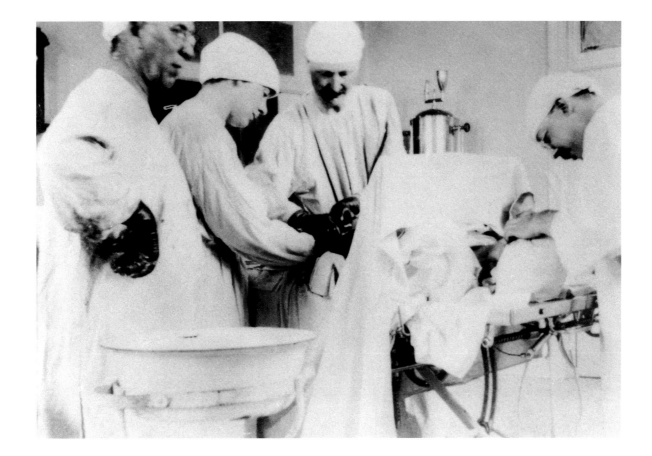

Opposite: At the cardiac catheterization lab at St. Peter's Hospital in Helena, a team of medical professionals performs a coronary angioplasty on a patient to reduce his chances of having a heart attack. Though doctors understood the principles behind the obstruction of coronary arteries as early as 1912, it was not until the late 1950s that cardiac catheterization was introduced. *Photo by John Reddy*

Above: A surgical team at Columbus Hospital in Great Falls performs medical miracles early in the century. Only in the 1890s did the practice of wearing gloves while performing surgery catch on. *Photo courtesy of the Cascade County Historical Society*

Above: Newsboys, cheerful despite the cold, embark on their rounds delivering the *Shelby Promoter* in 1966.
Photo courtesy of the Montana Historical Society

Opposite top: Christmas trees have long been a cash crop in northwestern Montana. Here, in October 1947, at the A. J. Thomas & Sons Christmas tree yard in Eureka, workers sort the trees by size and prepare them for shipping.
Photo courtesy of the Tobacco Valley Historical Museum

Opposite bottom: The Eureka Lumber Company was established in 1906 to mill timber taken from the woods of northwestern Montana. Loggers would topple the trees, haul them to the banks of Fortine Creek and the Tobacco River, and pile them there until river drivers could flush them to the sawmill in the spring flood. In 1907, when this picture was taken, the company built a dam on Fortine Creek to control the stream flow.
Photo courtesy of the Heritage Museum

rumbled massive machinery, revolutionary technology, eager workers, and outside influences to develop Montana resources. Eastern capital could finance any business scheme; every engineering problem could be solved; huge fortunes could be gained by developing Montana. What difference did railroad access make to Montana? Between 1880 and 1890, the state grew by 93,000 people, an increase of 237.5 percent!

Montana's participation in the Industrial Revolution depended primarily on the copper industry, which was centered in Butte, Anaconda, and Great Falls. For decades, Montana copper remained in great demand as telephone and electrical networks spread across America.

The dawn of the century brought a transition from frontier to modern corporate hegemony. The most vivid image is a shift from the open-range cowhand to the unionized smelter worker. Standard Oil's control of the Anaconda Copper Mining Company—and ultimately the state's entire economy—rendered Montana a classic "colony."

Anaconda's "Shutdown of 1903" paralyzed commerce across the state and demonstrated the extent of the corporation's control over Montana mining, refining, lumbering, railroading, merchandising, and other dependent industries. After a blackmailed Governor Joseph K. Toole called a special session of the legislature to adopt the Company's agenda, business in the state resumed.[5] "From the steps of the Silver Bow County Courthouse on October 26, 1903, "Copper King" F. Augustus Heinze angrily denounced this corporate demon:

> *These people are my enemies, fierce, bitter, implacable; but they are your enemies too. If they crush me today, they will crush you tomorrow. They will cut your wages and raise the tariff in the company stores on every bite you eat and every rag you wear. They will force you to dwell in Standard Oil houses while you live, and they will bury you in Standard Oil coffins when you die.*[6]

The "Shutdown of 1903" cast shadows all the way into the 1960s, as the Company built a powerful newspaper network to influence public opinion and openly ran twenty-four-hour-a-day "watering holes" to accommodate legislators during their biennial sessions.

From 1915 into the 1960s, the Anaconda Company allied itself with the Montana Power Company, an energy conglomerate that expanded from hydroelectricity into oil, gas, and coal. The control that these "Montana Twins" exerted over the state is the source of a 1960s gallows-humor anecdote. At the height of the Cold War, pundits remarked on the relative safety enjoyed by Montanans: "If the Russians attack us, they will come down through Alaska and Canada—but everybody knows that the Company won't let them into Montana!"

Since Anaconda's defection in the 1970s, it has become increasingly fashionable among Montanans to apologize for the Company's dictatorial dominance, writhed in economic spasm. In truth, the corporate objectives of the Company rarely benefited Montana communities or the long-term welfare of Montanans. The consequences of the Company's misuse and abuse of Montana's people and natural resources remain that corporation's most enduring legacy.

Montana's copper-based, turn-of-the-century economy integrated mining, smelting, timber, hydroelectric, and transportation industries to produce a free-wheeling capitalism. The era from 1900 to 1930 also featured turbulent labor relations.[7] Despite Company domination of the economy, Montana society remained in flux.

The transitional nature of the years from 1900 to 1930 is demonstrated by the homestead wave—the last true Montana "frontier" phase. The homestead boom, which sprinkled immigrants across the state's western

Opposite: The iceman cometh! Before refrigeration became commonplace, workers like this one employed by the Montana Transfer and Ice Company in Choteau, delivered blocks of ice to every Montana household with an icebox.
Photo courtesy of the Montana Historical Society

Above: The Ayrshire Dairy, which opened its doors in Great Falls in 1908, produced much of the milk, cream, and other dairy products used by area residents. In 1960, when this picture of the milk plant was taken, customers paid about 70 cents for a half-gallon of ice cream.
Photo courtesy of the Montana Historical Society

Right: Founded in 1917, the Bozeman Canning Company—proud producer of "Peas that Please"—employed local residents to can the peas that flourished in the Gallatin Valley. The cannery closed in 1958, a victim of blight, consolidation in the industry, and the rise in popularity of frozen vegetables.
Photo courtesy of the Montana Historical Society

forests and flooded them over the high eastern prairies, commenced in 1906. By 1917, the commensurate bust had begun.

The homestead boom relied on a federal policy offering free land to private citizens, as well as on massive publicity from transcontinental railroads, state governments, and local communities. Particularly fueling the homestead optimism were Jim Hill's "Highline" Great Northern Railway, the land-grant-rich Northern Pacific, and the upstart Milwaukee Road. This boom, like those associated with mining and lumbering, depended on one of Montana's seemingly endless natural resources—in this case, fertile soil.[8]

The homestead boom of 1906–1917, which brought an estimated 200,000 settlers to Montana, set the mixed farm-ranch pattern of Montana agriculture for the rest of the century by chopping large land holdings into tillable plots. A combination of abundant rainfall, rapidly expanding world markets, new farm technologies, conducive homestead laws, aggressive irrigation projects, and easy credit turned Montana's dry lands and river valleys into "a land of plenty." By 1908, Montana farm revenue had surpassed mining profits. Agriculture—through adaptation—has remained Montana's primary economic sector to this day.

Between 1900 and 1917, the state's farm acreage increased an astounding 2,325 percent! Then the inevitable bust hit. The evaporation of profitable World War I markets combined with long-term drought to precipitate bank failures and an out-migration of more than 100,000 disillusioned settlers from "the land of lost opportunity." Joseph Kinsey Howard—famous for his honyocker observation that "Rain is all Hell needs!"—captured the social consequences of this economic disaster when he wrote:

> *The dreams of great men often live a long time, as dreams. That of [Great Northern Railway mogul] Jim Hill, which he sought to bring to life in fact, became a witless nightmare. His trains rattled empty though dying towns. His neat little green fields were transformed as if an evil spirit had sped overhead, laying a curse upon them. Suddenly they were fenced deserts in which the trapped tumbleweed*

Opposite: This Montana farmer in the 1920s practices the system of dry-land farming outlined in *Campbell's Soil Culture Manual*, the homesteader's bible. After packing the soil, he breaks the top layer into a fine, loose mulch. H. W. Campbell assured farmers that this loose surface soil would collect what little rain fell on the semiarid plains, while the packed subsurface would store it like a reservoir for future use. *Photo courtesy of the Montana Historical Society*

Above: During construction at the East Helena smelter in 1938, a courageous—or foolhardy—worker stands on his head high atop the smelter's partially finished smokestack. The Great Depression likewise stood the Montana economy on its head, causing export prices to plummet and ravaging employment and personal incomes. *Photo courtesy of the Montana Historical Society*

Above: The smelter town of Black Eagle, which borders the city of Great Falls, is famous for its restaurants. In 1941, waitresses at the Unique Restaurant—celebrated for its hearty food and reasonable prices, including its 65-cent steak dinner—await the evening rush. *Photo by John Remmel, courtesy of the Cascade County Historical Society*

Opposite: In 1934, President Franklin D. Roosevelt reviews construction progress at the giant, earth-filled Fort Peck Dam, the largest New Deal project in Montana. By 1940, the year of its completion, the project had injected more than $100 million into the economy of the state. *Photo courtesy of the Montana Historical Society*

spun and raced nowhere all day. The little houses stood slack-jawed and mute, obscenely violated by coyotes, rats, and bats, and finally faded into the lifeless fields.[9]

The homestead bust combined with post–World War I declines in metals-mining and timber markets to plunge the state into a deep depression in the 1920s. In effect, production based on natural resources had been distorted by the overseas war, and Montanans paid the price for the postwar economic adjustment. Montana became the only state to lose population during "the Roaring Twenties." With the crash of the stock market on "Black Tuesday" (October 29, 1929), the rest of the nation learned what Montanans had known for a decade: "The tough times are here!"

BIG GOVERNMENT AND THE PROVINCES: 1930–1945

Much as the Panic of 1893 created a rent in Montana's economic fabric, the events of the Great Depression (1929–1940), the New Deal (1933–1941), and World War II (1941–1945) profoundly changed the state's economic and environmental patterns. Throughout these periods, in all western states, the federal government emerged as the primary source of spending and regulatory programs. It became the dominant player on the western financial stage.

The Depression in Montana merely intensified conditions that had begun in 1917. Plummeting prices for agricultural products, metals, lumber, coal, and petroleum ravaged Montana employment and income. Montana grain, which had brought $2.45 a bushel on the world market in 1918, fell to twelve cents a bushel in 1931. Recurring drought forced many farmers to leave the state—and the grasshoppers moved in.

International copper prices dropped from eighteen cents a pound in 1929, to eight cents a pound in 1931, to five cents a pound in 1933. In 1937, Montana suffered the highest unemployment rate in the country: twenty-two percent of its work force. State and local governments, as well as private charities, proved ill equipped to handle such an all-consuming crisis.

President Franklin Roosevelt's "New Deal" programs proved a godsend to Montanans. This wave of governmental experimentation combined relief, reform,

Above: During World War II, Camp Rimini near Helena was a training ground for sled dog teams and their drivers. These sled handlers and their malamutes, huskies, and other Eskimo breeds saw duty in search-and-rescue operations throughout the Arctic and helped to evacuate the wounded during the frigid Battle of the Bulge in Belgium in 1944, about a year after this photo was taken. *Photo courtesy of the Montana Historical Society*

Opposite: In the 1970s, more than 12,000 people were employed in Montana's lumber industry. This photograph was taken in 1976 at the Ksanka Lumber Company mill near Eureka. *Photo by Richard C. Shirley, courtesy of the Montana Historical Society*

and recovery projects. Average New Deal aid to each American ran about $250 total, but each Montanan received $710—second only to the $1,130 received by Nevada residents. Montana (like other sparsely populated western states) reaped such a windfall because of its low population density, its sizable tracts of federal land, its low incomes and high unemployment, its heavy reliance on natural-resources extraction, and its large dam projects.

Every sector of the Montana economy benefited somehow. For example, agriculture benefited from direct subsidies and price stabilization; mining revived as a result of federal copper purchases and the Silver Purchase Act of 1934; unions regained the "closed shop"; banks accepted the stabilizing support of the federal government; and the unemployed and the dependent took advantage of the Works Progress Administration (later known as the Works Projects Administration), the Civilian Conservation Corps, the National Youth Administration, and Social Security.

Perhaps the Public Works Administration and the U.S. Army Corps of Engineers most graphically symbolized the federal presence in Montana. These agencies supervised the construction of the Fort Peck Dam, a project that employed thousands of workers from 1934 to 1940 and cost in excess of $110 million. Yet, more important than the material accomplishments of the New Deal was its success in boosting public morale.

One of the most subtle and permanent policy changes instituted by the New Deal involved public lands. The government withdrew federal land from settlement, purchased private land to add to the public domain, and initiated such federal land-management programs as the Taylor Grazing Act of 1934. This public-policy shift to the conservation of federal lands set a strong precedent for the rest of the century.

The New Deal brought not only short-term relief and recovery measures but also long-term, enduring reforms and capital investments. Montanans may have accepted this new federal presence with some reservations,[10] but the New Deal forever shifted responsibility for the state's economy. In effect, federal funds replaced private capital from eastern financial corporations as the

major generator of economic growth. The location of the "metropolis" remained outside Montana, but it began to shift from the old financial/influence centers to Washington, D.C.

As if on cue, the nation's abrupt immersion into World War II solidified the federal presence in the West. In addition, the war effort precipitated major social and economic changes. The establishment of a military-industrial complex in the West particularly benefited such areas as San Francisco, Seattle, and Denver. Montana's share of the economic windfall proved much smaller.[11] Nevertheless, the state received an Army Air Corps base at Great Falls (later called Malmstrom Air Force Base), a special-forces training center at Helena (Fort Harrison), and a detention center at Missoula (Fort Missoula).

More importantly, the war boosted the state's natural resource–based industries. Both lumbering and mining benefited from high demand; the production of coal and petroleum soared. Although tens of thousands of Montanans migrated to the West Coast to work in war-industry

Opposite: Victor Carlson works as a coal miner in the central Montana town of Roundup. Montana harbors 13 percent of the nation's coal reserves. *Photo by Michael Crummett*

Above: A mule train hauls copper ore deep in Butte's Rarus Mine early in the century. Even after ventilating systems were installed in the early 1920s, both the temperature and relative humidity in Butte's deepest mines stood at well over 90. *Photo courtesy of the World Museum of Mining*

factories, the state's agricultural sector thrived. Montana farms and ranches, aided by a series of wet years, produced the greatest yields since the second decade of the century. Between 1940 and 1948, net income increased by 188 percent for Montana ranchers, who were relying on fewer, larger units and greater mechanization.

The period from 1930 to 1945 brought unprecedented economic and environmental disasters to Montana and the West. Nevertheless, the state economy benefited substantially from Roosevelt's New Deal and surpassed earlier production successes during World War II. It emerged in the mid-1940s as a state heavily dependent on the federal government. That "new American federalism" has marked Montana for the rest of the century. Most directly, this shift to federal responsibility began to alter the state's longtime, private-sector, "colonial economy" tradition.

Opposite: Tourists have always been attracted to the majestic mountains of Western Montana. These hikers stop to appreciate the Mission Range, which towers over the Flathead and Swan Valleys. *Photo by Herman Schnitzmeyer, courtesy of Kenneth & Betty Vincent*

Left: Montana's first oil boom came in the 1920s, when much of the activity centered around the Kevin-Sunburst field in north-central Montana. In 1951, oil was discovered in the Williston Basin, which underlies much of Eastern Montana. Speculators, geologists, and roughnecks flocked to the region in search of "liquid gold." *Photo courtesy of the Montana Historical Society*

Below: In 1953, the Westerners clothing store in Missoula displays an impressive stock of Western-flavored leather goods, including hand-tooled purses and beaded moccasins, parfleches, and gloves. *Photo by the Stanley Color Laboratory, courtesy of the Montana Historical Society*

Above: An imposing 16-foot auger digs Minuteman missile silos in north-central Montana during the 1960s. Each silo consists of an 80-foot-deep tube, launch equipment, and a long-range nuclear missile. Air Force officers working 12-hour shifts control the launch equipment from a nearby underground chamber. *Photo by Ray Ozmon*

Opposite: Workers in 1969 construct a bridge across Lake Koocanusa, a 90-mile-long reservoir created when Libby Dam, built between 1966 and 1973, backed up the Kootenai River north into Canada. The bridge, just south of Rexford, is reported to be the highest and longest in Montana. *Photo by Richard C. Shirley, courtesy of the Montana Historical Society*

MONTANA IN THE COLD WAR: 1950–1970

Montana rode a national wave of prosperity into the post–World War II era. The federal presence expanded, influencing such diverse aspects of Montana life as Social Security benefits, airport subsidies, "multiple-use" dams, and the interstate highway program. In 1969, Washington spent $1.88 in Montana for every dollar Montanans paid in taxes.

In the Cold War era, the Montana agricultural sector responded to international demands by solidifying its reliance on a combination of livestock and crop production. Relying on strong federal farm subsidies and increased technology, Montana ranchers moved from family farming into agribusiness. Similarly, the lumber sector depended on a postwar building boom, new equipment and processes, foreign markets, and timber sales by the Forest Service to develop from a cut-lumber business into a true wood-products industry, manufacturing such secondary items as particle board, pulp paper, plywood, craft paper, and formaldehyde.

During the 1950s and 1960s, Montana's metal-mining/refining sector continued to prosper. Yet, as the Anaconda Company diversified and relied more on its South American copper properties, cracks began to appear in its armor. The Company sold its newspaper chain in 1959 and closed its "watering holes" for legislators in the mid-1960s. Because of the Company's evolving corporate strategy, Montana remained third nationally in copper production, trailing Arizona and Utah.

Petroleum—an industry founded in the state in the 1920s—became Montana's postwar success story. The development of the deep Williston Basin boomed Billings and produced refineries and pipeline networks across the state. In 1949, Montana's petroleum output for the first time exceeded the value of its copper production. Cheap oil and gas directly fueled America's postwar affluence, mobility, and leisure activities. This reliance became particularly evident in the national craze for automobile travel, recreation, and tourism.

Montana had been attracting tourists since the late nineteenth century—particularly to Yellowstone and Glacier National Parks and to established dude ranches. Yet the waves of automobile tourists that inundated the state during summers in the 1950s and 1960s set new records and created a significant state industry. As the West became "the new American playground," Montana profited from its Old West ambiance, open spaces, mountain scenery, clean environment, and relatively small population.

This sudden boom in tourism provided a forecast of Montana's economic future. During the 1950s and 1960s, the state did not share in the boom of postwar scientific-technological businesses that located near the wartime defense industries (for instance, in San Francisco, Seattle, and Denver). If anything, Montana drew further away from "the new corporate West," which emphasized hi-tech, service, and manufacturing sectors. The state became an even more entrenched producer, rather than processor, of raw materials. As a result, many ambitious young Montanans abandoned the state to seek employment in that "new corporate West."

As Montana adjusted to its postwar role in the national economy, the influence of the federal government increased. Whether establishing Glasgow Air Force Base, building Hungry Horse Dam, leasing federal lands for grazing, or sinking intercontinental ballistic-missile silos throughout central Montana, the federal government became the mainstay of the state's economy.

Through federal construction projects, outright subsidies, regulatory legislation, and a myriad of other social and financial ties, Montanans wed themselves to Washington, D.C. The state's small population base and its inability to develop dynamic urban centers solidified that reliance. U.S. Senator Lee Metcalf credited "federal expenditures, particularly defense spending involved in creating missile silos and bases, with sustaining the Montana economy"[12] in the postwar era. Some wary Montanans characterized this increased federal relationship as a pact with the Devil; others perceived it as the long-sought bridge to economic stability.

AN ERRATIC TRANSITION: 1970–1990

During the late 1960s, the traditional economic, social, and resource-use patterns of White Montanans began to shift. These changes, more than any other developments, colored events through the 1970s and 1980s. Increasing numbers of Montanans recognized the consequences of depleting the state's land-based "treasure chest." They embraced a national movement that established wilderness areas and designated wild-and-scenic river corridors. They created a movement to protect both the Montana landscape and—by doing so, they believed—the people who relied on the land for a living. Montana historian Harry Fritz described that tradition in his book *Montana: A Land of Contrasts*: "A new spirit of appreciation spread over the land. Montanans came to understand and realize the distinctiveness of their state, the grandeur of its mountains, and the vastness of its rolling plains—its quiet beauty. . . . Suddenly the greatest detriments to the industrialization of Montana, its isolation and boundless distances, were magically transformed into its proudest assets."[13]

At the time, Montana politicians—many of whom had benefited from a legislative reapportionment mandated in 1965—appropriated the popular sentiment. A new state constitution, adopted in 1972 and packed with

Opposite: Workers at Dan Bailey's Fly Shop, a Livingston landmark, concentrate in 1938 on tying the best flies in the world. The shop, which was established that year by a well-known fly fisherman, is one of the world's largest wholesalers of fly-fishing tackle today. *Photo courtesy of the Park County Museum Archives*

Above: The Industrial Towel and Cover Supply Company, founded in 1948 and headquartered in Livingston, still delivers towels, mats, and uniforms to Main Street businesses throughout the Greater Yellowstone region. The company's fleet of delivery trucks is shown here in 1962.
Photo courtesy of the Montana Historical Society

Right: The fanciful storefront of C. S. Johnston's blacksmith shop in Glendive leaves no doubt as to the building's purpose. A pile of discarded horseshoes on the left eventually reached as high as the roof of the building.
Photo courtesy of the Frontier Gateway Museum

significant changes from its 1889 predecessor, is particularly noteworthy for its protection of the Montana environment. In a milieu of activism, lawmakers adopted the Strip Mining and Reclamation Act (1973); the Water Use Act (1973); the Utility Siting Act (1973); the Strip-Mine Coal Conservation Act (1973); the Major Facility Siting Act (1975); and the Coal Severance Tax (1975).

Abruptly, Montana emerged as a national leader in environmental stewardship, consumer protection, and participatory democracy. This political, social, and economic revolution marked an extraordinary transformation for a state historically dependent on extractive industries, transcontinental railroads, a "captive press," and the "Montana Twins."

Amid the socio-political excitement of "the Montana revolution," the state experienced adjustments to its traditional patterns of commerce and industry. Most of these modifications developed in response to the dynamic Cold War economy. Thus, the 1970s and 1980s were remarkable for the velocity and impact of their changes. These jolts of economic dislocation—collectively labeled by analysts "the deindustrialization of Montana"—hit all of the state's traditional industries: transportation, mining, timber, petroleum, coal, and agriculture.

For example, the 1969–1970 merger of the Northern Pacific, Great Northern, and Burlington railroad companies into the Burlington Northern drastically reduced Montana spur lines, passenger travel, and railroad employment. The lack of rail competition increased when the Milwaukee Road declared bankruptcy in the early 1980s. Entrepreneur Dennis Washington's subsequent creation of Montana Rail Link illustrated the "no frills," pragmatic nature of Montana's reconstituted rail system.

Even greater shock waves devastated Montana's mining industry and its primary employer, the Anaconda Company. Following the nationalization of the Company's Chilean copper properties in 1971, it withdrew from its Montana mining and processing activities, slashing approximately 850 jobs in Butte and Anaconda in 1974 and another 1,500 statewide the following year.

In 1977, the Company sold its mining properties to the Atlantic Richfield Corporation (ARCO), which

closed the smelters in Anaconda (1980) and Great Falls (1981). ARCO terminated all of its mining in Montana in 1983—including Butte's Berkeley Pit—and laid off its last seven hundred employees. Suddenly the Company was gone. To many Montanans, the withdrawal left a distinct void—like the unexpected death of a rich uncle.

Some new mining companies subsequently appeared, but they were market-cautious, non-union, high-volume hardrock operations. A few companies resumed underground mining, while others developed enormous open-pit/cyanide heap-leach complexes. These operations all emphasized hi-tech automation, a smaller force of non-union employees, and a tight tie to international markets.

Among the Anaconda Company's other divestitures was the 1972 sale of its Western Montana lumber properties to Champion International. Champion watched a booming 1960s lumber market disintegrate during the 1970s and into the 1980s. From more than 275 sawmills in the state in 1970, the number fell to 137 in 1982 and fewer than 75 mills in 1992. Still, the lumber industry remained Montana's largest manufacturer, representing about fifteen percent of the state's economic base.

Similar roller-coaster runs affected Montana's petroleum and coal industries. The 1973 Middle East oil embargo generated an explosion of petroleum exploration and production in the state, and a second oil boom developed during the early 1980s. However, these peaks alternated with severe economic valleys, most often caused by political and global-market factors.

The state's most dramatic economic cycle involved subbituminous coal. In the early 1970s, a classic boom hit the Yellowstone Valley. Energy companies stripmined readily accessible seams for rail transport to coal-fired furnaces in Billings and power plants in the Midwest. Other conglomerates built coal-fired plants adjacent to mine sites to generate electricity that would be carried by massive power lines to Northwest markets. The mined tonnage of coal increased from 7 million in 1971, to 22 million in 1975, to 30 million in 1980. However, during the 1980s, the national energy glut

Opposite: Built in Great Falls in 1908, the Anaconda smelter stack was a monumental symbol of the Company's century-long dominance over the state. When engineers condemned it as structurally unsafe, a group of citizens fought to preserve it for its historical significance. They were unsuccessful, and, in 1982, the 500-foot stack was demolished. *Photo by Tom Kotynski*

Above: Workers painstakingly handcraft a canoe at Morely Canoes in the Western Montana community of Swan Lake. Small businesses—those employing fewer than 100 people—provide almost three-quarters of the jobs in the state. *Photo by Rick & Susie Graetz*

slowed the state's coal rush to a more measured pace.

Finally agriculture, the state's oldest economic endeavor, suffered some dramatic changes during the 1970s and the 1980s. Always the victim of national/international market fluctuations, high freight costs, and weather cycles, Montana agriculture concentrated on the production of wheat, beef, and barley. Wise farmers also were quick to adopt such specialty crops as canola.

During the 1970s, a wet cycle coincided with huge wheat sales to the Union of Soviet Socialist Republics (USSR) to create a genuine agricultural boom. Just as surely, the 1980s brought plummeting commodity prices, exacerbated by a severe drought that lingered from 1985 to 1990. The postwar trend to fewer, larger farms, a greater reliance on mechanization, and the emigration of ranch children intensified. For the first time since the 1930s, Montana suffered a serious wave of farm foreclosures.

Of Montana's basic industries, only tourism escaped the effects of the 1980s recession. Despite the Middle East oil crisis, tourism surpassed mining during the 1970s to become the state's second largest industry after agriculture. Throughout the 1980s, it grew at an annual rate of about six percent. Out-of-state travelers who spent about $100 million in Montana in 1972 increased spending to $650 million by 1989.

Montana's public mood, which had swung left to embrace environmentalism in the early 1970s, reacted to the economic dislocations of the 1980s by championing conservatism. A population increase of only 12,375 during the 1980s clearly reflected the grim economic situation.

With the Anaconda Company just a memory, economic and political power passed to the Montana Power Company, the state Chamber of Commerce, the new Burlington Northern, and a host of other conservative stalwarts. Influential trade organizations emerged, such as the Montana Mining Association, the Montana Bankers Association, the Montana Association of Realtors, the Montana Wood Products Association, the Montana Taxpayers' Association, the Montana Stockgrowers Association, and the Montana Farm Bureau Federation. By the end of the 1980s, nearly everyone in Montana—from both the right and the left—considered himself an "environmentalist," regardless of his position on developing the state's natural-resources base.

MONTANA TODAY AND TOMORROW

Montanans entered the 1990s with a modicum of hope, even as they recognized the state's integration into an increasingly competitive global economy. Outsiders continued to "discover" Montana, and the population grew by more than 88,000 between 1990 and 1998.

Reflecting national growth and prosperity, Montana's traditional industries stabilized somewhat, and the service, construction, and small-manufacturing sectors improved. Agriculture again boomed, and tourism continued its dynamic growth. The Montana electorate veered to the right and—as it had in 1968 and 1971—rejected a statewide sales tax.[14]

Nevertheless, one full century following the watershed Panic of 1893, the Montana economy continued to exhibit its basic turn-of-the-century characteristics:

1. The state still combines two distinct geophysical regions;
2. Montana is still vast and relatively unpopulated;
3. Montana's economy still relies on the extraction of its natural resources;
4. The state is still far removed from populous markets;
5. Outside forces still exert such an impact on Montana that the concept of a "colonial economy" remains valid; and
6. The federal government still plays a significant role in Montana.

Workers pour nearly pure molten copper into giant molds to make copper anodes at the Anaconda Reduction Works in Anaconda. The smelter closed and was dismantled in 1980, marking the abrupt end to an era in the history of Montana heavy industry. *Photo by Michael Crummett*

However, the intervening century has weakened some of these characteristics and strengthened others. For example, the state's traditional reliance on extractive industries—specifically mining, lumber, petroleum, and coal—has diminished considerably. Thus, the Montana economy currently reflects the gradual national evolution from goods to services (private, governmental, and commercial trade). This service-sector focus tends to be labor intensive, rather than raw-material or goods intensive. Montana's extractive industries will not disappear; they simply will provide an increasingly smaller percentage of both jobs and income.

A similar shift in emphasis is evident in the role of the federal government. Because federal agencies continue to administer thirty percent of Montana land—as well as regulate national defense, water, and interstate transport and communication—the federal presence has grown through the twentieth century. Montana shares this development with other states in the northern Great Plains/Rocky Mountain region.

Thus, national legislation that manipulates federal-agency budgets and alters agency mandates directly affects the state economy. Montana producers are further impacted by such international pacts as the 1993 North American Free Trade Agreement (NAFTA) and the 1994 General Agreement on Tariffs and Trade (GATT). Still, for every dollar of federal taxes collected in Montana in 1993, the federal government returned $1.40 in goods and services to the state.

One very apparent Montana characteristic survives into the 1990s, where its existence becomes even more glaring. The state continues to function without a "metropolis"—a significant center of concentrated population, investment and banking activity, dynamic political power, federal-government offices, and other decision-making institutions. Rather, the Montana hinterland remains under the influence of several regional metro-

polises, particularly Minneapolis-St. Paul, Denver, and Seattle.

The economic instability of the 1990s is most apparent in the constant restructuring of local economies and in dramatic demographic movements, both into and out of the state. This illuminates an important reality that Montanans must face, however reluctantly: Since the end of World War II, Montana simply has not shared in the general, dramatic economic growth of the American West. Rather, it has been lumped with such states as North Dakota, South Dakota, Idaho, and Wyoming in a "regional outback"—a hinterland that is destined to remain a hinterland.

During the second half of the twentieth century, Montana has enjoyed no general distribution of wealth. Its population growth has been sporadic but cumulatively slow. Its urban growth, while locally dramatic, remains insignificant. It is capturing and developing no concentration of new, innovative, highly productive manufacturing facilities. Nor has Montana enjoyed much growth in the hi-tech sector. What is more, Montana's inability to share in the national prosperity will continue, because the state's basic economy remains unstable. The state's economic future is not optimistic.[15]

The wisest contemporary economists argue that Montanans must face this reality. They contend that Montanans need to stop complaining about "value added" projects and about "the high cost of space." Residents need to accept Montana's "hinterland" status and place greater emphasis on strategies that will enhance that status: research-and-development institutes; strong higher-education programs; modest "niche" businesses that defy the great distances to populous markets; home-building real-estate developments; information-age endeavors; and resort and recreational facilities for the mobile, well-heeled American public.

These economists warn that it is pure folly for

Montana to cling blindly to its past extractive industries. For example, in the twenty-first century, metals mining will employ hundreds (rather than thousands) of Montanans, and it will simply supplement (rather than buttress) the state's economy. The exception to this regional demise of traditional industries is agriculture.

Americans always have perceived agriculture in a special light; even today, the farmer remains more "noble" than the logger or the retail clerk. National legislation and governmental programs reflect this favored status. Because of the nature of the Montana landscape, agriculture still sets the economic, social, and political cadence of the state.

Thus, the Montana economy will continue to undulate on the basis of weather cycles, international markets, transportation costs, and federal legislation. The ability of Montana farmers and ranchers to "read and react" to

the global economy and to integrate state-of-the-art technology into production methods will determine their ultimate success or failure.

The Montana economy of the 1990s continues in a state of flux. Much like the volatile state economy that emerged from the Panic of 1893, the current prosperity depends largely upon forces beyond the control of Montanans. However, if today's residents could discover a philosophical basis for cooperation—and a common understanding of which resources constitute Montana's most enduring treasures—they might develop a common plan to mitigate future impacts. As author Wallace Stegner has observed: "When Westerners fully learn that cooperation, not rugged individualism, is the quality that most characterizes and preserves the West, then they will achieve the real West and outlive its origins. Then Westerners have a chance to create a society to match its scenery."[16]

Through the course of the twentieth century, the patterns revealed by the state's commerce and industry argue strongly for less individualism and for greater cooperation. The prize of "quality of life" for Montanans and their progeny is worthy of the concerted attempt. As Montana historian K. Ross Toole has suggested: "Our land has become exceedingly precious and will become more so. We want no walls built around this state. What we want, above all else, is to leave our children and theirs the richest heritage we can. Twist and turn and seek profit for the short range as we may—the only real heritage we can leave our progeny is the clean and beautiful land we have now."[17]

Montanans may well prove successful in this quest to regulate their own future and to preserve the landscape that is the basis of their "quality of life." If so, the familiar term "next-year country" will carry a far more optimistic connotation in the twenty-first-century than it has in the twentieth.

Montana Population

Year	Population	% of change
1870:	20,595	
1880:	39,159	90.1
1890:	142,924	265.0
1900:	243,329	70.3
1910:	376,053	54.5
1920:	548,889	46.0
1930:	537,606	-2.1
1940:	559,456	4.1
1950:	591,024	5.6
1960:	674,767	14.2
1970:	694,409	2.9
1980:	786,690	13.3
1990:	799,065	1.6
2000*:	920,000	15.1

*estimated projection by the U.S. Bureau of Economic Analysis

THE WAYS WEST

TRANSPORTATION IN TWENTIETH-CENTURY MONTANA

In the Big Sky Country, where natural resources are rich and abundant but the distances to markets vast, transportation has always been crucial to settlement and development. Harlowton, in central Montana along the Musselshell River, is just one of many places where the shifting patterns of twentieth-century transportation have left their mark. Its creation, initial settlement, and early development depended on the railroad, which passed through the south end of town between the Musselshell River and the river bluffs, where most businesses and residences were located. Like many railroad towns in the first half of the twentieth century,

Harlowton boomed as the railroad and its associated commerce boomed. It benefited more than most, as a matter of fact, because it was a railroad division point, with machine shops and a large roundhouse. But those buildings now lie abandoned and in decay; even the tracks are missing. The railroad declared bankruptcy in the late 1970s. Harlowton is still a central Montana crossroads, the junction of two federal highways that followed the railroad tracks into town. But with the railroad days over and the interstate highway system bypassing them, Harlowton residents are charting a new transportation future, one free of the dictates of the railroad but also one without a modern link to national transportation corridors.

In Montana, people have often developed transportation so as to get to a place, take its riches, and then move on to the next place, leaving behind old paths and roads soon forgotten. During the fur trade era, Native

American trails and the extensive Upper Missouri River system provided the primary paths of settlement and development. The booming mining camps of the 1860s attracted a rush of settlers who followed the rivers or rough, dangerous roads such as the Bozeman Trail to Montana Territory. As the number of settlers increased and the mines profited, railroad companies were soon drawn to the territory, and on the rails would ride most of the settlers and prosperity of late nineteenth- and early twentieth-century Montana.

The first railroad to enter Montana was the Utah and Northern, a spur of the Union Pacific Railroad, which built into the territory and headed to the Butte mines in 1880. The territory's first transcontinental link was the Northern Pacific Railroad, completed in 1883, which passed through the Yellowstone Valley before it crossed the timber-rich Rockies. Its winding route was due to the state's topography and a generous federal land

BY CARROLL VAN WEST

Opposite: Determined Great Falls residents prepare to pit their prized automobiles against each other in a contest of speed early in the century. *Photo courtesy of the Cascade County Historical Society*

grant that allowed it to claim hundreds of thousands of valuable acres as it extended branch lines to rich resources, such as Red Lodge's coal mines. The third major company, the Great Northern Railway, proved to be the most important. Led by James J. Hill, the Great Northern in the early 1890s combined the earlier Montana Central and Manitoba lines into Montana's "Hi-Line," passing through the northern counties and western mining towns.

New construction, technology, and corporate maneuvering after the devastating 1893–1894 depression soon transformed Montana's railroads. To move the heavy freight between his Butte mines and Anaconda smelter, "Copper King" Marcus Daly dropped the Utah and Northern in favor of his own Butte, Anaconda, and Pacific Railroad, a twenty-six-mile line that opened in 1894. Later, in 1913, it became the state's first fully electrified freight and passenger line.

In 1894, the Chicago, Burlington, and Quincy (the Burlington Route) extended a spur from Wyoming to the Northern Pacific main line near Billings. As soon as

the first Burlington train reached Billings in October, the town boomed and quickly became a significant regional transportation center, linking the Burlington's Midwestern markets with the natural resources of the Northwest served by the Northern Pacific.

The alliance of the Northern Pacific and the Burlington was too much of a threat—and opportunity—for Hill to ignore. Control of the competing lines would allow Hill to dominate regional transportation and be a legitimate rival of the Union Pacific and Southern Pacific for control of the entire western railroad system. From 1894 to 1901, Hill worked with key capitalists such as J. Pierpont Morgan to gain control of both the Northern Pacific and the Burlington Route. Confident of his own abilities and convinced that the Northern Pacific, especially, was a poorly operated line, Hill wanted actual management control over all three railroads. No doubt Hill was a master railroad manager; the Great Northern Railway, observes geographer James Vance, "was the best engineered of all the American transcontinentals." In 1901, Hill formally solidified his empire by creating the Northern Securities Company, but the U.S. Supreme Court in 1904 found the corporation in violation of the Sherman Anti-Trust Act. Barred from a formal corporate alliance, Hill and his backers settled for financial control over the lines. By 1908, Hill had connected Great Falls and Billings by rail and established the Laurel railroad yards. His ascendancy was complete; two years later, he claimed

Above: A freight train skirts the Missouri River near Dearborn. *Photo by John Lambing*

Right: A train chugs across a trestle over Rainbow Falls and the mighty Missouri River before the construction of a dam there in 1910. Railroads provided the state's primary form of transportation until the widespread advent of the automobile. *Photo courtesy of the Cascade County Historical Society*

Opposite: Josephine Trigg, a close friend of cowboy artist Charlie Russell, used a bicycle to navigate the streets of Great Falls circa 1910. *Photo courtesy of the Cascade County Historical Society*

to have "paved the way for the new era" in western transportation.

Hill's dominance over Montana transportation faced challengers. Foremost was the Chicago, Milwaukee, St. Paul & Pacific Railway, known as the Milwaukee Road, which counted E. H. Harriman and the Rockefellers among its investors. In 1906, to better compete against the Hill-Morgan roads, the Milwaukee Road extended its main line westward; within two years, it opened its Montana section.

The Milwaukee Road possessed technologically advanced design standards unmatched by other Montana lines. It took control of Richard Harlow's Montana Railroad Company, which ran through the central part of the state, but otherwise it followed a new path, largely through undeveloped and unsettled country. In 1914, beginning at Harlowton and ending at Avery, Idaho, the Milwaukee electrified over four hundred miles of the line—the longest stretch of electric railway in North America.

The railroad network of 1908 would serve as the state's basic transportation infrastructure until modern times. Railroad officials then faced another daunting challenge: finding people and freight to move over the thousands of miles of new track. One promising solution was immigration, especially by farmers who would use railroads to move produce to market. The promise of dry farming and irrigation, less restrictive federal homesteading laws passed in 1909 and 1912, and massive railroad promotional campaigns convinced hundreds of thousands of homesteaders to search for new beginnings in the Big Sky Country. Between 1909 and 1923, 114,620 homesteaders filed claims. Most settlers arrived by railroad and depended on the rails to move their agricultural products to regional, national, and international markets. The Great Northern, Northern Pacific, and Milwaukee Road each operated aggressive publicity campaigns to lure the newcomers. Hill especially became an effective voice for progressive agricultural practices. In 1913, the Soo Line entered the promotional fray by extending its western terminus from Ambrose, North

Dakota, to Whitetail, in northeastern Montana.

To serve the homesteaders and open new agricultural markets, all three major Montana roads constructed costly spur lines to tiny rural villages often composed of little more than huge grain elevators. So desperate were rural communities for a rail connection that they would literally pick up their buildings and move to a new location if the railroad relocated the line or built a new spur. Some new lines and towns were established late in the homesteading period. For example, the Great Northern built a spur from Harlem to Hogeland in 1928. The Northern Pacific's spur from Sidney to Circle dates to 1929, the eve of the Great Depression.

As the tracks extended across the countryside, scores of small towns and villages developed at almost every siding at regular intervals of seven to eight miles apart. Soon state officials heard demands for new and better roads to link the scattered towns to larger urban centers. Good Roads Committees were established in several towns; some remained active into the 1930s.

In 1913, the state legislature responded by establishing the Montana State Highway Commission. Improvements were slow in coming, resulting in some dangerous roads. For example, the original highway west of Libby, known as the Highline Road, was a one-lane road with steep grades and treacherous curves where it

Opposite: First introduced in 1929, the Great Northern Railway's Empire Builder was touted as the best-equipped passenger train in the nation. By 1955, the luxury line featured a coffee shop, diners, sleepers, air-conditioning, a public-address system, and domed observation cars. This train crosses the Blackfeet Reservation at Marias Pass, as it makes its run between Chicago and Seattle in 1966. *Photo courtesy of the Montana Historical Society*

Above: Early in the century, before the advent of air travel or modern highways, Montanans found the railways the most reliable and comfortable mode of transportation. This group of travelers enjoys a breath of fresh air and the receding view. *Photo courtesy of the Cascade County Historical Society*

Right: The Billings airport was a busy place even in 1948. Because the distances between Montana communities are so vast, air travel has been an important means of transportation since its inception early in the century. *Photo courtesy of the Western Heritage Center*

Above: In 1916, a crew grades a rural road at Bridger Creek in Sweet Grass County. Drivers had to make due with rough and often muddy dirt roads until 1921, when the first paved road was built between Butte and Anaconda. That same year, the Federal Highway Act provided matching funds for road projects.
Photo courtesy of the Montana Historical Society

Opposite: Built in 1936 and recently designated a National Scenic Byway, the Beartooth Highway climbs in breathtaking switchbacks to an altitude of close to 11,000 feet; its summit is called the "Top of the World." The first heavy snows often hit in early September, closing the 68-mile-long road between Red Lodge and the northeast entrance of Yellowstone. In this photo, taken in the spring, the winter accumulation has just been cleared away.
Photo by F. W. Byerly, courtesy of the Montana Historical Society

passed Kootenai Falls. One couple recalled that, when driving at night, the husband took the wheel while the wife walked in front, carrying a light and peering around sharp corners to be sure the road was clear. Tourists traveling between Spokane and Glacier National Park used the road more than local residents did. Indeed, the lure of tourism spurred early road development. Once Yellowstone National Park allowed automobiles within its borders in 1915, officials designated the existing road through the Yellowstone Valley as the Yellowstone Trail to entice tourist traffic.

A state highway map of 1920 shows an extensive, yet unpaved, road network. The first paved road was built between Butte and Anaconda in 1921, at a time when Montana contained 4,700 miles of trunk highways. Impetus for additional improvement came from the Federal Highway Act of 1921, which provided matching funds for road projects. Two years later, enough vehicles existed to justify state vehicle registration. Motor-carrier regulation came in 1931.

In 1926 and 1927, federal officials established a

national highway system, designating primary routes as U.S. highways. In Montana, these roads often followed the railroad tracks. US 2 paralleled the Great Northern's main line while US 10 followed the Northern Pacific. US 12 from Forsyth to Missoula largely followed the route of the Milwaukee Road, and US 87 between Havre and Great Falls went along the old Manitoba route. By the middle of the twentieth century, U.S. Highway 89 between Yellowstone and Glacier National Parks was a key tourist route. Another was the breathtaking Beartooth Highway (US 212), which was completed by the late 1930s.

At the time of the Great Depression, most roads remained unpaved, ungraded, and in generally poor condition. Spare tires and repair kits were required gear for anyone traveling the state's roads on a regular basis. Ironically, the unpaved roads were often served by modern steel, and even concrete, bridges. Almost three hundred vehicular bridges were built in Montana from 1900 to 1920, and another one hundred bridges were constructed in the next two decades. Several bridges and other highway improvements came from federal funding and labor provided by such New Deal agencies as the Federal Emergency Relief Administration, the Works Progress Administration, and the Public Works Administration.

As the state recovered from the Great Depression in the late 1930s, travelers on Montana highways encountered not only better bridges and roads, but also a new commercial landscape, especially along federal highways. There were auto camps, motels, service stations, garages, drive-in restaurants, and, beginning in the mid-1930s, state highway historical markers. Traveling by car had become more than a matter of getting from one point to another; it had become an experience to be savored.

To avoid the uncertainties and save the time of automobile travel, those with more financial means took to the air. In 1919, the Billings Air Service Station established the state's first flying school. In 1928, National Parks Airways launched the state's first commercial service, connecting Salt Lake City to Butte, Helena,

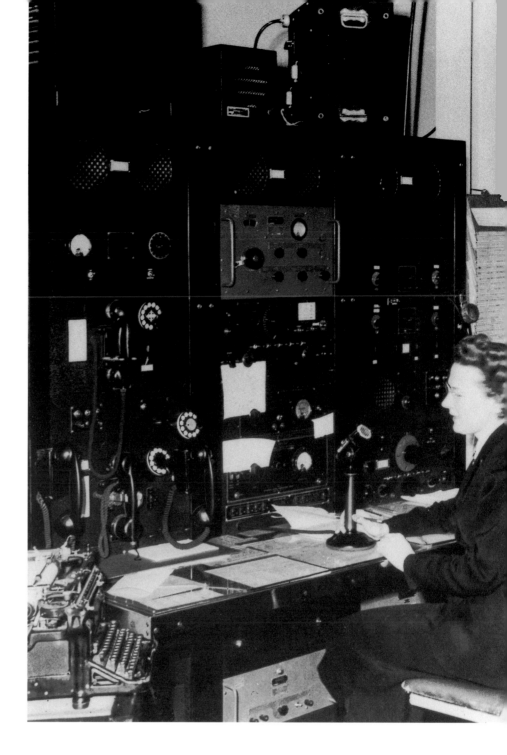

Opposite: Owner Arnold Swanson and his employees are ready to serve customers at Swanson's well-maintained Texaco station in Bozeman. As the automobile gained popularity, a whole network of motels, drive-in restaurants, garages, and service stations sprang up to cater to motorists. *Photo courtesy of the Gallatin County Historical Society*

Above: Mrs. Aili Domistrovich, an air-traffic communicator for the Civil Aeronautics Administration, guides airplanes into the Great Falls airport in 1950. *Photo courtesy of the Cascade County Historical Society*

Cromwell Dixon was only 19 when, in 1911, he became the first aviator ever to fly over the Continental Divide. Two days after his historic flight from Helena to Blossburg, at the top of the divide, the young daredevil died when his biplane crashed during a performance at the Inland Empire Fair in Spokane.
Photo courtesy of the Montana Historical Society

Cromwell Dixon in first
Presen

e to cross Continental Divide, Helena to Blossburg September 13, 1911.
o Montana Historical Library by Carl E. Kretlow.

Above: By the late 1930s, the Great Depression was beginning to lift and Montanans were eager to buy automobiles. Here, shiny new models fill the windows of the Dodge dealership in Havre. *Photo courtesy of the Montana Historical Society*

Below: A horse-drawn ambulance, seen here in front of Montana Deaconess Hospital, served the needs of sick and injured residents of Great Falls at the dawn of the century. *Photo courtesy of the Cascade County Historical Society*

Opposite: Neighborhood children on Terry Avenue in Billings pile onto a patient and stout-backed horse for a photo opportunity in 1926. *Photo courtesy of the Western Heritage Center*

and Great Falls. Missoula County's airport board dates to 1929. Two years later, commercial flights landed at Billings. New Deal agencies during the 1930s improved the state's urban airfields and built new terminals.

Another important transportation development of the 1920s was the construction of petroleum pipelines. In 1922, natural gas was discovered at Elk Basin, near the Wyoming-Montana border. The Ohio Oil Company promptly built a two-million-dollar pipeline to transport the gas from Wyoming to Billings. Pipelines supplied natural gas to many central and eastern Montana towns. Both the Montana-Dakota Utilities Company and the Montana Power Company aggressively marketed natural gas; by the 1950s, the state was annually producing over twenty billion cubic feet. In the wake of the Williston Basin strike, investors in 1954 opened the Yellowstone Pipeline between Billings and Spokane and the Butte Pipeline, which ran for 452 miles from near Poplar, Montana, to Guernsey, Wyoming. The energy crisis of the mid-1970s initiated another oil boom, leading to the construction of technologically advanced pipelines in the late 1970s and early 1980s.

Above: Young Courtenay Hill, grandson of railroad magnate James J. Hill, shows a budding interest in transportation himself as he takes an imaginary spin in the family Packard at Fort Peck in 1913. *Photo courtesy of the Montana Historical Society*

Opposite: Early in the century, the stern paddlewheeler *Klondyke* plied the waters of Flathead Lake, carrying passengers and freight from shore to shore. Its boiler was wood-fired.
Photo courtesy of the Montana Historical Society

The expansion of petroleum pipelines in the second half of the twentieth century was part of a vast modernization of the state's transportation infrastructure. The highway system changed the most. In 1948, the Montana Highway Planning Committee made plans to take advantage of funding from the Federal Highway Act, passed that year. After Congress approved the Federal Interstate Highway Act in 1956, civic and business officials across the state lobbied to have the new divided four-lane, limited-access highways come their way. Montana received three interstate highways. I-94 runs through the eastern half of the Yellowstone Valley. I-90 enters the state at the Wyoming border, extends to Billings, and then cuts west to Bozeman, Butte, and Missoula. I-15 is the state's primary north-south route, running along the spine of the Rockies, from Dillon through Butte, Helena, and Great Falls, and into Canada. The last interstate completed, I-15's final stretch between Basin and Butte opened in 1986, thirty years after the initial federal legislation.

State and local roads also were improved in the second half of the century. Most state roads were paved, although some remain gravel roads. Many county roads are little more than rough trails, almost impassable when wet. During my own extensive travels in Montana in the early 1980s, a county official in Jordan once warned me not to take certain local roads if it rained—or even hinted of rain—because my car would get stuck in the mud and muck until everything dried out. In 1996, Montana had 69,000 miles of public highways and roads, with 2,100 state-maintained bridges.

Airline traffic also has grown substantially during the past fifty years. The Billings International Airport expanded services during the oil booms of the 1950s and 1970s; it now is the state's largest. Regional carriers regularly serve the airports at Great Falls, Helena, Bozeman, Butte, and Missoula. Due to increased tourism, the Kalispell International Airport has grown significantly in the 1980s and 1990s. But federal deregulation of airlines has diminished service to all Montana cities and left smaller towns with infrequent, if any, service from commuter airlines. In 1996, according to the Montana Department of Transportation, there were 12 state-owned airports, 119 public-use airports, and 350 private-use airports in the state.

How did the once omnipotent railroads respond to the competition of modern transportation? They modernized their freight operations and consolidated already large companies into huge new corporations. Passenger service was the first to change. Immediately after World War II, companies tried to attract passengers with sleek, fast trains.

The Northern Pacific maintained extremely high standards for its dining-car service; those who recall the old trains also fondly remember such NP staples as the Great Big Baked Potato.

However, Northwest travelers continued to use cars and take airplanes. The beginning of the federal inter-state-highway system in 1956 and the 1957–1958 recession were the final blows. In 1961, the Milwaukee Road ended passenger service in Montana. Over the next decade, all Montana rail companies followed suit, and in 1971 the federally subsidized National Railroad Passenger Corporation, better known as Amtrak, assumed control of passenger service. Although threatened with federal budget cuts throughout the 1990s, Amtrak still operates passenger lines along the old Great Northern route, and travelers may stay at converted rail-

road facilities such as the old Essex bunkhouse, now the Izaak Walton Inn.

As passenger service from the private companies ended, freight business improved in Montana. The transport of coal dominated traffic along the Northern Pacific line, after a subsidiary of the Montana Power Company instituted large-scale strip mining at Colstrip, followed in the early 1970s by similar coal mines at Decker. Large coal trains regularly rumble east from Forsyth to their midwestern urban designations.

However, corporate restructuring has been the most significant railroad trend.

Throughout the 1950s and 1960s, officials sought federal approval to merge the Northern Pacific, Burlington Route, and Great Northern into one massive corporation. On May 3, 1970, the Burlington Northern

Railroad was finally approved, creating a system of over 24,000 miles of track from the three major Montana lines, along with the Spokane, Portland & Seattle Railway, added in 1970.

The Burlington Northern dominated regional rail traffic, and within seven years of the merger, the Milwaukee Road was bankrupt. In 1980, the Milwaukee abandoned its entire line from Miles City west. Six years later, the remnants of the Milwaukee Road became part of the Soo Line. The Union Pacific, which still operated trains to Butte, also expanded its system mileage by acquiring the Missouri Pacific and Western Pacific lines in 1981 and the Missouri-Kansas-Texas road in 1988.

The 1980s were also a time of expansion for the Burlington Northern. In 1980, it extended its rails to the Gulf of Mexico by acquiring the Frisco Line. The corporation established its headquarters at Fort Worth, Texas. In 1986–1987, it sold a large part of the former Northern Pacific line through Montana to two new companies. Montana Western Railway took over the fifty-two miles of track between Butte and Garrison. Montana Rail Link acquired 557 miles of the Northern Pacific main line from Huntley to Sandpoint, Idaho, along with seven Montana branch lines, creating a rail network of 940 miles. It is the property of Washington Corporations, led by the dynamic Montana businessman Dennis Washington.

In 1995, the Burlington's corporate restructuring reached dizzying heights when it purchased the Santa Fe Pacific Corporation and established the Burlington Northern Santa Fe Corporation. This railroad titan controls over 31,000 miles of track across twenty-seven states and two Canadian provinces, making it the largest rail network in North America. Its international railroad system certainly matches, if not exceeds, Jim Hill's most expansive dreams of a century ago.

Fast freights, open highways, modern pipelines, and powerful jets characterize transportation in Montana today. Yet, vestiges of the nineteenth century survive along the state's back roads. In 1995, three cable ferries still crossed the Missouri River in central Montana; at the dawn of the century, probably two dozen ferries had operated along the Missouri. The most isolated and least changed is the McClelland Ferry north of Winifred. Difficult to travel except in the dry months of summer, the access road and the ferry crossing are physical links to a forgotten transportation heritage, as well as poignant reminders of the changes in Montana transportation over the past one hundred years.

Today, we can compare the McClelland Ferry to transportation in our modern world and see clearly the differences between the nineteenth and twentieth centuries. One wonders, will Montanans of 2099 see the two-lane, paved federal highways of today and the crossroad towns such as Harlowton in that same poignant, nostalgic way?

Opposite: A United Airlines commercial jet approaches the state's busiest airport, Logan International, in Billings. Located midway between Minneapolis and Seattle, Denver and Calgary, Billings is a major transportation hub, as well as a business and convention center. *Photo by Michael Crummett*

SHAPING THE FUTURE

GOVERNMENT AND POLITICS IN TWENTIETH-CENTURY MONTANA

In his 1901 State of the State address, Montana Governor Joseph K. Toole outlined for legislators the problems

facing their young state. He deplored inequities in school funding, condemned corporate influence on elections,

and expressed confidence that he could negotiate a lower price than the forty-five cents a day, per person, that

the state paid to contract out care of its inmates at the prison in Deer Lodge. The Democrat also reported that

the Board of Sheep Examiners wanted to form a committee to investigate the effect of smelter smoke on livestock

in Deer Lodge, Powell, and Silver Bow Counties, as well as to study whether it contaminated neighboring

streams. In his address to legislators two years later, Toole endorsed the idea of amending the Montana

Constitution to provide for a state initiative and referendum. Of these forms of direct democracy, he said, "It

is our hope for the present, our refuge and safe harbor for the future."

For the next nine decades, Montana governors and legislators grappled with the same problems: school funding, corporate influence, prisons, and, beginning in the late 1960s, the environment—to say nothing of budgets, taxes, highways, and a host of other issues. State budgets for schools, higher education, and public institutions have often proved insufficient because of legislative frugality, the state's boom-and-bust economy, and still-simmering battles over Montana's unbalanced tax structure. Prison riots in 1959 and 1991 have helped draw statewide attention to overcrowding. In the 1970s, Governor Thomas Judge and reform-minded legislators such as Francis Bardanouve and Ann Mary Dussault led efforts to improve staffing and facilities at the state's isolated, neglected institutions.

After adopting the initiative and referendum early in the century, Montanans have used them often, especially after voters approved the 1972 state constitution, which lowered the number of signatures necessary to put them on the ballot. The new charter also made it possible to amend the state constitution via initiative rather than solely through legislative action and a public vote. Since 1972, Montanans of all political stripes have learned to use the initiative process, with some even paying people to gather signatures. Montanans used the ballot to give women suffrage in 1914, pass Prohibition in 1916, and

BY CHARLES S. JOHNSON

Opposite: In 1902, the year it was formally dedicated, the Montana Capitol stands alone on the eastern outskirts of Helena. Designed by a pair of architects from Council Bluffs, Iowa, its total cost was less than half a million dollars. Today, it is listed on the National Register of Historic Places.
Photo courtesy of the Montana Historical Society

repeal it ten years later. In 1912, they passed an initiative calling for the direct election of U.S. senators, thirteen years after Butte "Copper King" William A. Clark bribed state legislators to send him to Congress, only to have the U.S. Senate refuse to seat him.

Ballot measures have become a popular way to reverse unpopular decisions by policymakers. For example, environmentalists tried by initiative in 1996 to toughen Montana's water-pollution laws, a year after statutes were weakened at the behest of mining companies. In a campaign that overshadowed all other political races, the mining companies spent more than two million dollars to defeat the clean-water measure by a margin of fifty-seven to forty-three percent. Two years later, environmentalists got revenge as Montanans approved an initiative banning future cyanide heap-leach mining for gold and silver.

Until the 1950s or 1960s, the Anaconda Company (known formerly as the Amalgamated Copper Company and then the Anaconda Copper Mining Company) dominated Montana politics and economics. The company provided good-paying jobs, owned vast tracts of timber, and controlled most of the state's major daily newspapers until it sold them in 1959.

Later, Anaconda joined political forces with the Montana Power Company, the utility it created to supply its electricity, to become what some called "The Twins" or "Tweedledee and Tweedledum." Historians still debate the extent of their corporate influence, but their combined governmental lobbying efforts were daunting. Among these were the notorious "watering holes" for legislators, which offered free food and drink around the clock. Before the creation of the Legislative Council to draft all bills, the two corporations hired skilled lawyers to draft favorable legislation. Late in the twentieth century, Montana Power struggled to keep its franchise, as a new competitive environment for electricity and natural gas replaced its historical monopoly. In 1997, the company shocked the state by announcing its intention to sell its hydroelectric dams and coal-fired power plants. Atlantic Richfield had bought the Anaconda Company in 1977. Three years later, claiming that it was losing money, ARCO shut down its smelter in Anaconda and its refinery in Great Falls. In 1983, it did the unthinkable: it closed the copper mines in Butte, leaving behind the nation's largest toxic-waste, or "Superfund," site. The state has gone to federal court seeking $700 million for environmental damages.

As corporations such as ARCO reduced work forces and closed operations, Montana's organized labor movement dwindled, despite the efforts of such legendary labor leaders as Jim Murry, longtime chief of the Montana State AFL-CIO. Montana's historical reliance on union workers in the mines, smelters, and sawmills set it apart from more conservative neighboring states. It also helped keep Western Montana a Democratic stronghold, balancing the traditional domination of Republicans in the east. As union jobs disappeared, Missoula tycoon Dennis Washington was able to reopen the Butte mines without unions in 1985. This, coupled with an influx of well-to-do conservatives to the most scenic areas of Montana in the 1990s, eroded Democratic votes, threatening to turn Montana into a Republican stronghold like Idaho, Wyoming, and Utah.

Indeed, by 1997, a majority of the state's congressional delegation was Republican for the first time in eight decades. Republican Governor Marc Racicot was re-elected in 1996 with seventy-nine percent of the vote, and the GOP maintained a nearly two-to-one majority in the state legislature. The decline of the Democratic Party was illustrated by the fact that the lone Democrat willing to challenge Racicot in 1996 was Chet Blaylock, a distinguished retired legislator who filed after others

Opposite: Designed in the fashion of a 19th-century opera house, the spectacular rotunda of the Montana Capitol features a number of larger-than-life paintings and murals that depict scenes of the state's early history.
Photo courtesy of the Montana Historical Society

Right: A crowd swarms up the front steps of the new statehouse on the day of its dedication, July 4, 1902. The east and west wings were not completed until 1912.
Photo by W. H. Taylor, courtesy of the Montana Historical Society

refused. The seventy-two-year-old suffered a fatal heart attack just weeks before the election.

Throughout much of the twentieth century, Montana suffered from political schizophrenia. Voters most often sent liberal Democrats to Washington, D.C., while entrusting state affairs to conservative Republicans and the occasional conservative Democrat. The state constitution adopted in 1889 was designed to limit governmental power, and many state laws served to severely restrict the power of governors, making the office less attractive to capable politicians than a seat in Congress. As a result, throughout most of the first six decades of the century, Montana had generally lackluster governors with comparatively few powers—with a few notable exceptions, such as Republicans Joseph Dixon and Sam Ford. Some of these chief executives were personable, well-liked conservatives, such as J. Hugo Aronson and Tim Babcock, but they often accomplished little beyond holding the line on state spending.

That certainly cannot be said of the state's congressional delegation. Most Montana senators and representatives have wielded influence far greater than the state's tiny political base would seem to warrant. In the 1920s, the brilliant Democratic Senator Thomas Walsh exposed the Teapot Dome Scandal and was President Franklin D. Roosevelt's choice to be his first attorney general. Republican Jeannette Rankin, the nation's first congresswoman, was a well-noted suffragist and pacifist who cast votes against U.S. involvement in both world wars. Feisty Burton K. Wheeler started out as a liberal, running as Robert LaFollette's vice presidential candidate on the Progressive Party ticket in 1924. But later, he became a conservative Democratic senator and earned acclaim for stopping President Roosevelt's effort to pack the U.S. Supreme Court. Democratic Senator James Murray was a loyal New Dealer who fought successfully for federal aid to education but failed to win passage of a national health-care plan and was branded a Communist by the American Medical Association. Finally, there were Democratic Senators Mike Mansfield and Lee Metcalf. The wise, taciturn Mansfield was a foreign-policy adviser to numerous presidents, served as majority leader longer than any other American, and launched the Watergate investigation into wrongdoing by President Richard Nixon and his aides. Metcalf, an unabashed liberal, earned a reputation as a fighter for environmental laws and federal aid to education, as well as for his criticism of electric utilities.

Beginning in the 1960s, Montana government underwent a series of remarkable changes. Among them was reapportionment of the legislature, which ended rural Montana's political grip on the state. In 1964, the U.S. Supreme Court held that every state legislative chamber must represent "people, not trees or acres," in districts "as nearly of equal population as practicable." The 1889 constitution had provided one senator for every county. As a result, Montana by 1965 had one of the most poorly apportioned legislatures in the nation.

Left: A Montana voter emerges from a polling booth, having done her civic duty. The state traditionally has had some of the highest voter turnout in the country—a record 86 percent in the general election of 1968. *Photo by Michael Crummett*

Opposite: The Young Democrats of Yellowstone County prepare in 1934 to march—and beat the drum—in support of their party's candidates. *Photo by I. G. Petek, courtesy of the Montana Historical Society*

Tiny Petroleum County, population 894, had one senator, just like the state's most populous county, Yellowstone, with 79,016 residents. Governor Babcock resisted reapportionment and argued that "the theory of one person/one vote simply does not fit Montana." It took a lawsuit by a Butte woman, Phoebe Herweg, to force a federal court to reapportion the legislature. In an unsuccessful move to block reapportionment, the late Senator Dave Manning, D-Hysham, spoke for rural Montana when he said, "I do represent cows. I represent cows, acres, trees, coal, and a lifestyle."

Reapportionment shifted legislative power to urban areas. Montana's Indians are still underrepresented, as they made up six percent of the state population in 1999 but held only two of 150 legislative seats. Women, who

make up slightly more than half the state population, are also underrepresented, although they have scored gains since 1971, when Republican Senator Antoinette Rosell and Democratic Representative Dorothy Bradley were the lone female lawmakers. In 1999, a record thirty-seven women served in the legislature.

Once it was properly apportioned, the legislature tackled a host of "good-government" modernization issues, several of them under Democratic Governor Forrest Anderson, an old-guard pragmatist. In one move that has earned the state several billion dollars, Anderson and Representative Francis Bardanouve overcame the entrenched opposition of state bankers to set up the Board of Investments. It began investing idle state cash and pensions so that the money could earn interest instead of allowing it to sit interest-free in banks. Anderson also spearheaded reorganization of the state executive branch, after a constitutional amendment, passed in 1970, limited the number of state agencies to twenty. The 1971 Legislature implemented Anderson's plan, which empowered the governor to appoint department directors who served at his pleasure, just like members of the president's Cabinet. Despite Anderson's restructuring, cattle ranchers still had the political clout to insist that the Board of Livestock, not the governor, name the livestock director. Previously, Montana governors had been hobbled by dozens of boards, bureaus, and commissions, usually outside their direct control and dominated by special interests that ran parts of state government. As Republican Governor Joseph Dixon, Montana's most visionary chief executive, told lawmakers in 1921: "Let us nominate and elect the chief executive of the state, then give him full power to name his assistants in administering the various departments of the state government, and we will know exactly where to place our finger in locating blame or praise."

Adoption of the new state constitution in 1972 proved a pivotal event. By the 1960s, it was obvious that the 1889 constitution, primarily a vehicle to secure statehood, needed revision badly. In 1970, Montanans voted to call a constitutional convention and then chose one hundred delegates in a special election a year later. A GOP-backed sales tax on the same ballot was buried by voters, seventy to thirty percent, providing long coattails for Democrats running for seats at the convention. Democrats wound up with a fifty-eight to thirty-six majority over Republicans; six delegates were independents. Although the convention was not especially partisan, the Democratic majority, inspired

Left: During his tenure as Montana's 12th governor, Republican Sam C. Ford (1882–1961) led a successful effort to defeat a New Deal initiative that called for massive federal development of the Missouri River Basin, including a series of dams to provide power, reclamation, and flood control.
Photo courtesy of the Montana Historical Society

Above: Thomas J. Walsh of Helena (1860–1933) served in the U.S. Senate for almost 25 years and was famous for his aggressive and principled investigation of the Teapot Dome oil scandal during the 1920s. He was appointed attorney general by President Franklin D. Roosevelt but died before he could take office. *Photo by International News, courtesy of the Montana Historical Society*

Opposite top: In 1948, U.S. Senator James E. Murray (D-Montana, on left), joins President Harry S Truman (seated) on an aerial tour of country flooded that spring by the Missouri River. Murray (1876-1961) played a key role in the passage of many New Deal programs, including unemployment compensation, Social Security, and support for small businesses.
Photo by the United Press Association, courtesy of the Montana Historical Society

Opposite bottom: U.S. Senator Lee Metcalf (1911–1978), a native of the Bitterroot Valley, was best known in Congress as a leading proponent of wilderness and as "Mr. Education." A classic liberal, Metcalf fought against environmental pollution and, in his most ardent and sustained battle, for regulation of the private power industry. *Photo courtesy of the Montana Historical Society*

by the liberal mood of the early 1970s, produced a populist charter that *Time* magazine called "a model document." It eked by with a 50.6 percent margin, helped by bumper stickers inspired by independent delegate George Harper, a Methodist minister from Helena, who implored, "Praise the Lord and Pass the Constitution."

The new constitution made a number of important changes, including some aimed at the hidebound legislative and executive branches. Legislative reforms included a short-lived change to annual instead of biennial sessions and election of senators and representatives from smaller single-member districts rather than from an entire county. The change to single-member districts proved questionable, as state lawmakers, like congressional wardheelers, often paid the most attention to parochial needs of their own districts instead of the larger interests of the state. But the constitution contained a number of innovative provisions that are still being disputed and litigated, including the right to "a clean and healthful environment," a state right to privacy that has clashed at times with the public's right to know, the right to equal educational opportunity, and the statewide equalization of property taxes. Since 1972, policymakers have debated whether the new charter went too far, and the Montana Supreme Court, which has swung back and forth philosophically from conservative to liberal, has had to settle legal conflicts related to it.

While Montana's population has more than tripled since the start of the century, the state's vast physical size and comparatively few residents have proved to be both a blessing and a curse. The state lost one of two congressional seats in 1992, after failing to grow at the rate of most other states. That led to an election showdown between two political veterans: conservative Republican Ron Marlenee, a Scobey farmer-rancher who represented the eastern district, and liberal Democrat Pat Williams, a former Butte teacher from the western district. Williams narrowly won and represented the entire state for four years, until retiring in 1996. Conservative Republican businessman Rick Hill captured Williams's seat to join Republican U.S. Senator Conrad Burns and Democratic U.S. Senator Max Baucus in Montana's congressional delegation.

Leading Montana into the next century is Governor Marc Racicot, a moderate Republican and former attorney general who enjoys huge popularity. He is sometimes compared to former Democratic Governor Ted Schwinden, who was also very popular when he served from 1981 to 1989. Both men helped restore confidence in government after troubled administrations by their immediate predecessors. Racicot and Schwinden both enjoyed nothing more than traveling to small towns like those in which they were raised, taking government

closer to the people. Both men rose from the executive branch of state government and understood it thoroughly, unlike Republican Governor Stan Stephens, a talented Havre businessman and legislator whose administration got off to a horrendous start from which it never recovered after some poor Cabinet appointments. Just as some fellow Democrats condemned Schwinden as a closet Republican for his frugal fiscal policies, some GOP colleagues have accused Racicot of spending money as liberally as a Democrat. Racicot's critics, like Schwinden's, believe he ought to be bolder, take more risks, and chart a new course for Montana, rather than coast on his high popularity in the polls.

The interest groups seeking to influence Montana

officials have changed considerably over the years, particularly with the emergence of the education and environmental lobbies and with a change in corporate lobbying. The Montana Education Association and the Montana Federation of Teachers became strong lobbying groups after the legislature enacted a law in the 1970s allowing public bargaining by public employees. The two groups are moving toward a merger, which would form the largest union in the state. Such a merger might also change the anti–sales tax dynamics of the Montana State AFL-CIO, which now includes only the Federation of Teachers. Other major education lobbying groups include the Montana School Boards Association, School Administrators of Montana, and Montana Rural

Education Association. While they differ on labor issues, they often work with the state superintendent of public instruction to push for increased funding of education.

After watching volunteer Don Aldrich of the Montana Wildlife Federation lobby single-handedly for environmental causes during the 1971 legislative session, Missoulians Phil and Robin Tawney and others created the Montana Environmental Information Center to counter industrial lobbying and give the Wildlife Federation the assistance of a full-time staff in Helena. At about the same time, the Northern Plains Resource Council formed in Billings, organized by ranchers concerned about federal plans to strip-mine vast amounts of coal in Eastern Montana and erect numerous power

The state legislature gathers for a special session in 1992. When a pressing problem arises between regular sessions, which are held every two years, the governor or a majority of lawmakers can call a special session. Montana held 25 special sessions in the 20th century, all but eight of them after 1965. The sessions have dealt with everything from labor disputes and women's suffrage to balancing the state budget. The 1992 session considered reforming the tax structure and rejected a sales tax, among other things. *Photo by Ray Ozmon*

plants to generate electricity by burning the coal. The Greater Yellowstone Coalition was formed to protect Yellowstone National Park and the ecosystem surrounding it. Other influential groups that have surfaced in the past twenty-five years are the Montana Wilderness Association and state chapters of the Sierra Club, Audubon Society, and numerous other "green" groups.

Some corporations continue to have a strong influence over legislators. Montana Power Company has a powerful lobbying force and a strong community presence, as do other utilities such as US West and Montana-Dakota Utilities. Montana Power and US West successfully

pushed deregulation bills through the 1997 Legislature that could end their historical monopolies, despite the concerns of skeptics that individual consumers may suffer. The foremost lobbying group on tax matters remains the Montana Taxpayers' Association, with the Montana AFL-CIO providing a counter-balance with its opposition to a sales tax.

The Montana Chamber of Commerce and the state chapter of the National Federation of Independent Business lead the business pack in lobbying for corporations and small Main Street businesses, respectively. A host of associations represent specific trades, such as

Opposite: Delegates to the 1972 Constitutional Convention deliberate in the statehouse. Voters narrowly approved the progressive new constitution, heralded by many at the time as the most advanced in the country. It created single-member legislative districts, strengthened the right to personal privacy and a clean environment, and mandated a more open and responsive government. *Photo courtesy of the Montana Historical Society*

Above: President John F. Kennedy—the first U.S. president born in the 20th century—visits Malmstrom Air Force Base in Great Falls in September 1963, accompanied by Montana senators Mike Mansfield and Lee Metcalf. The local newspaper described the visit as one of the most exciting events of the decade. *Photo courtesy of the Cascade County Historical Society*

Right: Two-term Republican governor Marc Racicot, one of Montana's most popular politicians ever, has set the stage for the state's entry into the 21st century. Racicot's tenure as governor will end in 2000 because of term limits imposed by state voters in 1993. *Photo by Michael Crummett*

the Montana Bankers Association, Montana Mining Association, Montana Coal Council, Western Environmental Trade Association, Montana Wood Products Association, and numerous others. As legalized gambling has proliferated, so have the number of organizations formed to promote and oppose it.

Agriculture and livestock groups began cooperating more in the latter part of the century, abandoning some of their old rivalries. The Montana Stockgrowers Association and Montana Grain Growers Association are among the most influential agricultural groups, joined by the Montana Wool Growers Association and Montana Farm Bureau Federation. The Montana Farmers' Union, the lone left-leaning agricultural organization, is trying to rebuild after falling on hard times.

As the Montana population ages, the state chapter of the American Association of Retired Persons and the Montana Senior Citizens Association have gained influence. Religious lobbying groups testify frequently at the legislature, led by the Montana Association of Churches, which represents a number of mainstream Protestant denominations, and the Montana Catholic Conference. These church groups, which often take liberal stands on social issues, are frequently at odds with the Montana chapter of the Christian Coalition, a conservative organization formed by the Reverend Pat Robertson. No discussion of interest groups can ignore mention of the nonpartisan Montana League of Women Voters, a tireless bunch armed with detailed studies who never miss an opportunity to promote "good government."

Montana will enter the twenty-first century without many of its most experienced and talented legislators because of a term-limits initiative adopted by voters in 1992. The measure also requires top executive officers to leave their posts with state government after two consecutive four-year terms, although there have always been natural limits to the terms of those holding the top offices, such as governor and attorney general. Many experts are skeptical of the term-limit idea, but the public apparently is firmly behind it.

In the year 2000, new lawmakers and executives will face a decrepit tax system, overcrowded and costly prisons and institutions that are often sued for failing to provide adequate care, and an increasing stridency in the state's political debate, especially over environmental issues. Montana citizens, thanks to right-to-participate and right-to-know provisions of the 1972 state constitution and to the increased access they have to decision-makers via the Internet, have never had a greater opportunity to help shape the future.

Opposite: Max Baucus used an innovative technique to publicize his campaign for the U.S. House in 1974: He walked more than 600 miles across the western congressional district, from Gardiner to Yaak. In 1980, the Democrat was elected to the U.S. Senate, where he continues to represent Montana at the end of the century. *Photo courtesy of the Montana Historical Society*

Above: Elaborate gardens decorate the grounds of the Montana Capitol, which will enter the 21st century in the midst of an extensive renovation. The goal of the $14.2 million project, scheduled for completion in 2002, is to make the building safer, healthier, and more efficient. State officials also hope to undo some of the haphazard modernization of the 1950s and 1960s, restoring the building's original design and architectural integrity. *Photo by Donnie Sexton / Travel Montana*

Right: In 1989, Republican Governor Stan Stephens, surrounded by children dressed in the fashions of 1889, rings Montana's statehood centennial bell. *Photo by Stuart S. White*

A MIXED BLESSING

TOURISM AND RECREATION IN TWENTIETH-CENTURY MONTANA

You might say I acted just like a tourist, falling in love with the idea of Montana long before I met the real thing. I was nine years old, living in northern Indiana with my parents and brother, elbow to elbow in a sea of pint-sized houses, each one squatting on a lawn so small I could throw a baseball from my back yard and have it land in the mitt of a friend standing three doors away. Maybe it was those close quarters, that unfortunate lack of horizon, that set me up for the jolt I got on a warm day in September when I pulled the lid open on our mailbox to find a large envelope from the Montana Department of Commerce addressed to Mr. Gary Ferguson. And inside, this big, glossy brochure I'd sent for with a coupon clipped out of the back of my mother's Family Circle. *Page after page of outrageous Kodachromes, every one of them chock full of rock and timber and sky. Glacier National Park, Paradise Valley, the Beartooths—shots so wide and handsome they gave me vertigo,*

spinning my insides like the downhill curve on a roller coaster. It would be several more years before I finally found my way into Montana's mountains, before I first caught the spicy smell of her willow banks, felt the sting of snow pelting across her prairies.

Historians like to say that if you want to understand a culture, you first need to understand its mythology. The first step in knowing a place, they advise, is to unravel the stew pot of aspirations that drive the people—their hopes and visions, those things that hint at what they value most about the world. It may seem a strange notion, but one of the best spotlights for illuminating the mythology of Montana is tourism.

At its best, tourism was a meeting ground for those who wrestled lives from this powerful, overwhelming landscape and those who merely admired it from afar. You could see it, for example, in old ranchers locked in the hard times of the Great Depression, deciding to throw open their gates to dudes—sitting with them around the dinner table, recounting amazing tales of rodeo days and ornery bears and freight-train winters. And, of course, you could see it in the tourists themselves—so many of them, just like me, desperate to be dazzled, hoping for a glimpse of the promised land in the wink of a mountain sunrise.

BY GARY FERGUSON

Opposite: Montana's own version of Yogi Bear stops tourist traffic to beg for a handout in Glacier National Park in 1947. Since the 1960s, the National Park Service has prohibited the feeding of these wild and dangerous creatures. Not only can it result in injury or death to the person, but it can put the bear at risk, too. Animals that become habituated to humans often must be relocated or destroyed. *Photo by Don Boslaugh*

Below: In 1912, a group of vacationers relaxes in style at their comfortable "Pine Rock Camp" southeast of Helena. To ensure a pleasant stay, one camper even brought along her maid. *Photo courtesy of the Montana Historical Society*

Opposite: A carload of Montanans visits "The Grotto" in the badlands of Eastern Montana. Makoshika State Park, two miles southeast of Glendive, today preserves more than 8,000 acres of these spectacular badlands, which are carved by wind and water from soft mudstone, siltstone, and sandstone laid down by ancient inland seas. *Photo courtesy of the Frontier Gateway Museum*

THE PULL OF YELLOWSTONE

From a financial standpoint, tourism in the early part of the century was a slow horse. Most out-of-staters forged their impressions of Montana from railroad brochures—lavish, myth-spawning publications that portrayed the state as an intriguing, if somewhat brutish, curiosity. The kind of place best experienced from behind the window of a Pullman car, Scotch in hand, clickity-clacking up the rails on the way to the one real attraction in the entire region, Yellowstone National Park.

Given the high cost of getting to Yellowstone by rail, it just wasn't a journey that many American families could hope to make. But that hardly stopped residents of the area from becoming tourists themselves. The old notion that rural people weren't prone to travel for the fun of it just wasn't true, at least not around these parts. Every year, hundreds of Montana families hitched up their wagons, loaded up the kids among sacks of potatoes

and bed rolls and knots of jerky, and set out on fifty, a hundred, even two-hundred-mile trips down a weave of rutted roads, bound for Yellowstone. A 1911 report issued by the park estimates that roughly half of Yellowstone's visitors were local farmers and ranchers, almost all of them arriving in horse-drawn wagons. Those on tight budgets explored on their own—sleeping under the stars, fishing for dinner, cooking bags of beans in the park's thermal pools. Those with spending money could park their wagons at the gateways and shell out thirty-five dollars for a six-and-a-half-day guided tour by stagecoach. Coach campers stayed in modest tent villages, eating fresh trout while Mrs. Wylie shoed swarms of flies with her homemade swatters. At night, they

curled up under a couple of wool blankets (oftentimes alongside a complete stranger, since no one was given a bed of his own), often to be awakened by someone shouting and hurling chunks of firewood to keep the bears from raiding the mess tent.

If the diaries of the day and letters to friends and family are any indication, most locals fell in love with the whole experience. Notably, many of the men returned, hiring out their wagons and driving services to other tourists from the region. In 1909, when the acting superintendent of Yellowstone was directed to look into letting automobiles into the park, he cited these local wagon jockeys and their motor-shy horses as the perfect reason to keep cars out.

THE COMING OF THE AUTO

By 1910, America was neck deep in a serious case of auto-travel fever. But despite the unmistakable promise of tourism held in the swelling number of car owners, at the time Montana had less than a hundred miles of improved roads. The "Blue Book," a popular motorist guide of the day, was in Montana less an atlas than a manual for treasure hunts. Navigation was based on compass headings, not to mention somewhat vague suggestions about tracking your mileage with the odometer and making a hard left at the red barn, a right at the big stone house, straight on when you first see the church with the white steeple.

Furthermore, the enormous distances in the state, combined with a somewhat miserable tax base due to the small number of residents, kept Montana drivers hub-deep in honest-to-goodness adventure for decades. By 1930, the state of New York was boasting more than ten thousand miles of paved roads; Montana, on the other hand, had fifty. A wonderful glimpse into the challenges of auto travel during the 1920s can be found in the diaries of an indomitable Montana resident named

Opposite: Snow is slow to melt on the 52-mile-long Going-to-the-Sun Highway in Glacier National Park. Begun in 1916 and completed in 1932, the spectacular roadway is considered an engineering masterpiece. It climbs more than 3,000 feet, tunneling through rock and hugging sheer cliffs before it tops out at Logan Pass. Here, an incredulous motorist risks being buried in snow as she checks the depth of a bank along the Garden Wall in midsummer. *Photo by E. T. Scoyen, courtesy of the Montana Historical Society*

Above: Two happy hunters capture for posterity the deer they bagged during a hunting trip in northwestern Montana. Since the 1930s, many big-game populations in the state have increased significantly. Today, Montana is said to have the best big-game selection in the nation outside of Alaska. *Photo courtesy of the Heritage Museum*

Below: A weary and dejected traveler bemoans a flat tire he got near Augusta, circa 1935. During the first half of the century, Montana's mostly unpaved roads, notorious for their sharp rocks and gumbo mud, took a toll on both cars and drivers.
Photo courtesy of the Montana Historical Society

The University of Montana Grizzlies defend their home turf at
Washington Grizzly Stadium, which holds upwards of 18,000
vocally supportive fans. In 1995, the Missoula-based football
team won the Division 1-AA championship by beating Marshall
University, of Huntington, West Virginia. *Photo by Ray Ozmon*

Contented "dudes" savor a crisp summer night—and a few marshmallows—around the campfire in the high country of the Beartooth Range. *Photo by F. W. Byerly, courtesy of the Montana Historical Society*

Kathryn Stephen, who, along with two women friends, bought a used Ford in 1922, christened it Oliver Twist, and set out from the northwest part of the state to see the West. "Aunt Isa could not run a car at all," she wrote, "I learned after we bought it, and Iva, tho she had driven for several years on the Kansas prairies, boasted no experience on mountain roads." In the weeks before they left, the women's friends pleaded with them to enlist a male companion ("a man is so handy for pumping tires," explained one), but they would have none of it. On the second of June, they loaded up twenty feet of rope, a small ax, three pie tins, a couple of kettles and a toaster, fishing tackle, some clothes, and Aunt Isa's enormous blue telescope, and hit the road for Butte, ultimately bound for Utah, then Nevada, then California.

Things went pretty well, too, at least until it started raining at Monida Pass and the roads "turned smoozy with gumbo mud." Before long the three explorers—including Aunt Isa, who was well into her sixties—were down on their knees in the gumbo putting on chains; an hour later they had resorted to chopping sage with the hand ax "in a vain attempt to fill up the mud holes that gurgled around our four hubs." After several hours of this torture, someone finally came along with a team of horses, hooked up to Oliver Twist, and pulled him free.

Flat tires were also common fare; along one stretch, the women changed nine tires in three days. The tire pump was handled in shifts, each woman limited to no more than thirty strokes in a single turn. Even if you managed to keep your tires full of air, the rocks and ruts on many roads forced a snail's pace; in fact, there were days when Iva, Isa, and Kathryn were lucky to average six miles an hour. Brake linings burned out on mountain roads, and backs and shoulders ached from clutching the steering wheel. As in many cars of the day, the horn on Oliver Twist was driven from the engine. This meant that at slow speeds, in low gear, there was little in the way of noisemaking potential. Desperate for some means of warning oncoming traffic on mountainous hairpin turns, the women took to blowing madly on a referee's whistle. In the end, though, the shrill blast of the whistle was far more nerve-racking than the thought of a collision, so they gave it up.

By the 1920s, auto camps had sprouted across Montana, erected by communities as a means of encouraging the growing number of car campers to pitch their tents and spend a few extra dollars at the local grocery, hardware, restaurant, and mechanic. Most out-of-staters were thrilled by such facilities, trading information on which town had the best camps like hobos passing tips on friendly kitchens. But like many other Montanans,

Kathryn, Iva, and Aunt Isa were less enthusiastic. "We had an antipathy to the orthodox camp," wrote Kathryn. "They had always seemed so crowded and so—khaki! We objected to being permanently dun and indistinguishable among the dusty mob. We registered only when we needed to wash our clothes or ourselves, or when no more interesting place presented itself." And that wasn't often. Along their route, the women slept in a boathouse and on front porches, in haystacks and in a log cabin with a loft filled with pack rats, in canyons, out on the desert, and at least on one occasion, smack dab in the middle of the road.

DAWN OF THE DUDES

Are you feeling sick? Liver out of sorts? Tired when you get out of bed? Coffee tasteless? Toast half cold? Scold the kids? Snap at your stenographer and threaten to fire the office boy? Don't consult a doctor; there is a surer cure. Let old Doc Nature prescribe for you. . . Don't set the alarm clock. you will awake at daybreak without it and leap from bed wide awake, with more pep than you've had in months. For heaven's sake, don't shave! Merely neglecting to shave will help start the day right. At dusk you will be boyishly weary. At night you will sink softly into slumber, filled with the peace of the woods, trees, mountains, sunlight and flowing water. . . .

From a 1930s brochure by Karst's Rustic Camp
Gallatin Gateway, Montana

An awfully good case can be made that the dude-ranch experience, especially in the years from about 1920 through the early 1960s, came as close to ideal tourism as either Montanans or their guests have ever known. It was one of those delightful situations when tourists swept into the state, pushed by daydreams that reflected amazingly well the things held most sacred by Montanans themselves. Admittedly, most dude ranches catered to well-to-do Easterners and Canadians, so the experience wasn't exactly egalitarian. And yet by 1939 there were some twelve thousand summer guests laying down about three million dollars annually at ranches across Montana and Wyoming, the lion's share of which was fed back into local economies. It was dude ranching

Previous page: Like many Montana dude ranches, Karst's Kamp in Gallatin County catered to Americans and Canadians captivated with the state's wide-open spaces and fabled cowboy culture. *Photo by Albert Schlechten, courtesy of the Montana Historical Society*

Below: Skier Luke Stratford makes the most of a brilliant day at Bridger Bowl near Bozeman. More than a dozen downhill ski areas plus an abundance of steep slopes and deep snow make Montana a skier's paradise. *Photo by Bob Allen*

Opposite: With St. Helena Cathedral in the background, mountain bikers climb a steep track just outside Montana's capital city. The widespread advent of mountain biking in the 1980s has meant a growing crowd of people pedaling wherever pavement, dirt roads, or trails will take them. *Photo by Bob Allen*

that often got the credit for softening the blow of the Great Depression on the rangelands of Montana, Wyoming, and the western Dakotas.

In addition, when it came to championing the principles of conservation, the Dude Rancher's Association, which was kick-started in 1926 with the help of the Northern Pacific Railroad, was way ahead of its time. Its founding constitution called for members to "work with the federal government for the conservation and preservation of the parks and forests, and the wise conservation and protection of wildlife." By the late 1930s, the group was speaking out not only against further commercialization of the national parks, but more surprisingly, against the diversion of water from those parks for agriculture. These ranchers, reported a Montana newspaper in 1948, "will fight to regain the remaining heritage of a nation which heretofore had wantonly destroyed most of its original outdoor grandeur." Feisty Helen Brooke Hereford, who in the 1930s was toiling like a boilermaker running her guest ranch at the foot of the Beartooths, put it this way: "I'm not a sloppy sentimental sort of person, but what mountains and simple mountain life does [sic] to one is just hard to put in words, and is foolish to try. It is going to be a crime if the mountains are not kept natural as they are. They cannot be improved."

As a job, dude ranching was much like ranching in general, done as much for love as for money. With dawn there were cows to bring in and milk, then out into the pasture to round up horses for the guests. Fires to build, hot water to heat, and breakfast to prepare. Next, off with the ranch car for a hundred-mile round trip to the railhead or, in later years, to the airport, either taking guests out or bringing them in, then back to the ranch for hiking and riding and fishing with the dudes and "dudines," as female guests were called in the 1930s. In between, of course, there were ditches to clean and hay fields to irrigate, fences to fix, enormous vegetable gardens to tend, livestock to keep track of. After cooking and serving supper, there was the building of the bonfire, and if the moon was full or close to it, horses were saddled yet again for another ride up the trail. Finally, when

War II raging, the Bozeman Jaycees put out a brochure touting the advantages of life in the middle of nowhere. "Not a bad place, especially during these trying times when coastal towns are living under that worried complex of possible air raids." Such spirited efforts paid off. Just thirty years later, in the 1970s, tourism was the third largest industry in the state, bested only by agriculture and mining. By the 1990s, it had surpassed mining and was estimated to be worth a whopping $1.2 million a year. Visitation to Yellowstone National Park alone had grown nearly a hundredfold during the twentieth century, climbing from 32,000 people annually in 1910 to over three million in the 1990s. Communities around Glacier National Park, which had been hungry for visitors for some fifty years, were claiming tourist-related revenues of more than $260 million by the mid-1990s.

Clearly, one of the things that allowed tourism to flourish was the phenomenal rise in the use of automobiles. Those fledgling tourist camps that Kathryn, Aunt Isa, and Iva shunned on their journey in 1922 had by the 1960s bloomed into a vast collection of motor lodges and cafes, as well as a wide array of roadside attractions, including everything from mine tours to zoos to fishing-boat rentals. Whereas most out-of-staters used to arrive in Montana by railroad, more than eighty-five percent were coming by automobile by the 1960s. At that time the State Highway Commission, which was in charge of tourist promotion before the Department of Commerce assumed the job, took it upon itself to coach towns on how to better tap this growing pool of visitors. In retrospect, some of that coaching seems rather quaint, especially given the sophisticated marketing methods of today. For example, one brochure sent to towns across the state in 1960, titled "The Tourist School," suggested that motel owners start naming rooms after Montana points of interest and that restaurants yank menu covers showing cactus and ocean scenes and replace them instead with shots of home-state scenery.

As you might expect, as the financial stakes of tourism soared, so did the willingness of politicians and tourism officials to play hardball when it came to getting

all the guests had come and gone for the season, you could relax—cut ten or twelve cords of wood, round up your livestock, fix more fence, and oil and repair your saddles and bridles and harnesses so that you could start all over again come spring.

THE LATER YEARS

Tourism continued to gather steam as the century unfolded, slowing only during national emergencies such as the Depression and the first and second world wars. Even during those times, regional spin doctors did their best to turn lemons into lemonade. In 1942, with World

Opposite: A contented hunter, unruffled by dismal weather,
wades a creek with quarry in hand. *Photo by Denver Bryan*

Above: A successful angler prepares to release a wild trout in the
Bighorn River. Montana boasts 12 "blue-ribbon" trout streams,
including the Bighorn. They are known throughout the world
for their beauty, ease of access, and healthy populations of
sporting wild trout. *Photo by Michael Sample*

Opposite: Park ranger Gordon Edwards leads a party of hikers up Sperry Glacier in Glacier National Park in 1955. Since the 19th century, the 50 or so glaciers in the park have lost up to half of their mass as the climate has grown warmer and drier. Many others have melted completely. Blackfoot Glacier is the largest in the park; it covers about 1,000 acres. *Photo by Aunda Ann Cole, courtesy of the Montana Historical Society*

Above: Helena's Broadwater Hotel and Natatorium, a classic Victorian resort complete with a giant swimming pool heated by thermal springs, fell on hard times in the early 20th century. Here the hotel is shown at its grand reopening in 1939, after being transformed into a casino. When authorities cracked down on gambling in 1941, the Broadwater closed its doors for good. *Photo courtesy of the Montana Historical Society*

and keeping Montana visitors. When in 1967 *Redbook* magazine had the audacity to assign the name "Big Sky Country" to Arizona, California, Nevada, New Mexico, and Utah, Montana tourism promoters went ballistic. The mayor of Billings, in a letter that by today's standards fairly reeks of political incorrectness, wrote a letter to the magazine's editor, passing himself off as an Indian leader known as "Chief of the Big Sky Country." In this letter he suggests that scalping parties were being formed to deal with *Redbook's* plagiarism and theft. "Guthrie gave this name—The Big Sky Country—to our Montana land, it was ours for keeps, and we have no intention of letting anyone steal it. I might also advise you," he went on to say, "that only four times has the American Army ever been truly licked, and all four times it was Montanans who administered that threshing—at the Big Hole, the Rosebud, the Fetterman Massacre, and the Custer-Sitting Bull Battle. And as Custer can attest—

Above: A classic red tour bus, known locally as a "jammer," carries visitors up Going-to-the-Sun Highway and over the Continental Divide in Glacier National Park. By the 1990s, tourism had become the second largest industry in the state, with Glacier one of the most popular attractions. *Photo by Scott Spiker*

Opposite: Visitors to Glacier National Park savor the heart-stopping view across St. Mary Lake. Nicknamed the Crown of the Continent, Glacier encompasses more than 1 million acres of exquisite terrain. *Photo by Aunda Ann Cole, courtesy of the Montana Historical Society*

when we lick 'em, they stay licked. So if you think we will take this sneaking thievery lying down, you underestimate the courage of my fellow tribesmen."

THE ROLE OF RECREATION

In Montana it's often difficult to separate tourism—whether by residents or out-of-state visitors—from outdoor recreation trends in the nation as a whole. For example, fishing, especially fly fishing, has long been popular with Montana residents. (In 1940, an organization known as the Montana Boosters suggested that in addition to the words *oro y plata*, meaning gold and silver, the state seal should also include the word *ichthyo*, meaning fish.) By the 1980s and 1990s, fly fishing had become the recreation of choice for millions of other people, as well; the fact that Montana was blessed with some of the best trout streams on the planet did an awful lot for the pocketbooks of those who would make a living running fly shops, offering guide services, or managing riverside motels and lodges. Similarly, the explosion of popularity in downhill skiing in the 1970s and 1980s dovetailed nicely with a state where there's no shortage of either elevation or snow. The mom and pop ski hills that had been serving locals since the 1960s were soon joined by full-service destination resorts such as Big Sky and Big Mountain. Even snowmobiling, which once seemed the exclusive pleasure of residents, had by the late 1980s grown into a major source of revenue for towns such as West Yellowstone and Cooke City.

It's worth noting that these recreation trends have greatly influenced the style of how people travel in Montana. Whereas in 1960 more than half of the state's travelers didn't bother to plan where they would spend their next night (visitors to dude ranches being the obvious exception), the popularity of activities such as fishing, skiing, golfing, and float trips resulted in more and more people staying in one place for several days. As the twentieth century draws to a close, it is the destination town or resort capable of offering these varied kinds of recreation that seems best positioned for the future.

Opposite: Snowboarder Jason Shutz slashes down Avalanche Gulch at Bridger Bowl. The recent popularity of snowboarding has breathed new life into Montana ski resorts, as a whole new generation discovers the pleasure of hitting the slopes. *Photo by Bob Allen*

Above: Rafters battle whitewater on the Gallatin River near Big Sky. The Gallatin offers some of Montana's finest whitewater, as well as an abundance of technical rapids, tight turns, big rocks, and large waves. It is recommended for experts. *Photo by Donnie Sexton / Travel Montana*

Right: Every winter, the frozen expanse of Canyon Ferry Reservoir, near Helena, draws ice boaters from all over America. *Photo by Denver Bryan*

PACK TRAIN OFF OF THE HIGH COUNTRY

Above: A pack train laden with supplies heads through the Montana backcountry. Numerous outfitters and guides across the state are willing to lead the way to some of the best places to hunt and fish. *Photo courtesy of the Montana Historical Society*

Opposite: Ben Lamb, a Yellowstone National Park employee, lands a trout on the Gardner River. Though only a small portion of Yellowstone spills over into Montana from northwestern Wyoming, Montanans tend to consider the park their own year-round playground. *Photo by William Bull, courtesy of the Montana Historical Society*

At the same time, many places in Montana have been experiencing a dramatic increase in both full- and part-time residents—a trend that includes retirement populations as well as so-called "modern cowboys," people who can conduct business from virtually anywhere using a vast array of information technologies. Large numbers of people in both groups have moved to the state for what they describe as quality of life. As often as not, a big part of that quality of life includes being able to shoulder a pack and hit a mountain trail, wet a fishing line, swing a golf club, or glide down a ski hill.

As the twentieth century draws to a close, many Montanans—especially those living in areas heavily impacted by resort development—have come to think of tourism as a mixed blessing. An important part of the economy, to be sure, but one that seems increasingly fraught with risks. The risk, for example, of being overwhelmed by people so intoxicated with scenery that they are willing to pay anything for it, sometimes inadvertently pushing out the men and women who carry the history of the very place the newcomers claim to love. In other words, a fear that the characters of Montana, and thus the character of the place itself, will be traded away for sacks of gold. Equally frightening to many is that the

mere possibility of those tourist dollars will tempt communities to try to re-create themselves according to what they imagine others want them to be, that tourism will become less a matter of sharing than pretending.

Real dangers, to be sure. Maybe that's why on occasion we would be wise to take a minute to look back across the twentieth century and reconnect ourselves to those precious times when tourism really worked. Times when visitors wanted nothing so much as the chance to rub shoulders with something real. The days when locals thought the best way to catch tourists was with the same values that had fed their own sense of place for so many years. "Here men in leather pants have ridden into morning, tending herd while a new day burst on the roof of the world," said a 1930s brochure from a working guest ranch near Bozeman. "Here the noon breeze has swirled the smoke of branding irons. Here tired ponies have squirmed at loosened girths to wheel into the sage for supper. And here the cook has bellowed out the back door and banged the irons. Forty years of it. And the stars still pop like hot bullets, and coyotes still rim the silences with wailing."

Left: Hunkered in a blind, patient hunters wait for ducks on a bitterly cold Montana morning. Geese, swans, cranes, mourning doves, and snipes are other popular targets of waterfowl hunters. *Photo by Denver Bryan*

Above: A skier pauses circa 1940 to enjoy the view before descending a run near Whitefish. Skiing has been a popular sport in Montana since the 1930s. Big Mountain, one of the state's premier ski resorts, opened near Whitefish in 1947. *Photo courtesy of the Montana Historical Society*

Opposite: At the West Yellowstone Rendezvous Ski Race, Nordic skiers lean forward, eager for the crack of the starting gun. Cross-country skiing is a growing sport in Montana, and the state boasts more than two dozen designated cross-country ski areas in six national forests. *Photo by Jeff & Alexa Henry*

BLACK PATTI
TROUBADOURS

A NIGHTIM

SISSIERETTA JONES
BLACK PATTI
THE GREATEST SINGER OF HER RACE

A WOMAN IS ALWAYS AS OLD AS SHE LOOKS.
BUT A MAN IS AS OLD AS HE FEELS"

CHAUNCEY
OLCOTT A ROMANCE OF
ATHLONE
IN HIS NEW PLAY
BY
AUGUSTUS
PITOU
Manager

THE NEW DOMINION

ARIZO

LOWERY'S
GREATER
MINSTRELS

MISS NELL MACEWEN

THIS FADED ROMANCE

Art and Literature in Twentieth-Century Montana

"I have sometimes been tempted to believe that I grew up on a gun-toting frontier," Wallace Stegner wrote in Wolf Willow,[1] *his account of his childhood in a prairie homestead settlement he called Whitemud, in Saskatchewan, just across the Canadian border from Malta, Montana. Even at the age of six, Stegner had been prepared by the dime-novel mystique of the West to discover romance in what he later described as "this dung-heeled sagebrush town on the disappearing edge of nowhere, utterly without painting, without sculpture, without architecture, almost without music or theater, without conversation or languages or travel or stimulating instruction, without libraries or museums or bookstores, almost without books."*[2]

Ironically, Stegner grew up to become one of a handful of twentieth-century writers, including Bernard De Voto, A. B. Guthrie, Jr., and Joseph Kinsey Howard, who redefined that hazy region of the West of which Montana is a part, those high plains on both sides of the Northern Rockies which author William Bevis has described as "the region of cowboys, Indians, miners, homesteaders, beaver, and cattle, and wheat and gold and snow."[3] In the view of Stegner and those few others, of course, Montana was not the West of the dime novel, but a region of hardship and ruin. It had been endowed with spectacular scenic beauty and a romantic history, but it was isolated by distance and culture from the mainstream of America, exploited by out-of-state capitalists for its natural resources, drained of its cash, and finally reduced by entrepreneurs to one of the last unspoiled pieces of real estate in the United States.

It has become almost commonplace during the past fifteen years to hear Montana described as a colony, not only because of its economic dependence upon the rest of the country, but because it has become a fashionable retreat for the famous and wealthy, a place (to paraphrase Bevis) of outfitters and guides, chocolate-covered wild mountain huckleberries, great private fishing and big-game hunting, handcrafted log homes, glitz, and world-class powder snow. It has also become commonplace to hear of a late twentieth-century literary renaissance in Montana.

The two concepts—Montana as a colony of the distant East and Montana as the fostering mother of a literary renaissance—are worth considering together. The art and literature of a colony, as we know, typically begin and sometimes continue for centuries as imitations of the art forms of the home country. Just as the metaphysical poets

By Mary Clearman Blew

Opposite: In 1905, the Bozeman Opera House hosted more than 50 live performances, including plays, light opera, vaudeville shows, and a concert by John Phillip Sousa. With the advent of motion pictures a few years later, theaters offering live entertainment quickly lost their audiences. The Bozeman Opera House was demolished in the mid-1960s.
Photo courtesy of the Gallatin County Historical Society

Opposite top: Bob Scriver (1914–1999) consults his pet deer, Muley, in his studio at Browning. A connoisseur of wildlife, Scriver was admired both for his bronze sculpture and for his taxidermy. Perhaps the best-known example of the latter is the white bison Big Medicine, on display at the Montana Historical Society in Helena. *Photo by John Reddy*

Opposite bottom: Western paintings and sculpture bring high prices at the C. M. Russell Auction of Original Western Art, an annual event that draws art enthusiasts to Great Falls from all corners of the continent. Since its debut in 1969, the four-day event has raised close to 3 million dollars for the C.M. Russell Museum. *Photo by Stuart S. White*

Above: The National Symphony Orchestra, from Washington, D.C., toured Montana in 1996. It is shown here performing at the Wilma Theater in Missoula. *Photo by William Munoz*

Right: Monte Dolack, a printmaker and painter best known for his whimsical wildlife posters and cards, works at his craft in his Missoula studio. *Photo by William Munoz*

of seventeenth-century Puritan America imitated the English metaphysical poets, Henry Wadsworth Longfellow in the nineteenth century cast the Hiawatha of Iroquois lore in the ancient epic tradition of Europe, and John G. Neihardt in the twentieth century cast the Sioux warrior Crazy Horse in the same mold. A colonial art or literature will find its own unique vision only after the passing of years, and then only when it has great good luck in its artists and writers, as has happened in Australian literature and, most notably, in Latin American literature.

The new is always perceived through a filter of the past, but the first White travelers to lay eyes on what is now Montana were reduced almost to silence by the vast landscape, the sheer range of strange wildlife, the unfamiliar trees and grasses, and especially the human inhabitants. "Undescribable" is the adjective that turns up again and again in the Lewis and Clark journals, as it does in the accounts of other early travelers in the West, although of course the writers and painters immediately tried to describe it anyway. Predictably, they turned to European romantic aesthetics to explain to themselves what they were seeing.

During the early nineteenth century, the place that is now Montana was visited by John James Audubon, George Catlin, and the young Swiss landscape artist, Karl Bodmer, who carried his memories of Germany's Rhine River with its cliffs and castles to his paintings of the upper Missouri River. Bodmer invested the spectacular shapes of wind- and water-eroded rock with a Gothic sensibility drawn from European ruins. In a work like *The White Castles on the Missouri*, "seen by many Romantic Age observers as clear evidence that the western wilderness was so Edenic it continued to serve as God's architectural playground,"[4] the modern observer will be struck by the way the river bluffs overpower the miniaturized pronghorns on the sandbar. Anyone who is not convinced that sheer size and space overwhelmed Bodmer's vision of the Missouri should compare the animals of *The White Castles* with any of the stylized and cavorting sheep and elk from the ancient petroglyphs along the Snake or Columbia Rivers, where the animals are clearly a part of their gritty backdrops and clearly at home.

The White Castles on the Missouri dates from 1833, and a hundred and sixty years later one might expect that the art and literature of Montana would have outgrown the distortions of a European aesthetic. A hundred and sixty years ought to have been long enough for the breathtaking to become familiar, for a forbidding or overpowering landscape to become integral with the lives it sustains. By the last decade of the twentieth century, one might at least hope that the arts in Montana and the Rocky

Opposite: H. G. Merriam launched the creative-writing program at the University of Montana in 1919. Now recognized as one of the best in the nation, the program has produced such well-known Montana writers as Dorothy Johnson and A. B. Guthrie, Jr., as well as such contemporary literary talents as James Welch, Deirdre McNamer, Ralph Beer, and Paul Zarzyski. *Photo courtesy of the K. Ross Toole Archives, the University of Montana-Missoula [UM79-4].*

Left: Montana author Dorothy Johnson (1905–1984) captured the mythos of the American West in unforgettable stories like *A Man Called Horse, The Hanging Tree,* and *The Man Who Shot Liberty Valance*—all of which were made into classic Hollywood films. *Photo courtesy of the Montana Historical Society*

Below: Pulitzer Prize–winning author A. B. Guthrie, Jr. (1901–1991), taps away at a new novel in his Choteau study in 1988. Guthrie is best known for his classic novels *The Big Sky,* about the early fur trade, and *The Way West,* about the Oregon Trail. *Photo by Stuart S. White*

Mountain West would by now have torn off the blindfolds of colonialism and attained the unique vision that contemporary Latin American writers have achieved. But to draw the comparison of literature in Montana with the writing coming from, for example, contemporary Chile, or Montana's art with contemporary Mexican art, is to underline not how far we have come but how far we have to go.

It is easy enough to understand why the first White men to set eyes on Montana fell back on words like "strange," "ghostly," "chaotic," "unintelligible," and "undescribable" to tell an educated eastern audience what it was they were trying to see. It is also understandable that the first White women who came to live in Montana kept themselves focused closely enough on inner space and the immediate tasks at hand that they almost, but not quite, held the landscape at bay.[5] But it is easier to explain the current vogue for Western art and literature, indeed to cite some remarkable achievements of painters and writers in Montana, than it is to explain why we haven't gone much further than we have.

Montana writers in the twentieth century owe a great deal of their success to the early efforts of H. G. Merriam. To the extent that one individual can influence the literary fortunes of an entire region, that one person is Merriam. Following his appointment as an instructor

Opposite: Bill Ohrmann, a Drummond artist, displays some of his Western sculptures. In the closing decades of the 20th century, Western art—and all things Western—were enjoying huge popularity. *Photo by Jill Brody*

Above: Blackfeet artist John Louis Clarke (1881–1970) lost his hearing after contracting scarlet fever as a small boy. His Blackfeet name, Cutapuis, translates as "Man Who Talks Not." Eloquent in his chosen profession, Clarke created lifelike figures of Montana wildlife in clay and wood. His murals depicting Blackfeet life still hang in Browning and Great Falls. *Photo by Joyce Turvey, courtesy of the Montana Historical Society*

Above: Charlie Russell (1864–1926) painted his masterpiece, *When the Land Belonged to God*, for Helena's exclusive Montana Club in 1915. The state legislature later purchased the painting, and it now takes pride of place in the Mackay Gallery of the Montana Historical Society in Helena.
Photo courtesy of the Montana Historical Society

Left: Les Peters, shown holding a painting by Great Falls artist Olaf C. Seltzer, directed the C. M. Russell Museum when this photo was taken there in 1961. The Great Falls museum, built in 1953 and twice expanded, honors and collects the work of the famous cowboy artist Charlie Russell and his contemporaries.
Photo courtesy of the Montana Historical Society

Opposite: Bob DeWeese (1920–1990), one of Montana's most beloved and influential contemporary artists, wears his "Gangster Tie." Arriving in Bozeman at mid-century, DeWeese, together with his painter wife Gennie, introduced generations of young Montana artists to new aesthetic approaches.
Photo by Michael Crummett

of English at the University of Montana in 1919, Merriam nurtured and encouraged a generation of regional writers, established the second creative-writing program in the United States, and founded the magazines *Frontier* and *Midland*, which gave his protégés an opportunity to showcase their work. One of Merriam's students was Dorothy M. Johnson, who appropriated the old dime-novel mystique and rendered its cowboys and Indians more stylishly than anyone before or since. Another was A. B. Guthrie, Jr., who delved deeper in time than the cowboys and reinvented a pristine Montana for wider audiences with his best-selling novels, beginning with *The Big Sky* in 1947 and *The Way West* in 1949, which brought another level of prestige to writing in Montana when it won the Pulitzer Prize for fiction in 1950.

The creative-writing program in Missoula has continued to imprint young writers with a vision of the West as traditional as Walter Van Tilburg Clark's or as iconoclastic as Leslie Fiedler's. During the 1970s, the powerful presence of Richard Hugo in the creative-writing faculty left an indelible stamp on a younger generation of poets that includes Robert Wrigley and Sandra Alcosser. Since 1972, William Kittredge has dominated the program with his revisionist essays on the West, his short fiction, and his editing, with Annick Smith, of *The Last Best Place: A Montana Anthology*, which itself has become a state icon.

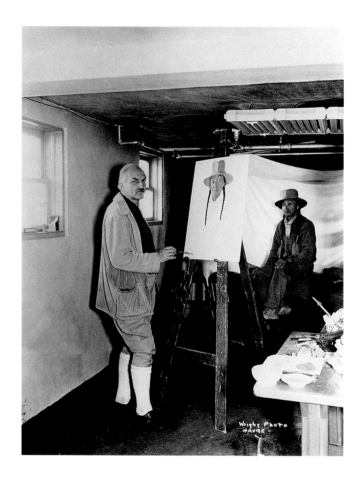

Another, and ironical, reason why literature and the arts in Montana and the West have received so much recent national attention is the phenomenon of the native writers, painters, and sculptors who have repudiated the sad romantic concept of the vanishing Indian and in recent years have re-emerged to claim their own ground. James Welch, a Blackfeet who was a student of Hugo's and was told by Hugo to write about what he knew, has brought prestige to Montana with his critically acclaimed poems and novels. The Oneida poet Roberta Hill Whiteman also studied with Hugo, and the playwright William Yellow Robe and the fiction writer Debra Earling are among the most promising of current young Native Montana writers.

National interest in literature about wilderness and the West also has been stimulated by the growth of the environmentalist movement. Although some environmental writers have tended to remythologize and idealize Montana as the "last best place," the new "green"

politics also has helped to focus attention on the nature writing of David Quammen and Rick Bass. Then, too, the environmentalist movement nicely complements the idea of Montana as fashionable subject matter. The screenwriters and novelists Tom McGuane, James Crumley, and James Lee Burke have been living in Montana and writing about Montana too long to be called outsiders, but in the past ten years a new crop has sprouted of romance novels and trendy mysteries, whose characters tend to be newcomers to Montana who run art galleries, admire the scenery, and sneer at the locals.[6]

Some of the same reasons also explain the popularity of Western art, which can in part be measured by the amount of money that goes through Great Falls every year in connection with the C. M. Russell Auction of Original Western Art. Just as the style of many Montana writers continues to be conservative,[7] many of the state's painters and sculptors continue to work in the romantic tradition inherited from Catlin and Bodmer and permanently associated with Montana through the renown of Charlie Russell himself, the self-taught artist who ran away from his home in St. Louis at the age of sixteen to become a cowboy and who rendered the faded glory of Indians, fur trappers, road agents, and bronc busters in a nostalgic palette of yellows and deep blues.

The accuracy of Russell's detail, his attention to the minutia of saddle riggings and beaded moccasin patterns, make his work as much artifact as art. Russell, who hit his stride in 1911 and reached the height of his career during the 1920s sold a painting to the Prince of Wales, believed that he was being faithful to an irrevocably lost past, and indeed his heartbreaking colors still stand as a eulogy to the First Nations and to the twilight of the open range. Perhaps it is Russell's very popularity that has made it so hard for us in the last decade of the twentieth century to see that, although he might have got the moccasin patterns right, the present is always with us and we live in the past at our peril.

Twentieth-century regional writers and artists have had reactive choices. They can more or less accept the myth of the West and costume their characters in faded

Opposite top: The German-born artist Winold Reiss (1886–1953) spent many hours painting vivid portraits of Blackfeet elders at Glacier National Park. Reiss came to the United States in 1913. Besides painting portraits (he is also known for his extraordinary portraits of the Black residents of Harlem) he achieved notoriety for designing the Crillon, the "first modern restaurant" in New York City. *Photo courtesy of the Al Lucke collection, Montana Historical Society*

Opposite bottom: At the Archie Bray Foundation for the Ceramic Arts, an internationally renowned arts center in Helena, a group of Montana potters inspects vases, plates, and bowls they have thrown for an exhibition in Calgary, Alberta, in 1957. The Archie Bray was founded in a brickyard in 1951. *Photo courtesy of the Montana Historical Society*

Above: World-renowned potter David Shaner of Bigfork checks out a load of his elegant pots, fresh from the kiln. *Photo by Michael Crummett*

Opposite: Inspired by the work of Pablo Picasso, Val Knight (1905–1990) of Great Falls embraced modern painting relatively early. Knight was a co-founder of Gallery 16, an artists' cooperative in Great Falls. *Photo by Michael Crummett*

Above: Robert Morrison, a longtime professor of art at Rocky Mountain College in Billings, demonstrates the witty marionette he designed and made as a self-portrait. Also known for his paintings and calligraphy, Morrison helped found the Yellowstone Calligrapher's Guild. *Photo by Michael Crummett*

Dressed in full regalia, Montana Indians pose for an early film crew. The Montana Film Office was created in 1974 as a clearinghouse for moviemakers who want to shoot on location here. As a scenic backdrop, the state has reaped an economic windfall, attracting $20 million in revenue in 1993 alone.
Photo courtesy of the Montana Historical Society

glory, like Johnson's Indians and Indian fighters or Guthrie's mountain men or the assorted desperados that ride across the canvases of Ace Powell in a tradition that continues to flourish. Or they can devote themselves to repudiating the myth, as Guthrie did in his later novels, or as William Kittredge has done in his essays, or as Ivan Doig has done in his meticulously researched memoirs and novels about a hardscrabble Montana past and a tough present. Or they can invent new stories, which run the risk of being lost for lack of being heard. The latter was true of Montana writers such as Grace Stone Coates and Mildred Walker, who have recently been rediscovered thanks to gender studies, which have tuned our ears to alternative voices.

The whole scope of literature and the arts in Montana is, of course, gratifyingly enormous and a focus for the burst of creative activity throughout the western region. The Archie Bray Foundation, which opened in Helena in 1951, helped to establish the international reputation of ceramist Peter Voulkos and launched the distinguished teaching career of Rudy Autio at the University of Montana. The Yellowstone

Art Museum in Billings has been a showcase for a spectrum of artists and a stimulant for the thriving arts community in Eastern Montana. The town of Butte, rising from the ruins of its copper-mining past, also fosters a growing arts community. A recent flourishing of community-supported cultural institutions such as the Myrna Loy Center for the Performing Arts in Helena, the Alberta Bair Theater in Billings, the Bigfork Playhouse, and many new visual-arts museums has complemented older and renowned museums and galleries such as the Montana Historical Society in Helena, the C.M. Russell Museum in Great Falls, and the Museum of the Rockies at Montana State University in Bozeman. The growth of the Western Heritage Center in Billings and the Northern Lights Institute in Missoula also bears witness to the intense interest that Montanans take in the culture of their region.

Just as young novelist Deirdre McNamer has found a strong voice and a deep-rooted vision of the contemporary West, visual artists in Montana are exploring ways to connect the old and the new. Through an amazing range of media—lithographs, woodcuts, textiles, silkscreens, steel, acrylics, pastels, paint sticks—twentieth-century Montana artists seem freer than the writers to expand form, to abstract, to experiment, to demolish.

"What's immediately impressive about the contemporary [art] work is its unruliness…," writes acclaimed Montana fiction writer David Long. "Many of the visual elements you'd expect to represent Montana do appear, time and again: mountain meeting sky, empty two-lane blacktop, cattle and sheep, horses, grizzly…. But these elements come with spin. They're taken apart and reassembled in ways that undermine expectation. They give not one calculated shock but repeated shivers."[8]

Repeated shivers, yes, from the powerful lines and dominating shapes of Isabelle Johnson's landscapes in oils, to the detail and concentrated patterns in the woodcuts of Edith Freeman, who studied with Johnson. Reassembly, yes, in the textiles of Dana Boussard and in the pictographic paintings and drawings of Jaune Quick-to-See Smith.

Opposite: Sophisticated screen star Myrna Loy (1905–1992) was born Myrna Adele Williams at Radersburg, Montana. She got her first thespian experience in Helena amateur theatricals. Best known for her role in *The Thin Man*, Loy performed in more than 80 films. Helena's performing arts center, the Myrna Loy Center, honors her memory and accomplishments. Loy is shown here at her family's homestead in Radersburg.
Photo courtesy of the Montana Historical Society

Left: Missoula native Norman Maclean (1902–1990) was the author of the Montana classics *A River Runs Through It*, which was made into a film by Robert Redford, and *Young Men and Fire*, about the Mann Gulch disaster that killed a dozen young smokejumpers in 1949. Maclean had a long career as an English professor at the University of Chicago and wrote numerous academic essays. He was in his 70s when his first book was published.
Photo by Joel Snyder, courtesy of the University of Chicago

Above: Laconic movie star Gary Cooper (1901–1961), shown here on the far right during his high school days in Bozeman, was born in Helena and spent much of his youth in Montana. He went on to win Academy Awards for his roles in *Sergeant York* (1941) and *High Noon* (1952). In the late 1930s, Cooper was the highest-paid American entertainer.
Photo courtesy of the Gallatin County Historical Society

Opposite: On location near Great Falls in 1995, Ken Burns films his popular documentary on the Lewis and Clark Expedition. As the bicentennial of the expedition nears, Montana prepares to celebrate the discoveries the explorers made here. Perhaps the most ambitious tribute will be the Lewis and Clark Interpretive Center, which opened in Great Falls in 1998. *Photo by Stuart S. White*

Gordon McConnell, chief curator of the Yellowstone Art Museum, is able to speak with authority about the talent of today's Montana visual artists and the multiformity of their work:

> *I would include Theodore Waddell's paintings, which approach sublimity by transforming range land into expansive abstract expressionist essays. John Buck and Richard Notkin, whose powerful, often humorous, symbol-laden words reflect a disquieting time and unsettled minds. Patrick Zentz, who rehabilitates technology and craft with unique machines that respond to the environment rather than transform it. Clarice Dreyer, who transubstantiates ephemeral plant materials into poetic and poignant metallic garden architecture—birdbaths, birdhouses and gazebos. Freeman Butts, whose bold, painterly landscapes capture the lingering wildness and sensuality of this land. . . . Anne Appleby's minimal, color field paintings draw from extremely close observation of the subtle colors of plant life and landscapes as the cycles of nature uncoil.*

Any regional artist or writer begins with certain advantages: a narrowing down of the bewildering multiplicity of the American experience, a precise sense of place, a dramatic history on which to draw. The dilemma for the regional artist or writer, a quandary that is particularly poignant for native artists, is that, however centered they may be in their own territory, they write for an audience that is likely to perceive their region as marginal. This wider audience still looks for news of the exotic, the uncommon, still hungers for local color. The artist's risk is in being patronized as quaint, and those of us who write about the West will forever be, in Sherman Alexie's words, in the business of "fancydancing."[9]

And for better or worse, what is fashionable in one season may become passé in another. Consider the distaste expressed by that quintessential urbanite, Woody Allen, who, after listening to actor Sam Shepard improvise a speech about leaving Montana to go East to medical school, said, "Montana? Montana...? The word 'Montana' is gonna be in *my* movie?"[10]

In an essay that enraged many Montanans in 1949, Leslie Fiedler wrote, "When he admits that the Noble Savage is a lie; when he has learned that his state is where the myth comes to die... the Montanan may find the possibilities of tragedy and poetry for which so far he has searched his life in vain."[11] Since 1949, Montana writers and artists have struggled to find a way to come to terms with their bloody history across a landscape that they love and have tried to describe through a dissonance of individual voices and visions. Some have evaded the hard light of day by trying to pre-empt the native experience, the native point of view; some have tried to deny their complicity in the myth by identifying with the Indian as victim. Many, native and non-native, have given a lifetime to revision. One can hope that their work has laid a foundation for writers and artists to come.

"I was Country," sings Barbara Mandrell, "when Country wasn't cool." Whether its current vogue will prove cool for the arts in Montana remains to be seen. What is clear is that two centuries of White exploration and settlement of the grand scope of Montana have not been long enough to shake off an imagined romantic past, and that the painters and writers still search for what the carvers of the petroglyphs and the old Sioux and Cheyenne ledger artists already possessed: mythic and emblematic ways to connect life and endless space. And a vision sharp enough to sustain us all, beyond a colony's limitations, into the coming century.

SOURCES AND NOTES

BIG ENOUGH FOR MAGPIES

Advisory Committee on Predator Control. *Predator Control—1971*. Washington, DC: Report to the Council on Environmental Quality and the Department of the Interior, 1972. (Also known as the Cain Report, after committee chairman Stanley A. Cain.)

Atwell, Gerry C. "An Evaluation of Magpie Predation on the Ring-Necked Pheasant." Master's thesis, Montana State University, Missoula, 1959.

Bean, Michael J. *The Evolution of National Wildlife Law*. New York: Praeger, 1983.

Brown, Robert L. "The Population Ecology of the Magpie in Western Montana." Master's thesis, Montana State University, Missoula, 1957.

_____. "Magpie Ups and Downs." Helena: Montana Fish and Game Department Information Bulletin No. 3, n.d.

Brownell, Joan Louise. "The Genesis of Wildlife Conservation in Montana." Master's thesis, Montana State University, Bozeman, 1987.

_____. "Wildlife Law Enforcement—The Early Years." *Montana Outdoors*, Vol. 20, No. 4 (1989).

Burlingame, Merrill G., and K. Ross Toole. *A History of Montana*. New York: Lewis Historical Publishing Co., 1957.

Cahalane, Victor H. "The Evolution of Predator Control Policy in the National Parks." *Journal of Wildlife Management*, Vol. 3, No. 3 (1939).

Craighead, John J., and Frank C. Craighead. *Hawks, Owls and Wildlife*. New York: Dover, 1969. (Reprint of 1956 edition published by Wildlife Management Institute.)

Curnow, Edward E. "The History of the Eradication of the Wolf in Montana." Master's thesis, University of Montana, Missoula, 1969.

Diettert, Gerald A. *Grinnell's Glacier: George Bird Grinnell and Glacier National Park*. Missoula, MT: Mountain Press, 1992.

Dolph, James A., and C. Ivar Dolph. "The American Bison: His Annihilation and Preservation." *Montana, the Magazine of Western History*, Vol. 25, No. 3 (1975).

Elrod, Morton John. *The Butterflies of Montana*. University of Montana, Bulletin No. 30, Biological Series No. 10. Helena, MT: Independent Publishing Co., 1906.

Everin, Walter A. "Predators—Enemy or Friend?" *Montana Wildlife*, Vol. 2, No. 1 (1952).

Ewan, Joseph. *Rocky Mountain Naturalists*. Denver: University of Denver Press, 1950.

Fischer, Hank. *Wolf Wars*. Helena, MT: Falcon Press, 1995.

Gildart, Robert C., with Jan Wassink. *Montana Wildlife*. Montana Geographic Series, No. 3. Helena, MT: Montana Magazine, 1982.

Hoffmann, Robert S., Philip L. Wright, and Fletcher E. Newby. "The Distribution of Some Mammals in Montana: I. Mammals Other Than Bats." *Journal of Mammalogy*, Vol. 50, No. 3 (1969).

Hornaday, William T. *Our Vanishing Wild Life*. New York: New York Zoological Society, 1913.

Opposite: The Missouri River, shown here near Ulm, flows more than a thousand miles from its headwaters at Three Forks to the North Dakota border, making it by far the longest river in Montana. *Photo by John Lambing*

Jack Horner, a world-renowned paleontologist with the Museum of the Rockies in Bozeman, has added immeasurably to our understanding of dinosaurs in the last couple of decades. His many accomplishments include the excavation in Montana of the first complete skeleton of *Tyrannosaurus rex* and the discovery here of the first dinosaur nests and eggs and the first clear evidence of how dinosaurs parented their young. *Photo by Stuart S. White*

_____. *Thirty Years War for Wildlife*. "Congressional Edition." Stamford, CT: Permanent Wild Life Protection Fund, 1931.

Koch, Elers. "Big Game in Montana from Early Historical Records." *Journal of Wildlife Management*, Vol. 5, No. 4 (1941).

Leopold, Aldo. *Game Management*. New York: Charles Scribner's Sons, 1933.

Linsdale, Jean M. *The Natural History of Magpies*. Pacific Coast Avifauna, No. 25. Berkeley: Cooper Ornithological Club, 1937.

Malone, Michael P., and Richard B. Roeder. *Montana: A History of Two Centuries*. Seattle: University of Washington Press, 1976.

McHugh, Tom. *The Time of the Buffalo*. New York: Alfred A. Knopf, 1972.

Moon, Gareth C. "Forest and Stream." In Burlingame and Toole (1957).

Mussehl, T.W., and F.W. Howell, eds. *Game Management in Montana*. Helena: Montana Department of Fish and Game, 1971.

Newby, Fletcher, and Robert Brown. "A New Approach to Predator Management in Montana." *Montana Wildlife* (August 1958).

O'Halloran, Patrick L. "Dynamics of a Reduced Magpie Population." Master's thesis, Montana State University, Missoula, 1961.

"Our Montana Environment . . . Where Do We Stand?" Helena: Montana Environmental Quality Council, 1996.

Picton, Harold D., and Irene E. Picton. *Saga of the Sun: A History of the Sun River Elk Herd*. Helena: Montana Department of Fish and Game, 1975.

Posewitz, Jim. "Animal Control." Labeled as "Fish and Game Department Position" in *Montana Outdoors*, Vol. 3, No. 4 (1972).

Presnall, Clifford C. "Changing Trends in Predator Management." *Transactions of the Twenty-First North American Wildlife Conference*. Washington, DC: Wildlife Management Institute, 1956.

Raymer, Robert George. *Montana: The Land and Its People*. Chicago: Lewis Publishing Co., 1930.

Reiger, John F. *American Sportsmen and the Origins of Conservation*. Norman: University of Oklahoma Press, 1986.

Robinson, Weldon B. "Population Changes of Carnivores in Some Coyote-Control Areas." *Journal of Mammalogy*, Vol. 42, No. 4 (1961).

Roe, Frank Gilbert. *The North American Buffalo*. Toronto: University of Toronto Press, 1951.

Roosevelt, Theodore. *The Wilderness Hunter*. New York: G.P. Putnam's Sons, 1893.

Ruff, Robert L. "A Study of the Predatory Effects of a Reduced Magpie Population on the Ring-Necked Pheasant." Master's thesis, Montana State University, Missoula, 1963.

Saunders, Aretas A. *A Distribution List of the Birds of Montana*. Pacific Coast Avifauna, No. 14. Berkeley: Cooper Ornithological Club, 1921.

Schneider, Bill. "Predator Control Confusion." *Montana Outdoors*, Vol. 3, No. 4 (1972).

Skaar, Palmer David. *Montana Bird Distribution*. Bozeman, MT: P.D. Skaar, 1975.

Silloway, P.M. *Birds of Fergus County, Montana*. Lewistown, MT: Press of the Argus, 1903.

Stuart, Granville. *Forty Years on the Frontier*. Edited by Paul C. Phillips. Cleveland: Arthur H. Clark Company, 1925.

Watts, C. Robert. "Changes in the Birds of Central Montana." *Proceedings of the Montana Academy of Science*, Vol. 40 (1981).

Willard, John. "Fish and Game." In Burlingame and Toole (1957), as a sub-chapter of Moon's "Forest and Stream."

Williams, Ted. "Beyond Traps and Poison." *Audubon* (March-April 1994).

OH-P;SHE-DU WOK-PAH (MUDDY WATERS)

1. *United States Census Records*. Washington, DC: Government Printing Office, 1900, 1910.

2. Michael L. Lawson, *Dammed Indians, the Pick-Sloan Plan and the Missouri River Sioux, 1944–1980* (Norman: University of Oklahoma Press, 1982), pp. 10-45.

3. David H. Getches, Daniel M. Rosenfelt, and Charles F. Wilkinson, *Federal Indian Law* (St. Paul: West Publishing Co., 1979), pp. 161-173.

4. Charles F. Wilkinson, *American Indians, Time and the Law* (New Haven: Yale University Press, 1987), p. 54.

5. Getches, *Federal Indian Law*, p. 69.

6. S. Lyman Tyler, *A History of Indian Policy* (Washington, DC: Bureau of Indian Affairs, 1973), p. 97.

7. Burton M. Smith, *The Politics of Allotment, The Flathead Indian Reservation as a Test Case* (Pablo, MT: Salish Kootenai Press, 1995), p. 5.

8. Ibid., p. 7.

9. Getches, *Federal Indian Law*, pp. 495-496.

10. Joseph Medicine Crow, *From the Heart of Crow Country* (New York: Orion Books, 1992), p. 121.

11. Francis Paul Prucha, *The Indian in American Society* (Berkeley: University of California Press, 1985), p. 56.

12. Tyler, *A History of Indian Policy*, pp. 125-150.

13. William L. Bryan, *Montana's Indians, Yesterday and Today* (Helena: Montana Magazine, 1985), p. 14.

14. *Crow Tribal Treaty Centennial Issue* (Crow Agency, MT: Crow Tribe, 1968), p. 41.

15. Tyler, *A History of Indian Policy*, pp. 151-163.

16. Ibid., pp. 202-239.

17. Getches, *Federal Indian Law*, pp. 92-93.

18. Tyler, *A History of Indian Policy*, p. 181.

19. K. Ross Toole, *Montana, An Uncommon Land* (Norman: University of Oklahoma Press, 1959), p. 137.

20. Wilkinson, *American Indians, Time and the Law*, p. 53.

21. 25 USC 450.

22. *Indian Self-Determination and Education Programs*, hearings before the Subcommittee on Indian Affairs of the Committee on Interior and Insular Affairs. United States Senate, Ninety-third Congress, First Session on S. 1017 and Related Bills, June 1 and 4, 1973, p. 66.

23. Ibid., p. 199.

24. *Revised Codes of Montana*, 85-20-201, March 1993, p. 935.

25. *Senate Journal of the Fifty-third Legislature of the State of Montana* (Helena: Montana Legislative Council, January 4–April 24, 1993).

EARTH, THE ESSENCE

Donald, David Herbert. *Lincoln*. London: Jonathan Cape Random House, 1995.

Howard, Joseph Kinsey. *Montana: High, Wide, and Handsome*. Lincoln: University of Nebraska Press, 1983.

Josephy, Alvin M., Jr. *The Nez Perce Indians and the Opening of the Northwest*. New York: Houghton Mifflin, 1997.

Malone, Michael P., Richard B. Roeder, and William L. Lang. *Montana: A History of Two Centuries*. Revised edition. Seattle: University of Washington Press, 1991.

NEXT-YEAR COUNTRY

1. The concept of an interactive "metropolis" and "hinterland" derives from Canadian scholarship. It defines "metropolis" as a dynamic population core that concentrates major industrial, economic, financial, and political power. This seat of capital and power exerts a strong influence over a large, surrounding area (the "hinterland") that contains few people, much space, and a wealth of natural resources.

   When applied to Montana, this metaphor identifies such "metropolitan" seats of power and influence as Minneapolis–St. Paul, Denver, and Seattle. Pertinent secondary "metropolis" examples include Spokane, Calgary, and Salt Lake City.

2. Joseph Kinsey Howard, *Montana: High, Wide, and Handsome* (New Haven: Yale University, 1943), p. 3.

3. The largest early separations that affected Montana involved 1890s forest reserves, 1907 national forests, and Indian reservations, whose establishment began with the Fort Laramie Treaty of 1851. The Montana Native American plays no significant role in this essay on the Montana economy of the twentieth century—a realistic reflection of the Indian's involvement in that economy. Reservation economics remains a distinct subject, beyond the scope of this essay.

4. The Sagebrush Rebellion (1978–1983) constituted a shrill opposition to the federal management of public lands in the West. It grew from local dissatisfaction with the Bureau of Land Management's handling of sheep-range land in Nevada in 1978. In 1979, Senator Orrin Hatch (R-Utah) introduced legislation to cede 544 million acres of federal land in thirteen western states to those states. During the ensuing debate, it became clear that the states were ill-prepared to maintain these vast public lands and probably would sell off the transfers. The proposal was fought and defeated by a broad-based, national, environmental coalition, which argued that the rebellion was an ill-disguised land grab, designed to give resource-users title to public lands. Strong opposition to the rebellion also coalesced in the West.

   This emotional, pro-development/pro-exploitation movement effectively was co-opted in 1981 by the Reagan administration, with the appointment of such radical-conservative western-lands managers as Secretary of State James Watt, BLM Director Robert Burford, and Environmental Protection Agency head Anne Gorsuch. However, resentment of federal land-control in western states survives in varying degrees, from state to state.

5. Heinze engaged in a five-year war against the Amalgamated (Anaconda) Copper Company, beginning in 1898. He used various means, including underground warfare, street debates, court action, and the press. In part by controlling key district judges, he thwarted the Company's dominance of the Butte Hill.

   With the loss of the Parrot Mine case in October 1903, Amalgamated shut down all of its Montana operations: mines, smelters, railroads, refineries, lumber camps, and stores. Fifteen thousand men, the majority of Montana wage earners, suffered as a result of the lockout and its ancillary effects. The state economy virtually stalled.

   Amalgamated then demanded that Governor Toole call a special session of the state legislature to pass a law permitting the transfer of a case from one court to another location simply based on a charge of judicial bias. Toole reluctantly convened the session, and it quickly passed the Fair Trials Bill. Anaconda resumed operations in the state. Heinze reeled from the loss and finally sold his Butte holdings in 1906.

6. Sarah McNelis, *Copper King at War: The Biography of F. Augustus Heinze* (Missoula: University of Montana Press, 1968), p. 82.

7. Labor events included worker-management warfare in Butte/Anaconda, Socialist regimes in several mining towns in the state, the spread of Industrial Workers of the World (IWW) membership in the timber industry, the hanging of IWW activist Frank Little in Butte in 1917, and the repeated occupation of Butte by state and federal troops.

8. Earlier Montana boom-and-bust agricultural cycles include the dramatic open-range cattle industry (1870–1887) and the

In 1923, Jack Dempsey, heavyweight champion of the world (back to camera), trains in Great Falls in preparation for his title bout with Tommy Gibbons. The boxing match, held in the oil boomtown of Shelby on the Fourth of July, was a financial flop, drawing fewer than 8,000 fans.
Photo courtesy of the Cascade County Historical Society

state's meteoric sheep production (1890–1912). In 1903, Montana led the nation in sheep raising.

9. Howard, *Montana: High, Wide, and Handsome*, p. 196.

10. In the face of the Great Depression and the New Deal, most Montanans dropped their "rugged individualism," born of their frontier heritage, to partake in the federal government's "planned society." However, as the Sagebrush Rebellion and the recent Freemen movement have demonstrated, substantial antipathy to federal control remains very much alive in the state.

11. The real disparity in war-supply contracts is seen in Montana's total of $25.3 million, versus $1.78 billion for Oregon and $4.5 billion for Washington. In 1946, critics charged that U.S. Senator Burton K. Wheeler of Montana had supported a campaign by the Anaconda Company to keep war industries out of Montana—thus preserving the state's fragile labor supply for the Company's use.

12. As quoted in Richard White, *It's Your Misfortune and None of My Own: A History of the American West* (Norman: University of Oklahoma, 1991), pp. 515-516.

13. Harry W. Fritz, *Montana: A Land of Contrasts* (Woodland Hills, CA: Windsor Publications, 1984), p. 127.

14. Montanans defeated a sales tax in a statewide referendum in 1971, and they reinforced that decision in 1993. Various legislative attempts to bring the sales-tax issue to the ballot have been thwarted almost biennially through the 1980s and 1990s.

15. Prospects for the Montana economy early in the next century seem limited—by the state's inherent "hinterland" characteristics, by its 150-year economic pattern, by its inability to diversify, and by rapid shifts in the global economy. With the exception of agriculture, Montana's mature, traditional, extractive industries remain in relative or absolute decline.

Although the long-term national shift from an industrial economy continues, Montana's small population base retards its involvement in this evolution. Thus the state's economy becomes more directly tied, for better or worse, to the federal government.

16. Wallace Stegner, *The Sound of Mountain Water* (Garden City, NY: Doubleday, 1969), p. 38. As quoted in "The War for the West," *Newsweek*, September 30, 1991, p. 35.

17. K. Ross Toole, *Montana History: A Telecourse* (Missoula: University of Montana Center for Continuing Education, 1977), Chapter 10, p. 10.

THE WAYS WEST

Hidy, Ralph W., et. al. *The Great Northern Railway: A History.* Cambridge, MA: Harvard University Press, 1988.

Hill, James J. *Highways of Progress.* New York: Doubleday, 1910.

Malone, Michael P. *James J. Hill: Empire Builder of the Northwest.* Norman: University of Oklahoma Press, 1996.

McCarter, Steve. *Guide to the Milwaukee Road in Montana*. Helena: Montana Historical Society Press, 1992.

Quivik, Fredric L. *Historic Bridges in Montana*. Washington, DC: National Park Service, 1982.

Schwantes, Carlos A. *Railroad Signatures Across the Pacific Northwest*. Seattle: University of Washington Press, 1993.

Vance, James E., Jr. *The North American Railroad: Its Origin, Evolution, and Geography*. Baltimore: Johns Hopkins University Press, 1995.

West, Carroll Van. *A Traveler's Companion to Montana History*. Helena: Montana Historical Society Press, 1986.

THIS FADED ROMANCE

1. Wallace Stegner, *Wolf Willow* (Lincoln: University of Nebraska Press, 1980), p. 4.

2. Ibid., p. 24.

3. William W. Bevis, *Ten Tough Trips: Montana Writers and the West* (Seattle: University of Washington Press, 1990), p. x.

4. Dan Flores, "George Catlin, Karl Bodmer and the Montana Dream," *Big Sky Journal* (Spring 1996), p. 43.

5. The thesis of Elizabeth Hampston's study, *Read This Only to Yourself: The Private Writings of Midwestern Women, 1880-1910* (Bloomington: University of Indiana Press, 1982), is that the diaries and letters of the first generation of women to live on homesteads on the western plains are characterized by what Hampston calls a "close focus," an attention to mundane detail at close range that shuts out the larger and more threatening landscape.

6. Scott Mainwaring, "Montana Mysteries: A Partial Bibliography," *Writing Montana: Literature Under the Big Sky* (Helena, MT: Falcon Press, 1996), pp. 272-281. Mainwaring reviews about fifty mysteries written in as many years that have been set in Montana.

7. Gregory L. Morris, *Talking up a Storm: Voices of the New West* (Lincoln: University of Nebraska Press, 1994), p. xvi.

8. David Long, "Straight to the Actual," *Montana Spaces*, ed. William Kittredge (New York: Nick Lyons, 1988), p. 173.

9. Sherman Alexie, *The Business of Fancydancing* (New York: Hanging Loose Press, 1992), p. 69. "A promise is just like money / Something we can hold, in twenties, a dream we reach / It's business, a fancydance to fill where it's empty."

10. John Lahr, "The Imperfectionist," *The New Yorker* (December 9, 1996), p. 79.

11. Leslie A. Fiedler, "The Montana Face," *Partisan Review*, 1949 (reprinted in *The Last Best Place: A Montana Anthology*, edited by William Kittredge and Annick Smith (Helena: Montana Historical Society Press, 1984), p. 752.

ABOUT THE EDITOR

Michael P. Malone has served as president of Montana State University in Bozeman for the past eight years and has taught history there since 1967. He is the author of nine books on the history of Montana and the American West, including *Montana: A Contemporary Profile*, *The American West: A Twentieth Century History*, and *Montana: A History of Two Centuries*. He has written numerous articles for historical journals such as *Western Historical Quarterly*, and *Montana, the Magazine of Western History*. He is on the editorial board of the latter publication. Malone holds a bachelor's degree in history from Gonzaga University and a Ph.D. in American Studies from Washington State University.

This grain elevator on the Hi-Line west of Chester has witnessed a dramatic evolution in Montana agriculture. Where once there were 160-acre homesteads carved from the prairie by hand and horse, today there are vast acreages harvested mechanically by corporations. *Photo by Chuck Haney*

About the Authors

Mary Clearman Blew was born in Montana and grew up on a small cattle ranch that her great-grandfather homesteaded in 1882. She holds bachelor's degrees in English and Latin and a master's degree in English from the University of Montana and a Ph.D. in English from the University of Missouri-Columbia. She taught and served as an administrator at Montana State University-Northern until 1987, when she moved to Idaho. Currently, she is a professor of English and director of the creative-writing program at the University of Idaho in Moscow. She has chaired both the Montana Committee for the Humanities and the Idaho Humanities Commission. Blew is the author of two short-story collections, *Lambing Out* and *Runaway*, and two memoirs, *All But the Waltz* and *Balsamroot*. She co-edited an anthology of women's writings about the Rocky Mountain West entitled *Circle of Women*.

Jeanne Oyawin Eder is a member of the Sisseton band of the Dakota Sioux and an enrolled member of the Fort Peck Assiniboine and Sioux Tribes. She holds a bachelor's degree in history from Carroll College in Helena and a master's degree in history from Montana State University. She is completing a Ph.D. in American History/Public History from Washington State University. Eder is the multicultural director at Western Montana College of the University of Montana. She lives in Dillon with her husband, daughter, son-in-law, and grandson.

Gary Ferguson has been a full-time freelance writer for seventeen years. His science and nature articles have

appeared in more than one hundred national magazines, and he is the author of thirteen books on nature and science, including the 1997 title, *The Sylvan Path: A Journey Through America's Forests*, which was a winner of the prestigious Lowell Thomas Award. *Spirits of the Wild: The World's Great Nature Myths* was selected by the New York City Public Library as one of the best books of 1996. Ferguson has appeared on more than one hundred radio and television programs in Los Angeles, New York, Seattle, Portland, Denver, and Chicago; his nature-oriented essays can be heard on National Public Radio. He and his wife live in Red Lodge.

Jim Gransbery was born in Butte and grew up in Dillon and Anaconda. He attended Carroll College in Helena and in 1968 received a bachelor's degree in history from Montana State University. He served four and a half years in the U.S. Navy as a hospital corpsman. After a sojourn in Spain, he returned to Montana and earned a master's degree in journalism at the University of Montana. He began his journalism career in 1976 at the *Havre Daily News*. Eighteen months later, he joined the staff of the *Billings Gazette*, where he has covered politics and agriculture since 1983. He is married and has two children.

Charles S. Johnson holds a bachelor's degree in journalism and a master's degree in history from the University of Montana. He has reported on statewide issues, politics, and people since 1971 and has reported from Helena on statewide political and governmental issues and people since 1974. He covered the 1972

Constitutional Convention, as well as every legislative session from 1975 through 1999, except for the session in 1979, when he was at Oxford University in England studying politics and economics on a Rotary International Fellowship.

Daniel Kemmis, director of the Center for the Rocky Mountain West, is the former mayor of Missoula, a former speaker and minority leader of the Montana House of Representatives, and a four-term state legislator. He is the author of two books: *Community and the Politics of Place* and *The Good City and the Good Life*. A graduate of Harvard University and the University of Montana School of Law, he was awarded a fellowship in 1998 at the Harvard Kennedy School's Institute of Politics. Also that year, the Center for the American West awarded him the Wallace Stegner Prize for sustained contribution to the cultural identity of the West. The previous year, President Clinton presented him with the Charles Frankel Prize for outstanding contribution to the field of humanities.

William L. Lang is a professor of history and director of the Center for Columbia River History at Portland State University in Oregon. He is the co-author of *Montana: A History of Two Centuries* (with Michael P. Malone and Richard B. Roeder) and author or editor of five other books on Northwest history, including *Great River of the West: Essays on the Columbia River* and *Stories from an Open Country: Essays on the Yellowstone River Valley.*

Mary Murphy is an associate professor of history and philosophy at Montana State University in Bozeman, where she teaches courses on the history of the American West and American women. She is the author of *Mining Cultures: Men, Women, and Leisure in Butte, 1914-41* and many other essays on regional history.

David Quammen is the author of eight books, including *The Song of the Dodo*, which won the John Burroughs Medal and several other awards. His most recent book is *Wild Thoughts from Wild Places*, a collection of essays published by Scribner in 1998. For fifteen years, Quammen was natural-science columnist for *Outside* magazine, and he still travels frequently on magazine assignments to places such as Madagascar, the Amazon, and Wyoming. He lives in Bozeman.

Laird Robinson, a Forest Service expert on the Mann Gulch fire, shows reporters the site of the 1949 tragedy near Gates of the Mountains. Twelve young smokejumpers and a district guard died horrifically when a wildfire they were fighting exploded out of control. *Photo by Stuart S. White*

Carroll Van West is the author of *Capitalism on the Frontier: The Transformation of Billings and the Yellowstone Valley* and *A Traveler's Companion to Montana History*. Since 1985, he has been a member of the Center for Historic Preservation at Middle Tennessee State University. He also is the senior editor of the *Tennessee Historical Quarterly* and editor-in-chief of the *Tennessee Encyclopedia of History and Culture*. His books on

Tennessee include *Tennessee's Historic Landscapes* and *Tennessee History: The Land, the People, and the Culture*.

Dave Walter has worked at the Montana Historical Society in Helena since 1979 and is currently the society's research historian. He graduated from Wesleyan University in Connecticut and in 1994 was named an honorary doctor of humane letters by the University of Montana. In 1998, he received the Montana Governor's Award for contributions to the humanities. He has taught college-level English and Western history and is the author of several books, including *Christmastime in Montana, Today Then, Will Man Fly?*, and *Montana Campfire Tales*.

Elite Forest Service smokejumpers prepare to do battle with one of the many blazes that ignite the West each summer. Thousands of young men and women have endured the rigorous training at the smokejumper center in Missoula since it opened in 1954. The first fire jump was made in Idaho in 1940 by Earl Cooley, of Hamilton, and Rufus Robinson of Kooskia, Idaho. *Photo courtesy of the Montana Historical Society*

ACKNOWLEDGMENTS

A great many talented people helped produce and compile the information and images that comprise *Montana Century*. The publisher would like to thank the following contemporary photographers, whose exceptional work not only enlivens the pages of this book but captures for future generations the memorable moments that are Montana history in the making:

Bob Allen
Joanne M. Berghold
Don Boslaugh
Jill Brody
Denver Bryan
Daniel J. Cox
Michael Crummett
Gene Fischer
Jeff Foott
Rick and Susie Graetz
Chuck Haney
Jeff and Alexa Henry
Donald M. Jones
Tom Kotynski
John Lambing
Richard Mousel
William Munoz
Tom Murphy
Ray Ozman
John Reddy
Michael Sample
Donnie Sexton / Travel Montana
Steve Shirley
Scott Spiker
D. R. Stoecklein
Salvatore Vasapolli
Scott Wheeler
Stuart S. White
Jim Wylder

The publisher also gratefully acknowledges the patience and indispensable assistance of the staff of the Montana Historical Society photo archives in Helena— Lory Morrow, Bonnie Morgan, Becca Kohl, Tom Ferris, and Jerry Cooper—as well as the following archives and individuals, all of whom generously loaned photos from their collections:

Boslaugh Family
Brandt Family
Butte–Silver Bow Public Archives, Butte
Cascade County Historical Society, Great Falls
Frontier Gateway Museum, Glendive
Gallatin County Historical Society, Bozeman
Heritage Museum, Libby
K. Ross Toole Archives of the University of Montana, Missoula
MonDak Heritage Center, Sidney
Montana State University Archives, Bozeman
Park County Museum Archives, Livingston
Peter Yegen Museum, Billings
Vivian Purdy
Tobacco Valley Historical Museum, Eureka
University of Chicago
Kenneth and Betty Vincent
Western Heritage Center, Billings
World Museum of Mining, Butte

Finally, the publisher would like to thank the following dedicated individuals for their invaluable research assistance:

Ken Graham
Rick Newby
Joan Shirley
Karen Sire
Noelle Sullivan

Index

Opposite: Dawn intensifies the splendor of Bighorn Canyon, a national recreation area south of Hardin. *Photo by Scott Wheeler*

Opposite: Photographer Evelyn Cameron came to Eastern Montana from England in 1889 and spent the next three decades documenting the daily lives of her plucky and persevering neighbors, including these children, who enjoy a few moments of fun before heading back to their homestead chores. *Photo by Evelyn J. Cameron, courtesy of the Montana Historical Society*

Earthquake—Three Forks

Numerous earthquakes have rumbled through Montana in the past century, including the one that caused this fissure at Three Forks in 1925. Two of the most destructive were the 1935 quake that crumbled homes and businesses in Helena and the 1959 temblor that killed more than two dozen campers and created Quake Lake near Yellowstone National Park. *Photo courtesy of the Montana Historical Society*

Like a lighthouse in a coastal community, this grain elevator at Waltham, east of Great Falls, is symbolic of the area's economic mainstay. *Photo by Bruce Selyem*

M

Amateur ornithologist Ewen Cameron poses in his Eastern
Montana study with a mounted gray trumpeter swan. Once
common in Montana, the swan had become extremely scarce by
the time this photo was taken in 1914. Cameron sent his research
about these rare birds to the Smithsonian Institution. *Photo by
Evelyn J. Cameron, courtesy of the Montana Historical Society*

N

Opposite: An early motorist stops to immortalize the moment after climbing to the crest of the Continental Divide at Gibbons Pass in the Bitterroot Range south of Hamilton.
Photo courtesy of the Montana Historical Society

Right: Meriwether Lewis bestowed the name Gates of the Mountains on these "remarkable" cliffs in 1805. Though the construction of Holter Dam in 1913 has reduced the rush of water through the "gates," they remain a startling and dramatic landmark on the Missouri River north of Helena.
Photo by Ralph De Camp, courtesy of the Montana Historical Society

Opposite: An informal boxing match is a welcome diversion from the day's labor at an Eastern Montana sheep ranch in 1905. *Photo by Evelyn J. Cameron, courtesy of the Montana Historical Society*

Another one bites the dust…. *Photo by Joanne M. Berghold*

Previous spread: Although its name means "bad or stinking earth" in Sioux, Makoshika State Park possesses a strange and haunting beauty. Created in the 1950s, the park southeast of Glendive encompasses acres of otherworldly buttes, pinnacles, and spires, as well as the mysterious fossils of long-dead dinosaurs. *Photo by Michael Sample*

Left: The fourth largest state in the nation, Montana straddles two very distinctive geophysical regions: the Northern Rockies and the Great Plains. In both, land remains the base on which the economy is built, whether through agriculture, lumbering, mining, or tourism. *Photo by Joanne M. Berghold*

Next page: The Yellowstone, one of Montana's finest fishing and floating rivers, wends it way between the Absaroka and Gallatin Ranges in the picturesque Paradise Valley. *Photo by Michael Sample*